Systemic Perspectives in Mental Health, Social Work and Youth Care

Systemic Perspectives in Mental Health, Social Work and Youth Care describes the theoretical foundations of a systemic framework, or 'systemic lens', and how the counsellor, therapist, social worker or other health professional can apply these ground principles in therapeutic meetings with clients.

The book presents a wide variety of perspectives and interventions, multiple examples and practical methods applicable to professionals with a range of experience. A case study covering a diverse family of three generations is presented throughout the book to clearly illustrate systemic perspectives, concepts and practices. This accessible book will inform and enhance the therapist's practice and conversations with individuals, couples, parents, groups or networks, even in the presence of psychopathology, multi-stressors or complex networks.

This highly readable guide will be essential reading for systemic practitioners of all backgrounds, as well as professionals looking to understand systemic approaches, and for those working in social work, youth care or mental health who want to enhance their current practice.

Anke Savenije is retired but worked as a psychologist, psychotherapist and systemic therapist. She is the co-founder of The Amsterdam Institute of Family Therapy, a centre for systemic therapy, training and supervision.

Justine van Lawick is a psychologist, psychotherapist and systemic therapist. She is a co-founder of the Lorentzhuis, a centre for systemic therapy, training and consultation in Haarlem, The Netherlands. She is a senior trainer in The Netherlands and abroad.

Ellen Reijmers is a psychologist, psychotherapist and systemic therapist. She is director and head of the psychotherapy training programme provided by the Interactie-Academie, a systemic training and therapy centre in Antwerp, Belgium. She is editor in chief of the centre's professional journal, *Systeemtheoretisch Bulletin*, and a senior trainer and supervisor.

The Systemic Thinking and Practice Series
Series Editors: Charlotte Burck and Gwyn Daniel

This influential series was co-founded in 1989 by series editors David Campbell and Ros Draper to promote innovative applications of systemic theory to psychotherapy, teaching, supervision and organisational consultation. In 2011, Charlotte Burck and Gwyn Daniel became series editors and aim to present new theoretical developments and pioneering practice, to make links with other theoretical approaches, and to promote the relevance of systemic theory to contemporary social and psychological questions.

"This accessible and hugely engaging text sets out both to explain systemic principles for professional practice and to support the development of systemic thinking in practice. The book explores the different ways in which we look at and understand families and their relationships, and importantly, why we might look in the ways we do. The authors follow the generations of a particular family system throughout the text and with their lively writing style draw us into the family members' experiences – their loves, their challenges, their dreams, their hurts and misunderstandings, and their successes. The authors invite us into the safety of the therapeutic context with the family members and clearly describe the unfolding of the therapeutic process, as they weave together the intra-personal with the inter-personal, social and developmental contexts of life. I strongly recommend this book as a practical and foundational text for training in health and social care practice. The sub-title of the book is 'A Relational Compass' – a strong metaphor to guide us the reader through the complexities of family life and to help make them more understandable, manageable and open to change."

Arlene Vetere, *PhD, Professor Emeritus of Family, VID Specialized University, Norway*

"This brilliant practice-orientated book provides a systemic compass to help practitioners to stay on course, with clients and therapists together confirming, debunking and changing their experience(s) of reality. Exercises at the end of each chapter invite the reader to reflect on their own practice and the personal contexts that contribute to their responses during the therapeutic process. A fascinating exploration of the different lenses needed to work systemically with a wide range of families in diverse settings – highly recommended to anyone interested in systemic practice!"

Eia Asen, *Professor Dr. Anna Freud Centre, UK*

"I would like to endorse *Systemic Perspectives in Mental Health, Social Work and Youth Care: A Relational Compass* by Anke Savenije, Justine van Lawick and Ellen Reijmers. This English translation will have special relevance for mental health practitioners including psychiatrists, doctors, psychologists, psychiatric nurses, family therapists and social workers who seek to apply a systemic, contextual, and family-centred practice framework. It draws on an ever-increasing evidence-based literature that acknowledges the value of applying a 'systemic lens' across a range of psychiatric diagnoses and presenting issues. The dual theory and practice focus of the book including useful homework exercises will have appeal for both beginning and experienced practitioners especially the detailed illustration of therapeutic work with the Dufour family across several chapters as well as the inclusion of a wealth of practice examples to illustrate the finer points of systemic therapy. English language readers will appreciate the focus on context in therapy conversations between therapists and clients and other systems and the book provides a useful and easily understood map for systemic practice across a range of settings for individuals, couples, parents, families, groups and larger networks. The chapters on systemic work with families presenting with 'individual vulnerabilities' and complex mental health issues and the role of common factors in therapy change will be especially useful. In summary this book will have wide appeal for psychologists, therapists, social workers and counsellors in English speaking countries who wish to learn more about applying a systemic approach in a range of mental health contexts."

Dr Glenn Larner, *Senior Clinical Psychologist and Family Therapist, Sydney, Australia, and Editor-in Chief of Australian and New Zealand Journal of Family Therapy*

Systemic Perspectives in Mental Health, Social Work and Youth Care

A Relational Compass

Anke Savenije, Justine van Lawick and Ellen Reijmers

Routledge
Taylor & Francis Group

LONDON AND NEW YORK

Designed cover image: Mila Van Goethem, *The family*, 2018

First published in English 2023
by Routledge
4 Park Square, Milton Park, Abingdon, Oxon OX14 4RN

and by Routledge
605 Third Avenue, New York, NY 10158

Routledge is an imprint of the Taylor & Francis Group, an informa business

Published in Dutch by Boom Uitgevers Amsterdam, 2018

British Library Cataloguing-in-Publication Data
Names: Savenije, Anke, author. | Lawick, Justine van, author. | Reijmers,
Ellen, author.
Title: Systemic perspectives in mental health, social work and youth care :
a relational compass / Anke Savenije, Justine van Lawick, and Ellen Reijmers.
Description: 1 Edition. | New York, NY : Routledge, 2023. | Series: The
systemic thinking and practice series | Includes bibliographical
references and index.
Identifiers: LCCN 2022031649 (print) | LCCN 2022031650 (ebook) | ISBN
9781032223117 (paperback) | ISBN 9781032223100 (hardback) | ISBN
9781003272038 (ebook)
Subjects: LCSH: Family counseling. | Family social work.
Classification: LCC HV697 .S33 2023 (print) | LCC HV697 (ebook) | DDC
362.82/53--dc23/eng/20221020
LC record available at https://lccn.loc.gov/2022031649
LC ebook record available at https://lccn.loc.gov/2022031650

ISBN: 978-1-032-22310-0 (hbk)
ISBN: 978-1-032-22311-7 (pbk)
ISBN: 978-1-003-27203-8 (ebk)

DOI: 10.4324/9781003272038

Typeset in Times
by KnowledgeWorks Global Ltd.

Contents

Preface

This book is aimed at mental health and social care practitioners who work with families, family members, partners, parents, adults or children, at times with individual psychiatric diagnoses or embedded in complex networks, and who want guidelines to practice systemically. Systemic practice means considering the context in which people live and in which problems and symptoms occur. This includes both the context of immediate relationships and the influence of the socio-economic environment and culture. Conversations with multiple people such as family members, close contacts or others may occur and is considered crucial in many treatment programmes. Alternatively the practitioner may have conversations with individuals and attend to significant others in the client's life and the people involved in the problems.

In conversations with individuals many professionals are unsure how to bring to the fore people who are not physically present in the session or they find talking with multiple people complicated. However everyone in the room *and* absent influential others have their own ideas about what is the matter and what needs to happen. And emotions can run high for family members and others involved because their relationships matter. Keeping oversight, taking into account different perspectives, not becoming overwhelmed by the severity of the problems or not becoming stuck in the hectic pace of the conversation is for the professional a challenge.

Systemic practitioners can choose from various perspectives and several interventions. Given this broad spectrum of options we felt it crucial to formulate global guidelines that can function as a common thread in systemic work with individuals, couples, parents, groups or networks.

This book is practice orientated. But good practice requires a clear theoretical framework: a 'systemic lens'. This lens consists of presumptions that form the basis of systemic work and colour the practitioner's perspective, positioning and actions. A systemic lens implies a specific way of looking at relationships and daily interactions, but also at problems in relationships, the role of the practitioner and what is likely to effect change. The systemic lens guides interventions. What this means for day-to-day practice is the major focus of this book and illustrated with many practical examples and applications, supported by various skills and techniques. As such the book is a *compass* to help practitioners stay on course and adopt or maintain a reflective position.

Structure

This book consists of 12 chapters. In Chapter 1 we describe the different lenses that can be used when looking at families, illustrated with the three-generational Dufour family. Examples from this family further illustrate the history of systemic therapy in Chapter 2. The principles that collectively form the 'systemic lens' are described: thinking in terms of connections, attending to the difference between intention and effect, considering feedback, relational processes, polyphony and sources of support and resilience. Chapter 3 focuses on how professionals too are influenced by the contexts they live in and work in.

In Chapter 4 we look at what preceded seeking professional help, the motivation of people to request professional input and what may be reasons to involve family members or other people in the therapeutic process. Again, this is illustrated with the Dufour family amongst other examples. Chapter 5 pays attention to factors the practitioner knows about but are generally not mentioned in conversations with clients, for example, that the introduction starts much earlier than the actual therapy, the influence of the referral and the significance of the space in which conversations take place.

In Chapter 6 we outline in practical terms how relationships, problems and the problems' contextual embedding can be systemically mapped. Throughout the therapeutic process professionals assume a specific positioning. Three major positioning approaches in systemic practice are discussed in Chapter 7. Chapter 8 follows with an overview of the various settings possible in systemic work: individual, with couples, parents, families, groups and bigger networks. We consider possible reasons and implications of choosing a specific setting and how changes in setting, if carefully chosen and prepared, can support the therapeutic process.

Chapters 9 and 10 focus on how systemic frameworks and positionings can be sustained in difficult circumstances. This is first applied to the work with people who present with mental health vulnerabilities or psychiatric diagnoses in Chapter 9. Chapter 10 provides ideas about working systemically with families with multiple or complex problems.

Chapter 11 describes a wide variety of skills and techniques that support the actions of systemic practitioners. And finally, in Chapter 12, we focus on the important theme of change, including the common factors that contribute to change in therapy and factors specific for systemic interventions. Given that what effects change remains partly elusive, the professional has to remain alert for the effects of their actions and the multitude of influences that may play a part in the change process.

About the translation

The original book *Systemisch werken. Een relationeel kompas voor hulpverleners* was written for a specific audience, namely Dutch and Flemish professionals who want to work systemically but function in a differently organised working environment which makes this challenging. This includes social workers, psychiatric nurses, psychologists, doctors and psychiatrists. Consequently we wanted to present the core values of systemic practice in a useful and practical way for professionals unfamiliar with the systemic approach.

The book has been successful in The Netherlands and Belgium. We are grateful to Routledge for publishing it in translation and hope it will be of value to English speaking professionals too.

It comes as no surprise that we came across issues during the translation process.

We changed typical Dutch first (and some last) names into more familiar English names. An example: a common female first name in The Netherlands is Joke. She became, for obvious reasons, Agnes. Additionally some regional or place names were described in more detail because their specific contextual connotations (such as a poor farming area in Flanders and in the south of The Netherlands) have no meaning for English readers.

We were unsure how to name the helping professional. The term 'systemic therapist' is allocated in The Netherlands and Belgium to professionals who have completed a post-graduate degree in systemic therapy. The audience we aim for is staff in mental health services who are eager to work more systemically but, due to a variety of reasons, are unable to commit to the full training programme. This may be their personal choice or they have insufficient qualifications or no support from their employer. The most fitting term appeared to be 'systemic practitioner', alternated with 'therapist', 'professional' and 'practitioner'. When we refer to professionals who mainly work with parents, we use the term 'parenting coach' or 'parent coach'.

In the process of writing the original book, it became clear that mental health and social care is organised differently in The Netherlands than in Belgium. That in itself was a challenge. The same applies to the translation in English. For example child protection services are organised (and named) differently in the United Kingdom, Australia or New Zealand, and different from Belgium and different again from The Netherlands. They have in common though the duty to protect children who live in situations detrimental to their development.

We endeavoured to make the Dutch edition, originally aimed at both a Flemish and Dutch audience, accessible to professionals who may not be proficient in reading English. Therefore the references reflect a considerable proportion of Dutch literature or translations into Dutch. In this edition translations in Dutch from English have resumed their original reference and the reference list was updated and complemented with works in English.

Our discussions about the translation problems we encountered were very interesting. Each time we had to find a translated term acceptable as 'real' English, without compromising the content and the intention of the Dutch text. Many thanks to our translator Veerle Poels who figured out those matters with patience and precision supported by invaluable lexicon and syntax input from Chris Sides.

The fact that systems theory, its conceptual framework, terminology and mode of practice are applied in many countries and many languages and the book therefore translatable is for us a source of joy.

Last but not least

At the time of writing, February 2022, the world is gripped by a pandemic. This influences our usual way of living and connecting with each other. It is no longer an option to invite people to our home, to see clients face-to-face or to make house calls. It has brought turmoil and division, not only in our society but also in families and individuals, both young and old. This has already changed our way of practising. What its influence might be long-term is unknown. At the moment we somehow have to relate to uncertainty and this could be long-term. The hope is that the pandemic also leads to creative new solutions, including for the huge problems the world is currently facing. Systemic practice means that we attend to the influence of such contextual tensions, uncertainties and possibilities on people and on relationships between people. It is important to be able to think in terms of systems and recognise the interactions between micro, meso and macrosystems. Currently this is for many all too palpable. It is this theory that forms the foundation of this book.

The original book was complemented by an online learning environment consisting of illustrations such as short videos about the pioneers, additional literature, documents or websites and practical exercises. For this edition, one exercise per chapter was selected from the online extensions and can be found at the end of each chapter instead.

Our hope is that this book provides a compass for practitioners who want to work systemically and that it may lay a foundation to expand their expertise and skills befitting their personal style, their clientele and their work setting.

Series editors' foreword

We are very pleased to introduce *Systemic Perspectives in Mental Health, Social Work and Youth Care* which is a translation of a very well-received book written by the very experienced Dutch and Belgian systemic clinicians and trainers, Anke Savenije, Justine van Lawick and Ellen Reijmers.

The book provides a wonderfully clear introduction for practitioners working in mental health, social work, youth care and other allied professions who are wanting to learn and develop a systemic approach to their work. It is an extremely well written and accessible text which lays out the ideas which are central to a systemic approach and demonstrates the ways they are applied in different situations and settings.

The authors' considerable clinical and training experience has enabled them to distil the gist of complex systemic ideas and to communicate these in straightforward and readily comprehensible ways. The book offers practitioners a clear framework for thinking and a connected range of skills and techniques to incorporate into their practice, whether working with individuals, families, organisations or networks. Placed centrally as the heart of the matter is the elaboration of interactional relationship building with multiple family members and other significant persons and a demonstration of ways to maintain multiple perspectives without which the work would not be possible. Each of the concepts are further illustrated through short practice extracts and examples. The authors also proffer some key questions for practitioners to keep in mind to aid them to continually review their work and to respond to feedback from those with whom they are working, thereby sustaining the systemic processes of their work.

Each chapter ends with an exercise which invites the reader to immediately apply the ideas to a situation of their own. In this way the book aims to be alongside practitioners to enable them to begin to introduce a difference to their own thinking and practice.

This book was written to reach those practitioners who may not have access to systemic trainings for a number of reasons, and will enable them to start to use the ideas, as well as to engage their colleagues and supervisor to help them develop these further. It should also prove very useful for access and introductory systemic courses. It also strikes us that individuals and families themselves will find the book extremely illuminating and could encourage them to begin to find different systemic perspectives to consider any challenges they may be facing and with ideas about how they might find a way through even without the aid of a relationship with a practitioner.

We are delighted to have this book in our series.

Charlotte Burck and Gwyn Daniel

Chapter 1

Does 'the family' exist?

Introduction

In photos and in popular magazines a family is usually depicted as a white middle-class household consisting of a father, a mother and their own two to three children. It is an image shared by many, an image that applies to the nuclear family as was the norm in the mid-20th century. Nuclear families still exist, but there is more variety in types of families. There are solo-parent families, three-generational households, blended families with step-parents, families with two mothers or two fathers and adoptive families. And relationships between people from different cultures and different social classes have become more frequent. Because of this diversity we can no longer speak of *the* (nuclear) family. Family relationships, family dynamics, living circumstances, experiences and backgrounds of family members differ between families and within families.

Families are social configurations, societal connections in which members care for one another physically, emotionally and materially. Family members may or may not have biological links, live together in a house with one or more generations or live in different places, even different countries. Each family and every partner relationship are embedded in a wider family of multiple generations. Families are always connected with other families. Marriage or partnership creates new ties, and adoption, donorship, foster care or a new love interest connect families as well. It is impossible to draw clear boundaries around a nuclear family, a couple or an extended family. Furthermore family relationships are dynamic; influenced by events and time they evolve.

In this chapter we will introduce a family: three generations of the Dufour-de Soek family. Important principles of systems theory are illustrated with examples from the Dufour-de Soek family to ground professional intervention and help practitioners with developing and maintaining a systemic perspective.

DOI: 10.4324/9781003272038-1

As the years have passed some members of the Dufour-de Soek family have accessed professional help. For that reason the family is introduced at a point in time some years ago.

Meet the Dufour-de Soek family

This is the family of Dirk Dufour and Agnes Dufour-de Soek. The family is gathering because son Thomas and his wife and children, who live abroad, are visiting the family in The Netherlands.

At the front in the middle are Dirk and Agnes, then 67 and 64 years old. Dirk and Agnes met at a fairground, respectively, aged 20 and 16. They married two years later. They both come from a Catholic family with many children. Their fathers were employed as labourers in the Philips factory in Eindhoven and their mothers were housewives.

Agnes hails from the Belgian Kempen, an agricultural area bordering The Netherlands. Poverty and scarcity of jobs drove many to work and live in the Dutch city of Eindhoven because of the Philips factories. So did Agnes's family. Many of her family still live over there. Agnes was four years old when they relocated. Dirk has lived his whole life in a small village close to Eindhoven. His parents' families still live in Kempen. Dirk and Agnes now live in a suburb of Eindhoven.

Dirk is a thoughtful man. He attended night classes and tertiary courses to qualify as an accountant, the first in his family with a higher degree. Since his retirement, he keeps busy as the bookkeeper of the theatre company he has been a member of for many years. At home he enjoys gardening, reading

Figure 1.1 Dufour-de Soek family portrait

the paper and following the news on TV. He does not talk much. Agnes is 64 years old. She studied home economics for two years and worked until the children were born. She has remained socially active in her community and at the children's schools. Currently she is a volunteer at the library. She is creative and sings in a choir. She babysits the grandchildren regularly. Agnes speaks her mind and likes to share her opinions with others. In the past, Dirk and Agnes went camping regularly, but that has stopped now as they're older. Sometimes they join organised bus trips, for instance, to Germany. Although their children have been christened, the church no longer plays an important part in their lives.

Dirk and Agnes have three children. Their eldest daughter, top left in the picture, is Kim (44). She works as a nurse in a regional hospital. Kim takes after her mother. She takes care of her appearance, works hard and is practical. Next to her is her husband Tony (47). He is a physiotherapist in a private group practice. He takes part in a lot of sports and is training for a triathlon. He is an easy-going man. They live not far from Kim's parents.

Standing left of Kim and Tony is their daughter Vera, who is 23 years old. She has studied communication science and started her own company developing websites. She works hard but likes the freedom of working for herself. Her partner Kira (32) is standing next to Vera. Kira's mother's family is from Indonesia and a substantial part of her family lives in The Netherlands. Vera and Kira are married and Vera is six months pregnant. The baby's biological father is a friend, Jaco, who studied at university with Vera. Kira tried a few courses at university without success and now works in hospitality. She has a daughter, Ratna (8), from a previous relationship. Ratna is a temperamental girl. In the picture, she is standing in front of her mother.

Sitting in front of Kim and Tony is their son, and brother of Vera, Ken (21). Ken is studying industrial design in Delft. He is an active member of the rowing club and his rowing team has won multiple prizes. Ken visits the family infrequently. He is currently not in a relationship.

Standing at the top right is Rose (42), Dirk and Agnes's second daughter. She has been in two long-term relationships and has been living in Amsterdam for the last two years. She has a close group of friends and teaches textile technology at a high school. Physically she resembles her father.

Standing in the middle of the top row, to the right of Tony, is Thomas (40), Agnes and Dirk's son. He studied economics and currently works for the World Bank. He has travelled extensively and considers himself more a world citizen than a Dutch citizen. Next to him is his Ghanese wife Akua (38). She works for village projects in Africa. Thomas and Akua live in Washington and have two sons: Kofi (14) and Rudo (10). They are standing in front of Akua and Rose.

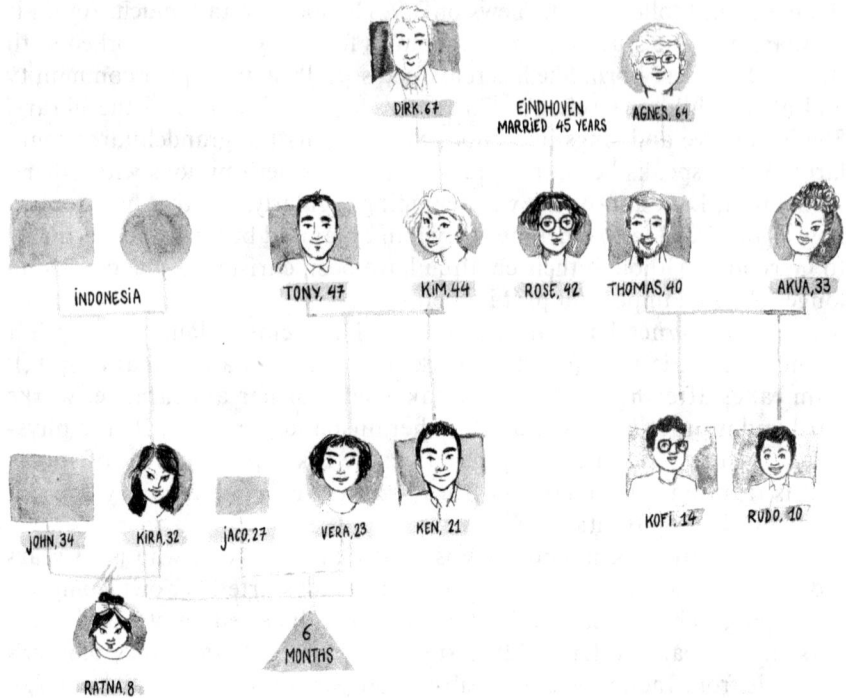

Figure 1.2 Genogram Dufour family

Different lenses

Many ideas circulate about families and how they ought to function. These include views about what a normal family is, what ought to happen in a family, what good parenting is and good partnership, how children ought to develop and how parents ought to contribute to this. Those views are derived from popularised scientific theories and distributed via media, literature and advertising. Schools and institutions that work with families uphold similar, rather traditional views that convey set standards to which families ought to adhere. In this context we can speak of reification, in other words, the changing of the concept or idea of a family into a reality, an object. Ideas about families become fixed, concrete, unchangeable facts (Cottyn, 2008). This obscures the situation that we are dealing with perspectives.

For example in the present day, much attention goes to the parenting of children. Tips and advice on how to bring up children so they develop into responsible and successful adults are handed out to parents. Good parenthood means that you look after your children's well-being and ensure that your child is securely attached. That is the norm and consequently a fact.

Norms like this influence what can and cannot be noticed, thought, or felt and become so to speak the sole lens people look through. Parents are held responsible for the way their children grow up. Consequently parents often experience a lot of pressure, feel guilty or believe they are failing.

The complexity of families is lost when only one lens is applied. Many reciprocal influences and context factors affect family relationships such as the child's and the parents' temperament, the relationship between the parents, with brothers and sisters and with the family, the socio-economic circumstances and the neighbourhood and culture in which the child grows up.

Context is an important systemic concept (Bateson, 1972). Nothing happens in a vacuum. Children, adults and families are embedded in diverse contexts which influence their development. In turn people and their relationships influence the context (Pearce & Cronen, 1980). This continuous process of relational influences has no specific beginning or a predictable outcome. For instance, difficult behaviour of a child can be *related to* (which is different from 'caused by') parenting or talent, to high expectations about academic performance, to influence of friends, maybe to the fact that their sister trumps them in everything, the loss of their grandmother, the unemployment of their father, waiting for a residence visa or to cramped housing.

This complexity is reduced in everyday life because it's impossible to see at a glance how everything is connected. People perceive reality from a particular angle. They order their perceptions and hence create a foreground and a background. Some things they see, others they don't. Some things are considered to be a cause, others a consequence. Watzlawick et al. (1967) described this as the *punctuation [of the sequence of events] axiom*, illustrated with the well-known ambiguous picture in which a vase or a woman's face is recognised, but never at the same time.

Another important premise of system's theory is that people order reality in a particular way. Consequently each perspective brings specific aspects into focus and not others. We look at the Dufour family through different lenses. Because families are socially positioned and part of broad societal developments belonging to a particular era, we focus first on the broadest lens, the sociological lens. We discuss factors such as socio-economic circumstances, the work situation, male-female relations and the position of children in a family. Societal developments and perspectives create what is or isn't taken for granted. They are the wide undercurrent beneath daily exchanges and actions. The community's norms, values and beliefs trickle through stories from neighbours, friends and colleagues about the Dufour family. Such outsider perspectives make up the second lens on the Dufour family. Then follows the third lens: the family's own perspective. Often family members describe themselves and their family in general terms, based partly on societal views, on perspectives from outsiders and on stories and important values of the family. Finally the family is described from the perspective of each individual family member. Each person has stories about their family and specific memories that are influenced by all other lenses, and by the unique contexts of each individual.

The four lenses provide different ways to understand family relationships and each constitutes a context that influences how a family is perceived and how family members describe themselves. The selected lenses each form a reciprocal context for one another. The sociological lens offers an overview of norms and values in time and place that echo through the stories of people who look at the family from an outsider position. The perception of outsiders influences in turn how family members experience their own family and give it meaning and vice versa. The different lenses also influence how a helping professional views the family.

We chose to use the wide-angled lens of the sociologist first and gradually narrow this down to the close-up of personal meaning-making. We acknowledge that other perspectives are conceivable.

The point is to illustrate that how families are perceived depends on the lens used and that switching lenses can lead to a richer and more dynamic picture of families. This is called *polyphony* ('many voices'), another central concept in systems theory.

The sociological lens

Sociologists are interested in broad societal structures and connections. de Regt (2014) describes how since the 1960s families changed significantly, both factually and ideologically. More variation occurred in the composition and structure of families and interaction dynamics eased. What was expected of men and women, mothers, fathers and children, how they were expected to behave and how tasks were apportioned also became more varied (Hochschild, 1989). de Regt summarises those change processes with the following overarching concepts: secularisation, democratisation and equalisation, individualisation and informalisation. These processes are associated with changes in the job market, increased welfare, the growth of the welfare state, increased access to education, emancipation processes and immigration (de Regt, 2014).

In the second half of the 20th-century women joined the labour market en masse. The roles of men, women and children changed. Contraception allowed for more sexual freedom. More attention was given to child development and children were protected more. Child labour became unlawful. Children were given a voice. Rules were no longer enforced top down by authoritarian parents, but families held discussions and negotiations (Brinkgreve, 2012).

A sociological lens helps to see wider connections. Many behaviours that are attributed to individual family members are actually more strongly connected to a specific period. If Dirk is described as someone who doesn't talk much, he will say that he was taught not to do so. He makes the connection with how it was in his family of origin. Let's not forget that in the previous century it was uncommon for most families to talk about personal problems or feelings. Another well-known example was the assumed relationship between psychiatric problems of young people and overinvolved mothers and absent fathers in the second half of the last century, because this was the dominant family model at the time (Hare-Mustin, 1978).

Looking at the Dufour family through a sociological lens, it becomes evident how societal changes had an effect on this family's development. Dirk and Agnes belong to the generation immediately after the Second World War. They grew up in the rebuilding era. The nuclear family, in other words a father, a mother and children, was the dominant family structure. Secularisation had been set in motion. While their parents were devoted church goers, this is no longer the case for Dirk and Agnes. Though both came from large Catholic families, birth control was part of planning their family and they were content with having three children. A democratisation process was initiated in the Dufour family. What father says no longer goes. The parents consulted their children and their voices mattered. Parallel with the democratisation process, an upward movement of their socio-economic status happened. Dirk completed tertiary studies and became an accountant, and so surpassed his own father on the social ladder. This led to more prosperity. Agnes attended home economics, was a mother and homemaker and outside of the home was very active socially. All their children continued this trend and attended tertiary education. Roles and tasks stereotypically allocated to men and women shifted. In the generation of Dirk and Agnes's children both men and women work, and childcare and domestic work are no longer the exclusive responsibility of a woman. In several domains, boundaries shifted. Sexual liberation, living together prior to marriage or not getting married at all becomes normalised. More people travelled and Dirk and Agnes's youngest son marrying a Ghanese woman and living in Washington fits in this picture. The socialisation of women and men changes, women who study are a reality, and two women having a child, as is the case for Dirk and Agnes's grandchildren, is no longer an exception. The cohort of single people grows. Two people remaining loyal to one another 'until death do us part' is no longer a given. Divorce, second relationships and blended families are now a large and significant part of society. Our example is Kira, the partner of granddaughter Vera, who left her husband for her new love, a woman.

Dirk and Agnes live in a neighbourhood where many families in similar stages of life came to live. At that time they were all young families with fathers working in the Phillips factory and mothers taking care of the children. The neighbourhood was crowded with children playing outside. The prosperity of the neighbourhood grew over time. People owned cars, houses were renovated and families took summer holidays. Today the children have left, many schools are closed and the fathers have retired. The neighbourhood has aged and social activities and public amenities have been adjusted accordingly. This influences Dirk and Agnes's daily life. Initially they lived in a young, lively and active neighbourhood which is now a quiet, peaceful suburb. They miss the children who used to play on the street but feel grateful for having neighbours they have known for such a long time.

The outsiders' perspective

Outsiders share a family's life through the neighbourhood, school, work, church, sports club, hobby club and other relevant areas. They describe a family as they experience them through the relationship they have. The perceptions of outsiders reverberate the beliefs, values and norms of those different contexts and the society.

Outsider perspectives can support families or add pressure. Neighbour Marion (67): 'Our children and theirs played together a lot and we often visited each other. In their house a lot was allowed, but it was Agnes who made the decisions and Dirk let it happen. Typical Agnes, she can be so dominant. Dirk just lets others walk over him, even more so since he retired.'

Bert (55) is a member of the theatre society and finds Dirk a very reliable man: 'He always attends and looks after the finances diligently. He doesn't like the limelight, but you can have fun with him, particularly when he brings his accordion. He is very proud of his children; I believe they've all done well. It's just his granddaughter, she has a child with another woman as her partner. We'd never expected that. I think Dirk feels embarrassed about it. I understand that.' What outsiders say reflects the social norms about a good upbringing, men-women relationships, how to behave, how to interact with others and whether you are a good family. Often these messages are implicit. Watzlawick et al. (1967) defined the *relationship aspect [level]* of communication. In interpersonal interactions it is not just about the words or what's been said or done (the content), but mainly about the relationship message that is relayed: this is how I see you, you (plural), us, myself. For example Agnes notices that Marion, her neighbour, makes comments in between the lines about her and her husband. She's offended because it feels like an attack on her and her family. She thinks her neighbour is nosy and that makes her impatient towards Dirk. 'Please, do a bit more', she tells him, irritated.

Jacqueline (35) is in the same choir as Agnes and has a different opinion: 'I find Agnes very social, she talks with everyone and never excludes people. One of the choir members was struggling and Agnes took her under her wing. I wouldn't do that, I come here to enjoy myself and nothing more. Agnes's children and grandchildren are her top priority. If she's unable to make choir practice, it's because of them.' This view of her confirms for

Agnes that they are indeed a good family and that she matters. Agnes felt something similar when in the past teachers spoke positively about her children. She feels it too when the doctor says that 'the Dufours believe that an ailment here or there will clear up by itself'. Impressions and perceptions about oneself and others are continuously exchanged in interactions (Laing et al., 1966; Reijmers & Cottyn, 2014; Watzlawick et al., 1967). These relationship messages can be pleasing and validating or critical and negating. The effect depends on what is accepted by the society and relevant reference groups, how the relationship is with the outsider in question and what is important to that person. The relationship messages always influence the way a family member experiences themselves, the relationships and the family. In turn this influences the relationships in the family and with the outside world.

The family

People react to the outside world and the norms and values channelled via conversations, social gatherings and the media. People want to be perceived in a particular way, for instance as socially engaged and caring, as enjoying life's pleasures or as an expert in art. Family members define their family through descriptions that circulate in family stories: 'that's a typical Dufour' or 'just like a de Soek'. In Dirk and Agnes's family, a 'typical Dufour' is someone slightly withdrawn and serious, but with a big heart. Dufours bottle things up and do things their own way, but they can be fun too. A 'typical de Soek' refers to being active, quick to organise and arrange and to being social and creative. Such descriptions imply norms, they exclude or include. The same applies with family descriptions. Members of the Dufour family make statements such as 'conflict between us is rare', 'we're there for each other', 'we don't bother others', 'we take responsibility when needed and we can have fun at times'. These reflect particular views and interactional habits shared by the family members: 'this is who we are and what we do'. Values and norms become anchored through descriptions like these: 'this is who we are as a good family'.

In this context the systemic literature talks about *family scripts*. Family scripts are 'the family's shared expectations of how family roles are to be performed within various contexts''' (Byng-Hall, 1995, p. 4). Each person brings scripts from their own family of origin into other relationships, which can bring stability or tension in those connections. Kim for example believes she is very similar to her mother, she has a similar practical approach, a huge sense of responsibility and is unable to do nothing. To her this fits her role as mother. Her husband Tony sees the role of a mother differently. His mother used to read and talk a lot with him and his brother. She was not practical at all and Tony really liked that about her. Kim experienced in her family of origin that husband and wife complement each other and don't argue much. Tony expects the opposite. For him disagreements and personal space are part and parcel of partner relationships.

Scripts can be found in family stories, in the myths that are told over and over in a family: about the grandparent who was a hero in the Resistance, about the aunt who managed six children on her own. Scripts and descriptions are not fixed but change over time and when relationships shift or events happen. An example: prior to having children, partners interact differently with each other. Parents do other things together and with their children depending on the age of the children. Children too value different things as they grow up (Govaerts & Splingaer, 2014). Times change and different issues come to the fore depending on the stages of life and family (Falicov, 1988; Splingaer, 2014). Since Dirk's retirement, Agnes would like him to participate more actively in family life, attend more to the children and grandchildren and occasionally cook or hoover. Her expectations are reinforced when she notices how other men of his age behave or when her son Thomas talks about his latest culinary success and when she reads how important it is for men to care for others.

The fact that ideas and expectations exist in families about 'this is who we are' doesn't mean that everyone attributes the same value or meaning to these ideas. Family members don't share the same experiences and meanings, they have different reference frames and different lives. In their interpersonal exchanges flows a constant stream of norms and values about themselves and other family members. 'Be caring' and 'don't argue' are very important values in the Dufour family. But Rose believes this is the reason why she struggles with conflict in relationships. For her not arguing is more a hindrance than a positive quality of a family or a partner relationship. She wants to avoid this in a future relationship. Resisting or avoiding repeated scenarios from your family of origin and the desire to do it differently is called a *corrective script* (Byng-Hall, 1995).

The individual in different contexts

People have multiple identities. Several contexts connected with culture, gender, generation, social class, work, home, friends and hobbies bring out different aspects of a person. Someone who is shy in groups can be loud at home. Many children behave quite differently at school than at home. Agnes displays other sides of herself when she is with her family than when she is with the choir. At home she organises everything, states how things are to be and can be impatient. With her girlfriends in the choir she listens more and is patient. These different identities are not separate from one another. Agnes believes she is a good mother and is content with her children. But when a choir member says she is so lucky that all her children and grandchildren live close by, Agnes misses her son in Washington and her daughter in Amsterdam and wonders why they moved so far away. That gnaws at her identity as mother.

Individuals can attribute a different meaning to so-called shared experiences. In this context inspiration from behavioural genetic research is interesting (De Mol, 2011; Dunn & Plomin,1991). Research shows that the environment in which children are raised is perceived and experienced differently by each child in the same family. Children have different temperaments, different characteristics and elicit different responses from their parents. A child can be similar to one of mother's favourite sisters, a father sticks up for his youngest son because he was teased by his older brother. The relationship dynamic influences other relationships, for instance between brother and sister. Parents perceive each child differently and respond to that. And children perceive their parents differently and respond accordingly. Because of these differences, a family becomes a different environment for each child and this in turn influences the child and the parents.

Multiple identity aspects and different meanings also play in the Dufour family. Thomas, according to his parents the clown of the family, has wonderful memories of his childhood: 'I had a really good upbringing. Lovely parents who accept you for who you are. I have always felt safe and supported at home. I was given a reasonable degree of freedom because they trusted me. I'd like to pass that on in the upbringing of my sons.' Thomas as son and Thomas as partner are two at times conflicting roles and contexts. When Thomas visits his parents, he behaves like the youngest child and loves being spoiled. He acts like a clown, makes his mother laugh and irritates his sisters. 'Akua and the children say that I behave weirdly in Eindhoven. Recently Rudo asked why I never make the same jokes when we're at home in America. I don't really know, it just happens. But Akua is annoyed when I behave like that at my parents'. She says I'm a mummy's child. That bothers me because I know my mum likes to care for everyone. Sometimes we argue about that.'

Rose doesn't share Thomas's good memories of their childhood. 'My older sister Kim bossed me around, she made me do all sorts of things. And Thomas was spoiled, he was allowed everything. I found him quite irritating. He teased me but my parents never saw it like that, they always protected him. My mother always nagged me about finding a good man and that I would make a wonderful mother. Apparently I am not good enough the way I am. It's a feeling I've always had with her.' When Rose hears repeatedly how special the four (grand)children of her brother and sister are, she feels excluded. This affects her sense of self in the family and the image of her family evolving over time. She lives in Amsterdam and has great friends. Most are singles without children and that provides a sense of kinship and normality.

Kofi (14), Thomas and Akua's son, voices it as follows: 'Last summer we visited mum's family in Ghana and that was so cool. Mum has lovely parents and many brothers and sisters. The whole day we spent outside, playing soccer. Or Granddad took us to the river and taught us to fish. Sometimes I feel bored in Eindhoven. There are not as many children to play with. I like it better in Ghana, but don't dare to tell my dad. My friends at school in Washington are jealous when I travel to Europe.'

In conclusion

In this chapter a number of different lenses have been covered, a small selection from the many perspectives possible. All those different perspectives influence one another and create a context for one another. Consequently everything is connected and in perpetual motion (Bateson, 1972). A systemic orientation helps to consider those interactions and to constantly contextualise. It invites the practitioner to look at the connections between beliefs, behaviour and relationships and the wider societal context, like the sociologist who observes and analyses. And it takes into account the smaller context of individual ideas and meaning-making. *The* family does not exist. With the help from the Dufour-de Soek family we highlighted systemic concepts and focussed on relationships, contexts, interactions and meanings. In the next chapter we delve deeper, into what a systemic framework entails, what its most important foundation principles are and what this means for the practitioner.

Exercise

Interview a family member, friend or colleague about their family of origin. Apply the different lenses as described in this chapter.

From a *sociological perspective*, questions can be asked about the area or neighbourhood where the family lived, ethnicity, socio-economic circumstances, social class, occupation, social mobility, family constellation, male-female relationships and migration if applicable.

Ask about *outsider perspectives*: how was their family perceived by others? For instance, by the families of the in-laws, neighbours, teachers at the school they attended as children.

How did they *themselves* perceive their family, as 'normal' or 'different'? Against what criteria was a family deemed to be 'normal' or 'different'? Did the interviewee agree with these criteria?

What was the influence of these perspectives on the interviewee?

Chapter 2

A systemic lens

Introduction

Systemic therapy is a challenging field of practice. The most important theoretical concepts deviate significantly from what is customary in other therapeutic models. In systemic practice many roads can be travelled, and many useful techniques are available. The therapist needs to keep in mind a multitude of viewpoints, opinions and feelings from clients and their significant others. Even when people close to the client are not always present in sessions, the reciprocal influence between people needs to be kept prominently in mind.

Systemic practice is usually associated with conversations with family members or couples. This is only partly true. In systemic therapy the therapist speaks indeed with multiple people, but more importantly adopts a systemic way of thinking and acting. In a way the practitioner puts on systemic spectacles to understand people's problems and to explore where change is possible. This systemic lens allows the professional to look at individuals and also at systems wider than couples or families, for instance, when due to a family member's problems complex networks emerge. These can include therapists, teachers, friends and others. Applying a systemic lens provides opportunities for the professional to work in various settings, such as individual, couple, family, group or network. This is discussed further in Chapter 8.

Immediate and extended families and partner relationships as social configurations are embedded in a societal context. By using the term *systemic* therapy it is easier to see that clients function not only within family relations but in social systems as well. The same is true for practitioners as we will see in the next chapter. So what exactly is this systemic lens through which the therapist looks? In this chapter we describe some fundamental principles of systems theory that bring about this systemic lens. But firstly we briefly visit the history of systems theory and systemic practice.

DOI: 10.4324/9781003272038-2

A brief history

Systemic practice is inspired by two important developments: the *practice* of working with families and *scientific research* in family relationships (Midori Hanna & Brown, 2018; Reijmers, 2014b; Vetere & Dallos, 2003). The first source of inspiration, the practice of working with families, hails back to the period around 1900. Social work at the time, busy with the demands of large poor working-class families, was at the origin of professional support for families. From the 1960s this way of working gained traction in mental health care. Social workers, psychiatrists and psychologists experimented with inviting families of psychiatric patients (Ackerman, 1966; Satir, 1972; Whitaker & Malone, 1953). Family focussed interventions and new ideas about change in psychiatric and mental problems were trialled. The second important source of inspiration was the scientific research on how severe problems in families originate and continue. The focus was initially on the interpersonal communication between family members. Around 1960 its theoretical foundation was based on cybernetics, the science of automated feedback processes. The idea was that human systems strive to maintain balance (equilibrium) or as described at the time, *homeostasis*. This balance should, as with mechanical systems, be sustained by information feedback. It was explained with the metaphor of a thermostat that regulates a heating system's constant adjustment to the environment in order to maintain a constant temperature. Influenced by the *General System Theory* the idea that living systems seek balance was abandoned. The biologist Von Bertalanffy (1968) stated that complex living systems are not driven only by seeking stability, but are also creative, change continuously and transform their organisation in many ways. From this perspective not only ecosystems but family systems too are perpetually evolving.

The pioneer therapists focussed their attention mainly on describing and analysing family interactions from the 'outside' with the therapist being an observer and expert. This changed in the 1970s and 1980s, influenced by societal and theoretical developments. Cybernetics as a founding theory of systemic practice came under fire. One of the criticisms related to the disregard for the social embedding of families and the social pressures on families. Its limited attention to individuals and individual meaning-making was also criticised; after all every 'system' consists of individuals. Another criticism pointed to the lack of attention for the variety in family systems (single parent families, blended families, grandparent families, families with LGBTQ or bicultural parents, foster families) and the wide diversity in partner relationships. Finally the idea that the therapist was a neutral outsider and the lack of attention to the importance of power and inequality in relationships, including the counselling relationship, evoked criticism too.

The philosophical stream of *social constructionism* in the 1990s was of great influence on social sciences in general and on systemic practice. To some extent social constructionism provided an answer to the criticisms described above. Its premise is that every idea, every expression and every action is embedded in a social context and therefore reality is constructed (Gergen, 2015). Many truths exist, not just one, depending on the angle taken, the position or role occupied and the relationships and contexts of participants. That practitioners cannot be outsiders became the guiding principle. The observer and the observed cannot be regarded as separate: therapists always co-construct.

The focus shifted further towards diversity, gender and power differences (Burck & Daniel, 1995; Goldner, 1985; Hare-Mustin & Marecek, 1988; Huijser, 1984) and so-called *dominant discourses* (White & Epston, 1990). The latter are beliefs that at a given time prevail in society and are so dominant that alternative interpretations are pushed aside. Examples of a dominant discourse in our society therapists often hear are the belief that 'fathers and mothers need to agree about how to bring up their children' or 'a good relationship is always a monogamous relationship'. When problems arise, individual causes or pathology are usually assumed, another illustration of a dominant discourse, alongside attachment theory, medical-biological explanations or trauma theory.

Perceptions guide actions

How we perceive the world is connected to how we relate to the world and how we act. This is a fundamental principle of present-day systemic practice. Colleagues who perceive their work environment as a threat will relate to each other and their job differently and do different things compared to colleagues who perceive their work context as supportive. A therapist who sees parenting problems as skill shortages will focus on different solutions than a counsellor who understands parenting problems as relationship problems. Simply put: the way we 'look' matters.

Systemic practice includes different approaches. Practitioners may focus predominantly on one of the following: the communication between family members, interpersonal behaviours, the structure and organisation of a family system or on the development of a family over time. Other approaches focus mainly on the future, on the effect of stories, on the experiences of the family members or on gender, race and culture (Midori Hanna & Brown, 2018; Savenije et al., 2014). These approaches can be considered as particular perspectives of reality, as lenses that zoom in on particular aspects of the interpersonal dimension as starting points for change.

Each framework focuses on the lens. In that sense theory is never objective: it co-constructs reality and guides actions. Theoretical premises always result in actual effects. When therapists are aware of their theoretical principles they can reflect on their effects on the therapeutic conversations. What follows are the foundational ideas of systemic practice. They form the framework shared by all systemic approaches. These premises 'showcase' reality in a particular way and consequently colour the actions and stance of the therapist, which in turn influences how clients see themselves and their relationships.

Systemic principles

Context is essential

Gregory Bateson, one of the founders of systems theory, stated: "Without context, words and actions have no meaning at all" (Bateson, 1979, p. 15). Context is thereby an essential yet broad concept. It can refer to a specific place, a space, an event or a situation, a history, a relationship and so on (Pearce & Cronen, 1980). The meaning of the sentence 'I am leaving' is quite different in the context of someone who is getting on the train than in the context of someone who just had an argument with their partner. In the previous chapter we described how the Dufour family can be viewed through different lenses. Each lens focussed on a different context to make sense of the family relationships and each time something new came into view. In theoretical terms: every context creates a different meaning. Many contexts resonate in each action or interaction: societal contexts such as culture, socio-economic class, ethnicity, sexual identity and religion, but also familial contexts such as the family of origin or the current living circumstances. Other influential contexts can be someone's temperament or values, their individual or relational history, their neighbourhood, work or school. Systemic practitioners try to keep an eye on all those contexts that contribute to problems being sustained and the problems changing. Alongside the contexts of the client's life their own contexts also play a part. We describe the contextual embeddedness of the practitioner in Chapter 3.

During a therapeutic conversation many contexts are present simultaneously and more visible or less visible. It depends on the therapist which contexts are brought to the fore.

In the chapter 'Something Has to Change' it transpires that Kim, Dirk and Agnes's eldest daughter is feeling down. Her problems could be related to her personality or to her marriage, the stage of life she finds herself in, the menopause, the changes at her work, the interactions in her family of origin, the societal ideas about women and so on. Depending on the context brought into focus in the therapy session, a different view of Kim's problems will emerge.

A systemic practitioner will highlight those contexts they hope will help the client to see their problems in a different, less self-blaming or other-blaming way and support change. This is called *contextualising*.

Everything is connected

Systemic practitioners think in terms of connections and interplay based on the fundamental idea that expressions, behaviour and relationships are characterised by reciprocity, by *circular patterns of influence.* In circular patterns cause and effect cannot be distinguished. This is founded on the systemic principle that all human behaviour, emotion or experience cannot be reduced to a single cause because of the many contexts and influences at play. *Circularity* is an important principle that differentiates systemic therapy and systemic practice from other therapeutic models.

Systemic practitioners avoid thinking in terms of cause and effect, such as Mr A's fear for attachment is caused by being abandoned in a traumatic way at a young age. Linear causality (cause-effect) is often illustrated by what happens when someone hits a ball: the strike determines the direction of the ball and how far the ball will go.

A simple illustration of circularity is that of a child (and not a ball) being hit by her mother.

> The mother slaps her child to stop the child's continuous whining. This could be effective: the daughter stops whining. But the effect could be that the girl starts crying, becomes angry, hits back or does something else. This in turn influences the mother's response which will influence the daughter's reaction again. It is also possible that the father had enough and gets angry, or perhaps he supports his daughter because he thinks Mum is too strict. Dad's reaction could be related to a bad night's sleep because he is facing redundancy at work. The relationships between mother and daughter, father and daughter and mother and father are embedded in a bigger family and that too can have an influence (van Lawick & Savenije, 2014).

Living systems are characterised by such circular patterns. Living systems such as people, families or societies are always open systems, never closed. *Open systems* do not have defined boundaries. They are changeable and have a complex relationship with the outside world. The Dufour family is not a closed system where each family member has only relationships with other family members. Their interpersonal relationships and each person's feelings and behaviours are the result of numerous interactions with a diversity of worlds outside and inside the family.

Circularity is connected to the concept of *equifinality,* another important principle in systems theory. Equifinality means that various causes can lead to the same result and goals and final outcomes can be reached in different ways. The approach of the therapist is influenced by thinking in terms of connections and the awareness that the multiple processes of influence and the effects can never be fully known. The professional does not make assumptions 'beforehand'; they don't impose their own interpretation but embody an attitude of curiosity and collaboration in the search for connections that enable new meanings. The position of the therapist is described in Chapter 7.

The difference between intent and effect

Pragmatics of Human Communication (Watzlawick et al., 1967) is a foundational work from the pioneer years of systemic therapy and is still relevant today. The authors discuss five communication axioms and associated communication problems. 'Pragmatics' refers to the *observable [behavioural] effects* of verbal and non-verbal communication. The focus on effects is still prevalent in systemic practice. A differentiation is made between intentions and effects. We are unable to control or determine what happens between us and others. Regardless of what we believe, feel or mean, the effects of communication are not in our control (De Mol et al., 2018).

> Agnes Dufour, Rose's mother, never had the intention to exclude her daughter. Yet when her mother proudly talks about the children of her eldest daughter Kim, this is the effect on Rose, who has no children.

Not being able to control effects also applies to non-verbal exchanges.

> The small tokens of attention Agnes gives to her son Thomas make Rose feel neglected. That is an unintended effect of Agnes's profound care for her youngest son which Thomas seems happy to receive.

This happens in therapy too. When the therapist makes a validating or constructive comment to the client, such as 'well done', this can be perceived as an acknowledgement by one client but as an insult by another client or be felt as a denial of the problems. Not just a comment or a question, but also clothing, a particular look, attitude, voice or tone can have unexpected effects. This doesn't mean that the professional can't have an opinion or has to be completely neutral. This is impossible and in fact undesirable. It means that systemic practitioners continuously monitor the effects of exchanges between clients and between themselves and the clients. This point highlights the importance of the therapist being aware of the effects of their own ideas, opinions or vocalisations in a particular situation. Practitioners construct hypotheses while talking with clients, which are presumptions about what is the matter and the significant influences. It is not a question of whether a hypothesis is correct but whether the hypothesis is useful and helpful. Cecchin, an influential systemic therapist, reminds us that "as long as [the practitioner] does not fall in love with the hypothesis, as long as he plays with it, or talks to colleagues about it, there appears no valid argument to prevent him from building a hypothesis" (Cecchin et al., 1992, p. 10).

Focus on feedback

Taking note of effects is closely related to the systemic concept of *recursivity*. Recursivity means that behaviour always provides information and elicits new behaviour. These feedback processes are an intrinsic part of human interactions and therefore also occur in therapy sessions. Whatever happens is influenced by what happened just before and influences what happened next.

> A simple example is of the husband who brings flowers home for his wife. His wife is not happy and says: 'I don't like lilies much.' The meaning ascribed to his wife's response determines to some extent the husband's response. He can become angry or stay quiet or feel dumb. He can return to the shop and buy another present. Whatever he does will have an impact on his wife. It provides her with information and her interpretation will influence her response (van Lawick & Savenije, 2014).

This circle of unending action and reaction is called a *feedback loop*. The more people are involved, as in families, the more complicated such feedback loops can become. Similar feedback loops are present in therapy. Therapy is a circular process of encounter, empathy, formulating hypotheses, intervening, evaluating, adjusting hypotheses and intervening again. In other words systemic therapy is feedback oriented. And the voice of the client is important here. This means that therapists have a conversation with clients, family members or partners about the effects of therapy and what the next step in the therapeutic process could be.

The importance of relationship and interaction

From the early years of systems theory the focus was on how people *react* to one another, on interactions, and the concept of communication proved useful. Communication always refers to verbal and non-verbal expressions. Communication theories then (Watzlawick et al., 1967) described sequences of interactions and patterns between people. The therapist looked for rules and disruptions in the way people react and how this contributes to the beginning and the sustaining of problems. This was innovative because the focus shifted from individuals to relationships.

Presently systemic therapy is still about *interactions* and *relationships*. The underlying idea is that people's functioning can be understood in the context of what happens between people rather than within them: the person's behaviour, emotions and meaning-making develop within relationships. Individual problems are hereby not ignored but the focus is shifted. The systemic practitioner takes an interest in all individuals who are part of a system. Individual people can experience problems differently and give different meanings to the same event. They do not share the same contexts and have different vulnerabilities and skills. All this influences their relationships and vice versa. Systemic practitioners take note of how people interpret and make meaning of other people's behaviour and respond based on these interpretations. These are called *patterns of communication.*

> An example of a communication pattern is Rose, the middle daughter of the Dufour family, who is feeling somewhat excluded and then withdraws because her mother appears to give more attention to her happy and active younger brother Thomas.

Such patterns can be very powerful.

> This pattern has existed for a while now and reinforces Rose's view and feeling that Thomas is favoured. When Rose withdraws, this opens up more space and care for Thomas. In turn this contributes to confirming and amplifying Rose's belief.

It is a pattern, without beginning or end. Everyone plays a part, but nobody is causing it. This is labelled a *vicious circle*. Vicious circles are perpetuated by what is called *punctuation*. People always see or experience the reality from a particular perspective or angle, or in other words, they structure or order the reality.

> Rose assumes that Thomas is favoured and that is why she's feeling so excluded. Thomas believes that Rose's aggrieved attitude affects the atmosphere, so he tries to lift the mood. Agnes feels rejected by Rose's sullen behaviour and prefers to focus on her happy-go-lucky son Thomas.

Each family member labels the behaviour of the other person as the cause of their own response. They apply a linear sequence to a circular process. Once such ordering is made, this becomes the frame for new information and reinforces the punctuation. This is fertile soil for punctuation quarrels or battles for truth.

> THOMAS: 'Don't be so cranky. What's the matter with you?'
> ROSE: 'What should be the matter? Don't you see how Mum has eyes only for you?'
> AGNES: 'Don't be so moody Rose, I love you all the same.'

And so begin endless discussions because of different punctuations, differing assumptions of cause-effect sequences that are perceived as true.

Stories matter

The systemic foundation principles discussed so far, namely the focus on context and exchanges, attention towards the difference between intent and effect, the focus on feedback processes and the importance of relationships and interactions, were founded in the early years of systemic practice. Around 1980 social constructionist narrative ideas were introduced (Anderson & Goolishan, 1988) that were strongly linguistically inspired. Next to interactions the therapist became interested in individual meaning-making and in people's stories, or *narratives* (Olthof, 2018). People make sense of themselves and the world through stories about themselves and others. They are influenced by the bigger and smaller narratives that circulate in society (White & Epston, 1990). Taking note of the stories people tell is another way to keep the focus on the interpersonal dimension and contexts. People who seek therapy often have a story about themselves or others that has become reduced. This is also called a poor or sparse story because of lack of variation.

> When Rose for instance can only see that she is missing out and that Thomas always has been and still is favoured by their mother, that story has lost much of its detail. This is influenced by many factors. What plays a role perhaps is that Thomas is the only son and the youngest, likes similar things as his mother and loves to joke around, while Rose is more serious. Another influence could be that their father withdraws regularly. Rose doesn't have children or a partner, but her sister and brother do. That makes her feel different, an outsider. Seeing that her single friends have good relationships with their parents strengthens her feeling that she is alone in this.

A poor narrative is often a *problem-saturated story* in which the person or others *are* the problem. That story comes with a specific plot: the person or others have to change.

> Rose's story could be: 'I have missed out, they don't understand me.' This could make her feel worthless. Her problem story could be: 'I am worthless' and her goal: 'to improve my self-confidence'.

All stories, including problem stories, stem from numerous small and big exchanges in people's lives. These can include comments from teachers, family members and friends but also the major stories in our society, the so-called *dominant discourses*, for example about what it means to be a man or a woman, about the importance of (great)parenthood and partnership, about what it means to be single. The systemic practitioner tries to change the structure of the story by shifting the idea of the person being the problem to the problem being the problem. The narrative systemic therapist Michael White (2007) described it as follows: "the problem becomes the problem, not the person" (p. 26). This is called *externalising* the problem. This approach allows for recognising the effects of the (individual) problem on relationships and identities.

> Rose could be described as someone who lacks confidence or someone who is cautious or scared of failing perhaps. In such description Rose seems to be the problem, while 'lack of self-confidence' is the problem. She has a problem, but she is not the problem. The interpersonal dimension is brought back into focus by exploring with Rose what this lack of confidence does to her, when it bothers her more and when less and how it affects her contacts with others.

Next the systemic practitioner tries to introduce alternative stories that are richer than the problem story. This is called thickening the story.

> For instance Agnes, Rose's mother, could talk about how to her, Rose has always been the independent one, someone who prefers to look after her own affairs. Her friends could point to how happily and fully Rose can participate in company.

Polyphony

In therapy it is of importance that everyone can express themselves and feel listened to, that the therapy is perceived as helpful and a context of polyphony is created in which significant people who are absent have a voice too.

Polyphony refers to the therapist's awareness that what people talk and not talk about is connected to a diversity of contexts. Polyphony also means bringing differences into focus. Voices can be harmonious or conflicting and some voices are louder than others. For example, for a couple that has just started living together, the voice of the partner's family can suddenly sound loud and clear ('that's not how you decorate your house') and contradict the voice of their close friends ('such a trendy original idea you guys came up with!'). Polyphony can create tension between partners: which of these voices are taken into consideration or ignored? Tension can also rise between a couple and their family or friends or within families. When people request professional help, the therapist's voice is added. Multiple voices echo within an individual too, some are loud, others softer, in harmony or in conflict. An *inner dialogue* is ever-present.

> Once a year Thomas and his family visit The Netherlands. They stay with Agnes and Dirk. Agnes takes this for granted and loves it. But the voice that says: 'how lovely' is contradicted by the voice that says: 'so much trouble and disruption, so many people and mess in the house'. Another voice says: 'I want to be the best host and mother-in-law' and another voice says anxiously: 'I can't talk with my daughter-in-law because she only speaks English.' Another anxious voice wonders whether her grandsons will enjoy Eindhoven and understand her Dutch enough.

A therapeutic attitude associated with polyphony is one of *multipartiality* or *multiple empathising*. The systemic practitioner has to be able to attune to the many voices that resound in a person and to speak with multiple people at the same time. There are always multiple therapeutic alliances. The practitioner is aware that they too belong to a professional care system with its own history and social embedding. The therapist listens actively and reflects on the diversity of voices that inform their own inner dialogue. Reflecting on the polyphonic inner dialogue, alone or with colleagues, can be helpful when the practitioner feels stuck (Rober, 2005, 2017).

Attention for process and change

People, relationships and contexts change. Individuals develop, families increase or decrease and change in composition, situations change, children leave school, people change jobs or partners. This all influences how we perceive ourselves and others, and our relationships. Individuals, families and partners don't live on an island but in changing societies. The social discourses in societies influence families, individuals and their self-perceptions too. Paying attention to dynamics and changeability implies a process-oriented vision and attention for the concept of time. This is reflected in the 'stages' in the family life cycle (Carter & McGoldrick, 2004; Falicov, 1988). It is the concept that family relationships change over time because people decide to live together, children are born, children grow older, children change school, eventually they leave the house. People retire, die or parents separate. Family transitions like this generate the need to let go (partially) of familiar ways of being and to replace old with new. Change can create pressure on existing relationships and can lead to crises and interpersonal or personal problems. In families and across generations relationships change over time too and again numerous factors are of influence. Relationships between men and women and parenting values of three generations ago are not the same as today's (de Regt, 2014). In the Dufour family we have seen that across several generations things can change, such as the education level, the socioeconomic status or the degree of urbanisation. This can cause problems or tensions in families.

> Thomas Dufour lives with his Ghanese wife Akua in Washington. They both have excellent jobs and Thomas and his family move in international circles. He can't share much with his parents about his life. He thinks of Dirk and Agnes as nice and unpretentious people. His father Dirk feels that distance. Dirk feels quickly irritated and tense when world politics are discussed; his son seems so opinionated then. At a time like that Thomas feels that his father doesn't really know what he does, reads or knows. Then being the clown feels more comfortable.

Changes in society and therefore in relationships, opportunities, expectations and dreams of people can evoke confusion too, for instance when someone looks at themselves with today's eyes in the context of the past.

> Dirk reproached himself later in life for having spent too much time at work and not enough with his wife and children. When he was working, he just accepted as his role being the breadwinner and often being away from home because of work. That was considered normal then, a good thing. But nowadays fathers are expected to do things differently. Dirk feels guilty, particularly when he sees what a caring father his son is.

However changes in the social and relational context can contribute to the decrease of problems, for example, when someone feels better after relocating, a change of jobs or a new relationship. The systemic practitioner remains aware of ongoing changes in relational and social contexts that influence the experiences of clients and professionals.

Focus on supports and resilience

From the beginning systemic therapists have emphasised the importance of sources of strength and support (Minuchin & Fishman, 1981). Resilience refers to processes in families enabling them to adjust to changing circumstances, to rise above problems, even learn or grow from adversity. Identified problems are therefore balanced with attention for non-problematic areas and for past and present sources of strength. The therapist also explores how clients dealt with problems in the past. Resilience is not a one-off phenomenon but a process with long-term and short-term perspectives (Hawley & de Haan, 1996; van Lawick & Savenije, 2014). A couple can move through several transitions without many problems, such as living together and having children, getting married, dealing with their adolescent daughter and so on. But they could get stuck at the stage when their children leave home. In each stage problems need to be overcome and relationships and roles need to be redefined. And people gather skills that could be helpful later during a more difficult transition. Attention for resilience is associated with the idea that solely focusing on problems or their causes is often unhelpful when trying to overcome the problems (De Shazer et al., 2021; Walsh, 2006; Watzlawick et al., 1974). Although therapists tend to focus on problems, the family's strengths rather than its vulnerabilities will determine whether therapy is helpful (Nichols & Schwartz, 2006). The systemic practitioner keeps an eye and ear open for when and how families do well and how they, then and now, despite the difficulties, were able to realise some of their dreams. What constitutes resilience is not fixed. It can be specific experiences, like positive memories they share, reading books, the comfort of a pet or skills such as the ability to reflect, be flexible, excel in sports or a hobby.

Akua and Thomas Dufour have had to overcome several problems as a couple. Their cultural backgrounds differ significantly which occasionally causes misunderstandings between them. The move to Washington required a huge adjustment. The pressures of work and travelling complicate family life. But the ease with which their sons integrated in school is a source of strength for both Akua and Thomas. Their shared drive to achieve and their interest in other cultures also provides strength in their relationship.

Next to resilience sources of support are important. Support systems can include friends or neighbours, a job well-liked, or being a member of a religious community. The systemic therapist enquires who or what the client can lean on. Sources of support can strengthen resilience. The loss or absence of supports, for instance, due to grief, migration or unemployment, can result in diminished resilience.

When they migrated to the USA Akua and Thomas had to leave their friends and families behind. People who provided support in the past are now somewhat alienated from them because they have been living abroad for so many years. In the meantime they have made new friends and have work colleagues who mean a lot. People in their networks share similar circumstances and understand the dilemmas they face as a family and as partners.

Resilience and sources of support can be considered buffering processes (van der Pas, 2014) or protective coats (Tjin A Djie & Zwaan, 2007). These are factors that protect people and relationships, support them in times of change and help them to manage the situation.

Professional help as co-construction

A systemic lens implies the principle that all reality is constructed. How someone perceives the world and the distinctions they make is not an absolute given but embedded in culture, time, society and community. Social constructionists state: reality is *co-created* by many (Gergen, 2015). This doesn't mean that reality doesn't exist or that reality can be reduced to 'it's only a construction'. It means though that what one calls reality is supported by institutions, practices and viewpoints. Reality as a construction is very real.

The systemic practitioner's hypotheses are not absolute truths either, but rather viewpoints and impressions supported in a specific community, perspectives of reality. This changes the role of the professional. They are not the experts who know *the* truth but are experts in continuing a dialogue in which alternative perspectives of the problems can be introduced. Their role is not to uncover the truth, but to unearth many truths. They explore those truths and enable discussion.

For the Dufour family this means that the therapist explores not one but several truths. The truths of Dirk, his children and grandchildren and the truths of his wife, friends and other family members. This isn't easy, particularly when perspectives are extremely different, or stories emerge about unsafe or crazy behaviour.

In conclusion

Systemic therapy can be considered co-constructing reality to generate different meanings for problems so that problems become less intense or prominent or disappear. It is a framework that guides the practitioner's actions. And action influences the framework as well. In a systemic framework the practitioner is not an outsider who observes and knows. The therapist is a *participant*, someone who co-creates reality. Clients and therapists together confirm, debunk or change their experience of reality. The presumption that practitioners always co-constructs makes them more aware of the effects of what they say or do and more attuned to feedback from clients. It results in therapists being curious about their clients' perspectives and meanings and how these came to be, are reinforced or debunked. They take note of contexts, connections, interactions and stories. They ensure that everyone feels heard and 'populate' the sessions with multiple voices. They highlight resilience and sources of support for people.

Exercise

Think of a conflict situation in a client's family or someone else's family. Describe this from the perspective of each individual and include each person's views about what is happening and the cause of the problems. What could each person's intentions be? What are the effects of each person's actions? Can you identify any patterns?

Chapter 3

The practitioner

Introduction

In therapeutic sessions the practitioner shows curiosity, interest and competency, but also needs "to be present as a 'self'" (Rivett & Street, 2009, p. 215). A therapist is not a blank canvas. Their responses to clients' stories and how they behave influence the conversation. The self and the context of the therapist influence their responses and choices. Practitioners have their own vulnerabilities and personal capabilities (Rivett & Street, 2009). They bring their own history, experiences and temperament to the therapeutic conversations, which contribute to their hypotheses and what they think, feel and do (Cecchin et al., 1994).

Jensen (2007) states that practitioners in the helping profession are not always aware of the role personal experiences play in the choices they make in a session. It is possible though they do realise this. For instance a therapist could notice they tend to argue with fathers, or they feel uncomfortable during a conversation but are not sure why. The influences the therapist notices require specific skills. They need to be able to reflect on the effects of clients on themselves, on their own contribution to the progression of the therapy, on their own pitfalls and strengths and connect these to different contextual influences. The practitioner may need to discuss these influences with clients or decide whether to do something with it.

In this chapter we highlight some important contexts that are influential in a practitioner's life: their family of origin, life experiences, current living situation, socio-cultural contexts such as colour, ethnicity, social class, gender, age, religion, the organisation they work for and the influence of societal developments. These areas help the professional in reflecting on how they function.

The family of origin

Therapists generally accept that the family of origin they grew up with and their childhood experiences are significant influences in their personal and

DOI: 10.4324/9781003272038-3

professional life. This refers to the influence of the family history, the family relationships, their own role and position as a child and the circumstances that have contributed to resilience or to problems. What the practitioner takes away from all this is firstly behaviour or the so-called 'family scripts', the family's scripted way of doing things, and secondly specific meanings, the 'family stories'. The family stories refer to the family's account of their actions in the past, what was spoken about in the family, what was said about the family and how did the family thinks and talks about issues (Byng-Hall, 1995).

Vivian is a young family counsellor with little experience. She has noticed in conversations with parents, usually older than her, that they regularly ask for her advice and impart to her a position of authority. An older colleague has quite the opposite experience. Rob, who has much more experience, feels immediately small and dumb in such conversations and often feels he is not taken seriously. Rob and Vivian talk about their roles in their respective families of origin. Both are the youngest child. Vivian's mother died when she was 14 years old. Her older brother had left home by then, and she became her father's support and advisor. Rob is the youngest of five children and felt he never transcended his position as the youngest. What he said was never taken too seriously by his older siblings or his parents.

Vivian and Rob had the same position at home, but completely different roles. Both their family scripts play a role in their current functioning as practitioners. How they subsequently behave and what its effect is, can vary greatly.

Vivian has noticed that sometimes she feels rather uncomfortable in that position, particularly when she is dealing with problems she doesn't have personal experience with. She now tries to be less 'authoritarian'. It helps, she finds, to ask explorative questions. Recently she mentioned to a family her inexperience with a particular problem. That was terribly frightening, but it turned out well.

Colleagues have often said to Rob that in sessions he seems to pay more attention to the youngest child in the family, giving that one more space to talk. They believe this can offer a wonderful yet complicated challenge for families. Rob also empathises with insecure fathers. Just recently he was surprised to receive a compliment from parents with whom he felt quite insecure, for his calm demeanour and how at ease they feel with him.

Many aspects of personal family histories resonate in how therapists view problems and how they respond. A professional can feel negative towards clients who bicker often and intensely because their parents did the same, or the therapist is not accustomed to quarrelling because it never happened at home. It is important that practitioners reflect on these family scripts to understand better what they value and what constitutes the foundation of their work. It provides opportunities to experiment, to try out different roles and behaviours in support of the therapeutic process.

Life experience

Like everyone else, therapists draw many of their beliefs and ideas from personal experiences.

> Vivian collects her clients from the waiting room. This is their second appointment. Mrs Peterson is referred for low mood. She has had breast cancer. This has been treated but she hasn't bounced back. In the individual intake session Mrs Peterson complained about her lack of energy and the lack of support from her husband and children. Vivian asked whether her husband could join them. He did, and last time they spoke about the influence of the cancer on both their lives. Vivian thought him very supportive, quite different from her own father who, when her mother was seriously ill, ignored the illness completely. From experience she knows that the illness disrupted everything at home and she has a lot of empathy for Mrs Peterson. She would like to include the children in the sessions because she remembers how difficult it was knowing so little about her mother's disease. As children she and her brother were excluded from it all. When Vivian thinks about it, she decides it is best to ask both parents what they each think about inviting the children along.

Rivett and Street (2009) describe how therapists' empathy relates to their own experiences of unhappiness, understanding that relational distress can have an impact and having experienced some painful events themselves. Based on their own experiences, practitioners make meaning of clients' feelings and experiences. One therapist believes that some emotions need to be tolerated because they are part of life, while the other therapist believes a solution is needed. The practitioner may have experienced in their own life history that resilience and trust in recovery are important ingredients. Each professional brings their own beliefs to therapy: 'when there is violence in the relationship, it's better to separate' or 'in relationship therapy secrets have to be revealed'. Personal norms can be backed by a team or supported by a theoretical framework or widely accepted in society. It is a challenge when the therapist realises their values belong to 'the context of the therapist', perhaps not endorsed by clients and often not helpful in therapy. In that case shelving personal opinions and asking contextual questions about these themes can be a way forward.

The cultural and social embedding of the professional

Mental health and social care practitioners are expected to work with people from diverse backgrounds and different cultures. However therapists are culturally and socially embedded too. Burnham (2012) is a systems therapist who is interested in difference and diversity. He uses the acronym GGRRAAACCEEESSS for the different dimensions that can be at play: gender, geography, race, religion, age, ability, appearance, class, culture, ethnicity, education, employment, sexuality, sexual orientation and spirituality. Sociologist Verkuyten (1999) calls this social ordering. When you hail from the province of Brabant in the south of The Netherlands, you belong to the group 'Brabanders' (geography). Most Brabanders used to be Catholic. If you were a protestant (religion) you belonged to a minority, the 'protestant Brabanders'. Systems therapist Falicov (2004, 2012) has published extensively about diversity. She describes how everyone has their own *cultural niche*: a combination of all the social orderings one is part of. In that sense each conversation with a client, family or couple is a meeting of cultures.

> Maria is a systemic practitioner. It is the first session with 25-year-old Zeynep. Maria and Zeynep are of similar age. Zeynep is Iraqi-Belgian. Her whole family lives here. She is the youngest, is not in a relationship and lives at home. She referred herself because she is anxious and depressed. She took sick leave from work. Zeynep feels she is the slave of the family, everyone asks for her help. Particularly her mother calls on her, but she has to babysit her brother's children too. She is scared to say anything. After the intake Maria muses that Zeynep becoming more independent and perhaps leaving home could be a good therapy goal. It seems appropriate for Zeynep's age. A colleague however questions this. She suggests assessing a bit more first, perhaps make a genogram. This could clarify how Zeynep is embedded in her family, what her goals are and whether what Maria perceives as normal is shared by Zeynep. Although Maria finds this cultural intervention a bit over the top, she decides to take up the suggestion. She needs to practise making genograms anyway.

Socio-cultural differences can clash. The values of families and family members can be incompatible with significant values of the therapist. This can lead to uncomfortable confrontations and position the practitioner on the horns of insoluble dilemmas.

Ingrid has been supporting a couple, Jerry and Rita, who are about the same age as herself. The goal of the intervention is to get their lives back on track because it can be quite chaotic at times. In the previous session they told Ingrid that Rita had unexpectedly fallen pregnant and the couple was at a loss as to what to do next: have an abortion because their lives are complicated enough as they are, or keep the child because Rita is eager to have children. Ingrid notices feeling uncomfortable around this topic. She clams up. She knows this is related to her religious beliefs. Abortion is for her a sin and prohibited. Her instinct is that she needs to discuss with the couple not to have an abortion. But she is aware this does not fit with her role and task as a therapist. She knows she can't talk about their considerations. Is she the right person to help this couple?

Therapists are limited in what they can cope with. When big or insurmountable differences in important areas of life appear as described above, it is appropriate to question whether the therapy can continue with this particular therapist. Immediately this raises the question whether this is an option within the organisation. And how to discuss this with Rita and Jerry? In a nutshell suddenly new dilemmas and questions arise. This concurs with the issue of when and how to discuss differences, who needs to canvass the topic and what does a therapist disclose about their own background.

As part of his job Rob frequently speaks with parents. Often these conversations are about problems the children have or the problems the parents have with their children. Regularly parents ask Rob whether he has children. He has indeed: a son and a daughter. He then tells them something about his children. What he doesn't say is that he lives with a male partner. They both are the children's parents, preceded by a long and complicated procedure. He believes his living situation is unfamiliar to most parents he works with. They could ask him all sorts of questions which he would find too personal as a therapist. He is similarly selective with colleagues. Although his decisions around this suit him, sometimes he feels guilty for keeping something important about himself secret.

What a practitioner tells clients is partly a professional position and partly a personal choice: one therapist will disclose more about their personal life than another. Just as the one family will ask more questions about the therapist than other families do: the therapist's age, whether they are married, have children or have personal experience with the problems in focus. Professionals can say something about it or not. The relationship between the clients and the therapist influences the extent of the therapist disclosing personal information. This is also the case for socio-cultural differences.

Burnham (2012) and Falicov (2004, 2012) consider it the therapist's responsibility to name socio-cultural differences at the start of therapy and to clarify that these can be discussed. Other practitioners prefer to wait until differences emerge in the sessions. This is the same for clients too: some clients feel seen and acknowledged when the influence of social and cultural backgrounds is discussed. Others could have the impression that the focus is always on being different and feel discriminated. The therapist may discuss socio-cultural differences and personal experiences or not. Whatever they do it remains important they stay alert for the effects on the therapeutic process.

The influence of training, vocation and organisation

Each theoretical framework, training, vocation and organisation where practitioners work harbours assumptions about mental health and mental illness, what is and what isn't appropriate for therapeutic interventions, how problems need to be dealt with and by whom. Boeckhorst (2014) calls this *frames*, a useful term. A frame can be seen as a lens or a sieve through which situations, interactions and problems are filtered (Coyne, 1985; Goffman, 1974). The frame of systemic therapy consists of looking at relationships, context, patterns of interaction and meaning-making. This is a different lens from looking for individual causes of problems.

A youth team consists of psychiatrists, psychologists, family therapists and child therapists. Different views and interpretations tumble over one another. Molly, who holds mainly family sessions and supports parents, often feels she is in contention with individual child diagnoses, descriptions of parents in terms of pathology or lack of child management skills. Her perspective is that parents find themselves in vulnerable positions which her team doesn't seem to take into consideration. She has to battle for the inclusion of parents as important partners in their journey. Everyone seems to know 'what's in the child's best interest'. In recent years the organisation has been restructured. Her profession has lost esteem and the voices of the psychiatrist and the main practitioner have gained importance. However her job has not become easier. It makes her feel hopeless at times.

Collegial frames can clash and practitioners may notice that the organisation's frame doesn't fit the frame of their training or professional group (Boeckhorst, 2014). Organisations and funding systems can become barriers for professionals who prefer to work systemically. Such clashes can have a negative impact on the professional identity of therapists. Frames are changeable too. Therapists need to adjust regularly to a changing professional landscape with changing procedures, routines and guidelines because of new insights, societal changes or political decisions. That is never easy. For the professional it is important to explore to what extent inconsistency between the frames of the organisation and the therapist fosters or hinders connection with clients.

Society as context

Beliefs exist in society about what is normal and what is (un)healthy. Those ideas have an effect on what therapists believe is normal or ordinary and relate in principle to everything they are faced with. For instance what is considered healthy or sick amidst the tendency towards an increase in individual diagnoses and more pressure to treat? Various beliefs circulate about couple relationships, men and women, raising children, diet, punishment, how long grief may last, how people are to behave after separation and so on. Those beliefs have changed considerably in the last few years, in a relatively short period of time when it comes to societal changes. Changes don't make beliefs less powerful. They keep a status of truth and influence what practitioners consider normal and take for granted. The position of children is an example. In the early years of systemic therapy, the focus was on parental authority and its reinstatement. In later years parents were expected to negotiate with their children and to reach consensus about what is acceptable and what isn't. In place of disciplinary strategies such as taking away privileges or temporary time-out the most valued discipline technique became: talk, talk and talk (Brinkgreve, 2004).

Vivian is meeting for the first time two parents and their two children, Nico who is 15 years old and Sara who is 7. The parents have been married for many years, but a few months ago, the father decided to leave his wife. While he is establishing a new life elsewhere, the mother is still in shock. In the session they address the relationship of the children with their father. Nico doesn't want to see his father and Sara doesn't want to visit him without Nico. Nico never replies to his father's messages and Sara doesn't respond to his cards, letters and invitations. Mother too has tried to talk sense into Nico but to no avail. Halfway through the session Vivian realises she is doing the same as the parents: she has been trying to convince Nico that restoring contact with his father is in his best interest. She's unsuccessful. Vivian becomes aware she's aligning herself with what is expected by society and by the parents: it's important that children maintain contact with both parents and Nico needs to be convinced of this. She is left feeling as helpless as the parents.

Beliefs and perspectives influence the focus of the therapist and the pressures, opportunities and barriers they experience. This can be illustrated with another societal evolution, the idea of 'a quick fix'. The belief that everything can be fixed, controlled or managed makes people expect that problems can be resolved quickly with the correct diagnosis and treatment. Often this generates excessive expectations of professional help and medication.

Rob works in an organisation to which many couples are referred, like Irene (64) and Martin (64). Irene sought help because of relationship problems. She finds interactions with Martin increasingly difficult and thinks he may be autistic. The general practitioner made the referral and the couple was on the waiting list for a while. In the meantime Irene has browsed the internet about autism and demands an assessment. Martin strongly objects because he doesn't believe he is autistic. Rob feels under enormous pressure. He would like to explore why and when the idea of autism surfaced. He wonders whether the approach of retirement and what this could look like plays a role. But Irene is not interested in Rob's hypothesis. She wants a diagnosis because only then the problems can be worked on swiftly.

For mental health and social care practitioners it requires skill to manage such pressures and expectations and simultaneously be aware of personal beliefs.

The internal dialogue

Rober (2005) describes how during a therapy session a continuous dialogue takes place between multiple voices inside the therapist. The internal dialogue relates to the happenings in the conversation and the associations and feelings these elicit in the therapist. Which associations arise is connected to the relationship context. In a therapeutic conversation between a Caucasian therapist and a Surinam family skin colour will play a role. In a conversation with a religious family religion as context will be more prominent. How and which issues are brought to the fore is also related to the practitioner as a human being and their contexts of influence. What they focus on, what they say and do, is the result of internal considerations. These considerations are not 'neutral' but associated with personal factors and the contexts in which the therapist moves. Whether this aligns with the clients cannot be determined beforehand.

An important skill of systemic practitioners is being aware and reflecting on the diversity of personal contexts that could play out in sessions. In systemic jargon this is called *personal contextual reflection*. This may be a natural ability or one the therapist gains in training and through life. Some therapists find it easier to engage in contextual reflection than others. Input from colleagues, peers or supervision can be helpful. Perhaps 'others' are crucial for contextual reflection because it surely happens that a professional is unaware of the influence of particular contexts. Polyphony can be regarded as a process in which many different voices need to be included.

In conclusion

In this chapter we described how a therapist works and lives amidst a spectrum of contexts that influence to a greater or lesser degree how a conversation evolves. Therapists' personal background and history, their living situation, life experience, socio-cultural niche and profession play a part in the therapeutic conversations, as do their professional training and work environment. Practitioners are also influenced by societal developments. All these influences affect what a therapist does, notices or experiences and what is neglected or remains invisible. Therefore they need to reflect on their own practice and the personal contexts that contribute to their responses in therapy. The therapist can then adjust their actions accordingly. Finally the practitioner also considers whether to bring personal experiences into the conversation and how best to do this.

Exercise

Draw a learning-life line from top of the page to the bottom. Indicate chronologically on the line learning experiences that have been important in your life, that influenced the way you see relationships and families or that have changed your view of the world.

Write down who played a role in this: family, friends, teachers, TV, idols, books, animals et cetera. How does this influence you in your work?

Chapter 4

Something needs to change

Introduction

When do people access mental health or social care? When do such services become involved in people's lives? When is professional help and support, whether mandated or voluntary, offered? What may be grounds to access systemic therapy? These questions are addressed in this chapter and illustrated by the Dufour family.

> Vera and Kira are at a loss.
>
> Six years ago Vera gave birth to her son Benny. Vera and Kira are very happy with their boy, but have increasing problems with Kira's daughter Ratna, who is 14 years old. Ratna has regular anger outbursts during which she destroys things or hurts Benny. Everyone thinks she's jealous. Kira and Vera have tried everything to calm Ratna down: they have given her extra attention and they have been strict, but nothing has made a difference.
>
> Kira divorced John when she met Vera. Ratna was four years old at the time. After the divorce John picked up Ratna regularly for outings. Ratna has wonderful memories of those times. But she also remembers that he often didn't show up even when he'd promised. A couple of years ago John left for Curaçao. He seldom makes contact.
>
> Vera and Kira's relationship with donor Jaco has become complicated. They had agreed that Vera and Kira would make all the decisions, including about Jaco's role in Benny's life. Kira adopted Benny and Jaco was to visit Benny regularly. But he's become more insistent on his role as a father. He wants to spend more time with Benny, take him to his family and on holidays. Because of the fights with Ratna he believes home is not safe enough for Benny. He said to Vera and Kira he would like Benny to live with him for longer periods. Vera and Kira objected strongly. It caused tension between the couple and influenced their partner and parent relationship. Kira is considering leaving Vera because the tension is too much to deal with; perhaps it would be better for Ratna.
>
> School has concerns about Ratna too. She is often aggressive and truants regularly. The school has asked the counsellor for assistance. After consultation with Ratna and Kira, the counsellor decides to refer them to a therapist who is more familiar with these kinds of problems.

DOI: 10.4324/9781003272038-4

Different times, different people

Both today and in the past people request professional help with mental health or social problems of individuals, partners or their children. However how problems are understood changes. Presently people have different ambitions or opportunities than a hundred years ago and family relationships are not the same. Society has an impact on people and their relationships. How problems are labelled has an effect on the way people understand themselves and others. In that sense, labels are never neutral.

de Swaan (1981) states that within changing relationships people decide 'which difficulties are grave, and which are intolerable, which ones must be lived with and which ones can be remedied and how. Some suffering may be conceived of as a punishment, some as an ordeal, a catharsis, a disgrace, a token of election, some as a consequence of fate, or of stupidity, some as merely sham. It wasn't until the past century that people came to describe some of the difficulties they encounter in living with themselves and with others as psychic problems' (de Swaan, 1981, p. 359).

de Swaan describes some social changes that have contributed to the start of a growing group of people, mainly women, who suffer from agoraphobia; this is the fear of going outside, of entering shops or of walking across crowded squares and places. It was an almost non-existent phenomenon in the beginning of the 19th century because women were subject to socially endorsed restrictions on their movement in public. They hardly left the house and if they went out, they were accompanied by a chaperone or family member. Modesty and domesticity were expected of them. The anxiety of the outside world wasn't seen as abnormal, to the contrary. Such restrictions of movement have now disappeared and women depend less on their husband or partner. But, de Swaan says, similar emotions once associated with movement restrictions are discernible in current agoraphobic reactions. But a socially accepted motive is absent, leaving an inexplicable and individual fear.

de Swaan describes how diagnoses, like agoraphobia, are embedded in broad societal developments and changing social relationships. This applies to other areas too. For instance, in the second part of the previous century a woman who devoted her life to caring for husband and children was the norm. Today such commitment is frowned upon. A woman who is considerate and devotes herself to others is now seen as someone who lacks boundaries and unable to look after herself. This could become a diagnosis of dependent personality and is related to the pressure on people to be independent, autonomous and successful.

In Kira and Vera's family the extra pressure to be good parents is connected to their being 'not a run of the mill family' and adds to the tension between the couple. Social pressures and relationship expectations, also influenced by messages dispersed by media, create new problem areas. These social and relational interplays are important in systemic therapy.

Seeking help

Over time problems and how problems are labelled have changed considerably, similarly the how and where of seeking help. Before professional help existed, people turned to religious leaders, visionaries, witch doctors or other esteemed advisers. Help and advice were also expected from the family, particularly when they were well off, or from dignitaries or church charities. From the 19th century help and support became more organised and mandated by industrial and government organisations (de Swaan, 1988). The motives were two-fold: to support poor people and to maintain the social order. Religious norms and civil ideals were guiding principles (van Os & Boerma, 2015). Families who didn't follow the norms were depicted in cartoons as chaotic, alcoholic, aggressive and adulterous. Remnants of those norms still exist in our current society.

In the meantime, professional help has changed significantly to being mainly secular and professionalised, offering a wide spectrum of approaches for individual problems, relationship problems and problems in families. In general it is now considered the responsibility of the government to provide this kind of help. Attitudes towards professional help have changed as well. But helping services have changed quicker than the taboo on asking for help. Until the second half of the 20th-century people were expected to deal with their own issues. Asking for help was considered a weakness. Presently in The Netherlands and Belgium many people find it acceptable to access professional help or therapy. For some groups in the population such as the elderly, older migrants or refugees from countries where mental health and social assistance is less available, the barrier remains significant.

The normalisation of a pathway to professional help is for most people connected with the belief that well-being, having a good relationship and lovely children is possible when enough effort is made with the right means (Dehue, 2014). People are less accepting of adversity as part of life and when personal, relationship or societal problems arise they soon look for a way to resolve the problems (Alon & Omer, 2006; De Wachter, 2014; Verhaeghe, 2014). This 'quick fix' ideology is strongly supported by the media in multiple ways. Consequently the norm related to asking for help has changed: people are expected to do something about their problems! People who struggle are bombarded with advice about what to do and how and what should help.

When Kim, Dirk and Agnes's daughter, complains about her sleep problems she receives multiple pieces of advice: a self-help book on positive thinking, herbal remedies, homeopathic remedies, more exercise, yoga, mindfulness training, aura reading, psychotherapy, sleeping pills, assessment at the sleep clinic, relationship therapy and more.

The pathway to professional help

Even with the growing pressure to address our own problems, many still hesitate to take the step towards professional help. Most people talk with friends, family or colleagues and try a few suggestions. It's not until they have exhausted their own abilities and resources that seeking professional help is considered. For some people it is normal to access therapy. Once the decision is made, the issue arises of how to choose from the various options on offer. The choice is often made coincidentally. A friend or family member speaks highly about a particular counsellor, a haptotherapist, a holistic healer or a psychotherapist. Perhaps the GP initiated the referral to a therapist or an organisation they have had positive experiences with or where there is no waiting list.

Ratna's school counsellor refers Vera and Kira to Marian, who happens to work systemically. The school counsellor often refers to Marian and never heard of complaints. The pathway to professional help is also connected to someone's social environment (Hoeymans et al., 2010). Every choice, accidentally or not, leads to completely different outcomes. A person can end up in a mental health service or private practice, in a place where only individual therapy is offered or where the whole family is always included or where a variety of treatment options is available. The focus may be on physical and medical aspects or psychiatric factors. It can be a place where practitioners keep a close eye (or not) on safety and pedagogic skills and so on.

Most mental health and social care services apply an individual perspective: they focus on individual diagnoses and individual solutions.

In Kira and Vera's family, for example, there are complex problems at multiple levels. This often leads to one or more individual intervention trajectories. Ratna for instance can be identified as the main problem and receive individual therapy. She could be referred to group therapy for anger management, like a social skills training for adolescents. In that case one or both parents are often included by offering separate parenting support. Kira can be offered individual therapy to talk about her own emotional and relational problems. Vera too can be treated individually, while Benny may be considered for play therapy.

In The Netherlands when specialised and intensive help is needed, an individual diagnosis for a child or adult is required before the intervention is reimbursed. A similar trend is noticeable in Belgium. It is rarely suggested that everyone involved meets first to talk about the concerns and what could be helpful. This is strange in a way, because problems never happen to one person in isolation, regardless of these being social, financial or psychiatric problems or physical illness. Although many care providers note the importance of including the family, the reality is different. From a systemic perspective clients' problems are always interwoven with relational patterns, possibilities and obstacles. A systemic practitioner will regard Ratna's problematic behaviour in a relational context, such as the demands from school, her girlfriends, her father who left and barely communicates, her mother who chose to be with a woman, her adopted little brother who appears to be the golden child and the tension and fights she witnesses between her mother and Vera and Jaco. All those complex relational dynamics influence one another.

Including others

As evident in the example of Vera and Kira, a person can coincidentally be referred to a systemic practitioner. However a potential client can make a well-considered choice to work with a systemic practitioner, particularly when it comes to involving significant others. Systemic therapy is an obvious choice for relationship problems or family problems. Other complex relational problems can benefit from systemic intervention too. When multiple professionals are working with one family, each with their own view and goals, misunderstandings or stagnancy in the intervention can occur. A systemic practitioner will be aware of this and has the skills to organise for instance network meetings. Another indication to include close others is when the problems have significant consequences for family members, for example when dealing with an unpredictable progressive illness and the person becoming increasingly dependent on their environment, such as MS, Parkinson's, dementia or cancer (Gualthérie van Weezel and Jong, 2014). Even in the case of individual mental health problems or psychiatric problems systemic intervention can be indicated. Professional help is then required and consultation with loved ones. Systemic therapy offers family members or partners an opportunity to discuss concerns with each other, think about feasible supports and who takes responsibility for what. Changing the setting of individual therapy to include others can be helpful as illustrated below by therapist Milan, who works at a GP practice.

Kim consults her GP about burn-out symptoms. The pressure from her work at the hospital is getting to her. She is home alone a lot. Vera and Ken have left home. To Kim and Tony this feels like an enormous transition. Tony has been exercising more. He is trying to encourage Kim to do the same, but she can't do it. Kim is also worried about her parents who need more help. She feels that her brother and sister leave most of this to her. The worries swirl in Kim's head, making her feel more and more miserable. She is not sleeping well. The GP decides to refer her to the mental health practitioner associated with the GP practice. Milan, the therapist, suggests they explore the theme of work pressure and how Kim could manage this differently. He also suggests having a joint conversation with Tony. 'Your worries exist beyond you. It could work better when you and your husband explore together how things could improve with you and between you. Together you're stronger,' he says. Kim becomes tearful, the word 'together' touched a nerve. She feels how she's missing 'together', how alone she feels. About two weeks later Tony and Kim have a session with Milan.

Milan chooses to have conversations with Kim *and* Tony because he knows that a problematic relationship could undermine people's physical and mental well-being, while a good relationship can provide resilience in dealing with problems.

In conclusion

The pathway to professional help and the type of intervention that emerges are related to the time and the context in which the request for help is formulated, to referral procedures of GPs and other referrers and to other random factors. People live in relationships and contexts. This foundation principle of systemic intervention offers many possibilities to understand people's problems, include others when needed and find starting points to ease the concerns.

Exercise

Have there been instances in your personal life that you've had contact with professional help for psychological issues? If not ask someone who has.

What preceded your action? What kind of advice was offered by people around you? What tipped the balance for you to seek professional help? How did the helping journey evolve? How do you see it in hindsight?

Were family members or others involved in the therapeutic process? If so how was that for you? If this was not the case would you have liked that to have happened?

What did you take from this into your work?

Chapter 5

The start of the working alliance

Introduction

An important aspect of successful therapy is the working relationship between the therapist and the client. The practitioner needs to attend to this from the first contact with the client. But what exactly do therapists need to have in mind? In this chapter four important areas are discussed: the context of the request for help, the material and physical environment, negotiating a therapeutic framework and creating a safe space to talk. A working alliance can be strengthened and lay a foundation for effective intervention when the practitioner takes into consideration what those factors mean and how they affect clients.

The context of the request for help

The first meeting between client and therapist is for the client usually not the first contact with helping services. Clients may have a history of earlier contacts with social or mental health care. They are referred or took the initiative themselves, and they have expectations. Before the first therapeutic meeting, clients have some knowledge about the procedures and the rules of the service. They received an appointment letter and perhaps completed some questionnaires. They may have been assessed by another professional before they meet with the therapist who will work with the client. All those points of contact have an influence on the therapeutic process and support or undermine the alliance the therapist seeks to establish with the client. The same welcoming ritual can make some clients feel welcomed and others reprimanded. They had the impression that the professional is taking their problems seriously or feel not understood at all. In the first conversation with the client the systemic practitioner will explore the context of the referral and its effects. This isn't an easy task and is complicated by the increased pressure on practitioners to be efficient with time and money (Nagtegaal & Van Stratum, 2017). Starting the first therapeutic session with immediately exploring the problems could lead to *contextual blindness*. The therapist then misses some important contextual factors that play a

DOI: 10.4324/9781003272038-5

part in how clients talk about their problems, whether they feel understood and how motivated they are for intervention.

The effect of procedures

Mental health and social care services and private practices have referral processes in place outlining how clients can be referred and are to be invited. This, together with the information provided or requested, influences the shaping of the working relationship. Protocols and procedures influence what clients think and feel about the service and the help offered. Long waiting times can scare people off or make them angry. The service can be perceived as bureaucratic or having little concern for their problems. Practitioners can come across as being thorough and professional. The client can be relieved that arrangements for therapy needn't be made straight away. Procedures influence the client's expectations of that first conversation. For instance because of prior questionnaires clients could assume that further assessment is unnecessary, and therapy is to start immediately. Or they prefer to disclose information in person at the first meeting because completing a questionnaire feels too intense.

The same applies to written invitations. Tone, content and language communicate how clients are perceived and approached and influence the subsequent conversations.

> You have been referred to our service because of behaviour problems of your son Dicky Storm. We would like to invite you, his parents, to discuss with us what the problems are and what interventions would be the most appropriate.

In this example the practitioners present themselves as experts who offer various interventions for the problem.

> You have referred yourself to our mental health service. We would like to have a conversation with you to hear what your concerns are and explore together how we can support you. We would like to meet as many family members as possible who are involved in your concerns. You can decide who you would like to bring with you to the first appointment.

Here the professionals present themselves as collaborative.

On 26 September our service received a referral from the police because of concerns about your daughter.

> I would like to visit you at home on 6 October at 2.30 pm to discuss these concerns. If you wish you can ask another professional or someone from your family or friends to be present.

In this letter the professional presents themselves as controlling.

The invites evoke various worlds and expectations to which clients will have different responses. The same can be said for other service procedures. Therapists who work in a mental health or social care service usually have no influence on referral procedures and somehow need to position themselves in relation to these. Having the awareness that these procedures influence the working alliance, the therapist can instigate in the first session a discussion about the clients' experiences of the intake process.

TINA: 'I thought it all took a very long time.'

THERAPIST BRENDA: 'I can understand that. I'd prefer to make an appointment immediately when people ask for help because they're calling for a reason. I know my colleagues agree. Unfortunately, we receive more referrals than we can respond to, so people have to wait for a while.'

TOM (TINA'S PARTNER): 'Well, I thought it wasn't that bad. When I had to see a medical specialist, I had to wait much longer and we're not an emergency, are we?'

BRENDA: 'It appears that you are confident that you can still manage together for a while, that's great to hear. Can you say a bit more about that, that you think that you're not an emergency? And (Brenda addresses Tina) can you say why the waiting felt so long for you?'

The initial invitation

When clients refer over the phone and get to speak immediately with the therapist, as happens in private practice, they often launch into talking about their problems and what is causing them.

KIRA: 'I'm ringing to make an appointment because my daughter Ratna's school advised me to do so. My daughter is very rebellious. I think some things are happening at school. She also finds it hard that her father is so far away and doesn't have much time for her and ...'

THERAPIST MARIAN: 'I am sorry to interrupt but I'm hearing that the school requested you to contact us because of concerns about your daughter Ratna. Shall we make an appointment so we can discuss together what the concerns are and explore whether we can assist you?'

Marian is choosing her words carefully to signal to Kira she has listened to her. She proposes how and where to discuss the concerns further. In the phone conversation she explores who needs to be present at that first meeting. This depends on the referral reason, the person who requests help, the therapist's judgement and the client's culture or living situation. For instance a nephew who lives with the family can be a significant voice and needs to be involved in family sessions. In other families, cultures or communities, grandparents, other family members or religious leaders such as an imam or an elder can be figures of authority. It is vital to explore during that first contact how significant these people are, what they think about the concerns and whether they need to be invited (Jessurun, 2010; Jessurun & Warring, 2018; Midori Hanna & Brown, 2018).

> MARIAN CONTINUES: 'Does Ratna know that you are seeking help for her?'
> 'YES', KIRA REPLIES: 'She knows that I am ringing, but she doesn't want to come to an appointment by herself.'

While Ratna knows about the referral, this is not always the case. Children don't always know that their parents are accessing professional help or a partner is unaware that the other partner made inquiries about couple counselling. Family members aren't always in agreement about seeking professional help or one party is unwilling to take part in therapy sessions. This too deserves exploration. The beliefs of significant others influence the intervention. Making space for hesitations is part of creating multiple working alliances (Rober, 2002, 2017). When people have agreed to invite other family members, the therapist will enquire in the joint session about each person's response to this proposal.

> When Milan suggests that Kim brings her husband next time, several thoughts cross her mind: it would be nice to not have to resolve everything myself, but also: what will Tony think of this, he probably thinks I am nagging him. On the way home Kim has more doubts: what can and cannot be said in the session? She's uncertain for quite a while, but eventually she invites Tony to come along next time.
>
> Tony doesn't mind going with Kim, but he doesn't say anything further about it. He too is worried: what did Kim talk about, why do I need to go, is there something wrong between us? Will the therapist listen to my side of the story?
>
> After greeting the couple in the waiting room, Milan attends immediately to the issue: 'Kim, I've had a meeting with you while Tony, we don't know each other. I suggested you come together because in my field of work I believe that worries are not a solitary experience. When someone in the family has a problem, the people who live with that person have the problem too. Usually they are concerned as well, and I like working with partners and family members.'

After this introduction Milan can explore carefully what Kim has shared with Tony about their first meeting. This is a first step in creating a working alliance with everyone involved. Direct questions at the start of the session such as: 'Did you talk at home about our first meet-ing?' could feel like an interrogation for the clients, intensify the tension and create distance. Kim and Tony didn't discuss anything, Kim was too scared to talk and Tony was too scared to ask. If Milan had asked them what they had discussed at home, both would have probably felt caught and blamed. Every question is an intervention, there's no such thing as a neutral question.

The referral

People are commonly referred by another practitioner or their GP as was the case with Kim. To address the complex issues in Vera and Kira's fam-ily the school enlisted initially a school counsellor who referred them to another service. The referral itself and how things progress from there have specific meanings for clients; they can be a help or a hindrance for the alliance (Midori Hanna & Brown, 2018; Selvini Palazolli, 1985; Selvini Palazolli et al., 1980b). For instance when the referrer sings the praises of the therapist as one of the best they know, it immediately creates high expectations. When a therapist feels stuck with a family and refers to a colleague, that negative experience can influence the alliance with the new therapist (Brok, 1990). Clients who are referred always wonder what the referrer believes the issue is and why they have been referred to this spe-cific service or practitioner. A referral can make people feel taken seri-ously or dismissed. Clients can be referred by child protection services: 'otherwise we need to consider taking other measures'; by school: 'other-wise we can't continue with your son'; by their partner: 'if you don't come with me now, I want a divorce'. This all needs attention. When the school counsellor refers, as in Ratna's case, it is possible that the belief exists within the school that problematic behaviour of a child is caused by the home situation, while the parents believe their child is not well supported at school. The therapist can become stuck between parents who are convinced the school is failing and the school counsellor who believes something is not quite right at home.

Vera and Kira wonder why the school counsellor doesn't find out first what's happening for Ratna, what is worrying her so much. Kira believes that stuff is happening at school too. The school counsellor has a full diary and finds the situation with Ratna too complex. She is relieved to hand it over to a colleague who really needs to work with the family, because that's where the problems are.

Each person attributes meaning to the referral. If the therapist ignores what the referral means for each person, they align themselves with the school's view without knowing what the family members think. Inviting the referrer to (a part of) the first meeting can help to clarify the meaning of the referral for the clients and the professionals. This can foster the transition and make space for a constructive alliance with the new therapist.

Previous experiences with professional help

Some clients have a short or long history of contacts with professional services. Clients who found prior interventions helpful will be more open to a new trajectory than clients with negative and disappointing experiences. Attending to this is crucial for the therapeutic alliance. Clients and therapists together can explore what has been helpful or unhelpful, the various opinions in this respect, what clients absolutely don't want to happen and what their current goals are. Not all practitioners deal with pre-session information the same. Some prefer to read the file beforehand to be prepared for the first meeting, while others prefer to meet clients for the first time open-minded and not influenced by prior information. In both cases it is important the therapist mentions what their approach is.

When Milan meets Kim for the first time he says: 'The GP has collected quite a lot of information about you, but I always like to get to know someone first before I delve into the file information. I prefer to hear from you first why you are seeking help.'
  Or:
MILAN: 'We are meeting for the first time, but I've read a few things about you in the file from the GP. Do you know what's in your file?'

Clients are appreciative of the therapist summarising in lay terms their understanding of file information, referral letters or questionnaires. It can clarify whether clients recognise themselves in the information or would like to correct or explain something.

The material and physical environment

The influence of environmental factors on the alliance is often ignored in mental health practice. It is seldom a topic in training or study manuals. However aspects of the material and physical environment are meaningful. Watzlawick et al. (1967) stated that all behaviour is a form of communication. Is a space looking tidy or messy, how does the light come in, the smells, the accessories, they all influence the first and subsequent meetings between therapist and clients. The material environment reveals something about people. People express themselves through their home interior, the car they drive and the jewellery they wear. Therapists reveal themselves through objects in the therapy room. A mental health service leaves a particular impression with the building, the neighbourhood and its workspaces (Harris et al., 2002; Van den Berge, 2001). A small survey about the influence of a psychologist's therapy room showed that a room decorated with a personal touch in contrast to a sparsely decorated room contributed to more disclosure and depth in the conversations and resulted in the therapist being more appreciated (Reerink, 2010). Therapy rooms need to be spacious enough when more than one person is invited for a joint session. "Too small a room, in other words when the 'psychological territory' is too small, can be stress inducing" (van Meekeren & Baars, 2013, p. 169). Often appreciated are plants and objects that impart something about the therapist, are familiar to clients or reveal something about the service's philosophy. Pictures reflecting the diversity in the practice's clientele can make clients feel welcome. However what is appropriate is not set in concrete. A therapist who displays a photo of their family on their desk can charm some clients but alienate others. Presently practitioners have to change rooms often to maximise the use of the building. It is helpful when such spaces are decorated in a way that makes many people feel comfortable. A poster, a lamp, toys for the children, comfortable chairs all hint of the atmosphere the therapist is hoping to create: anyone can sit here, children are welcome, people need to feel comfortable. This can be challenging in times of austerity. With a few small adjustments the professional can create an atmosphere of hospitality, for instance, with colourful prints on the wall or with a supply of paper and pencils, toys or puppets.

> MIRANDA: 'I was tired of the sofa in my therapy room. For a decent conversation I prefer to sit at a table. I hadn't expected that the new round high wooden table would have so much effect though. Some clients have opened up, children participate while they're drawing and people fill their own glasses of water. As if the table provides both safety and connection. I am going to paint the table with white board paint so we can all draw on it.'

External features and physical appearance

Clothing too is communication. A practitioner who dresses in shorts and sandals in the summer can be an embarrassment to parents who take pride in how they and their children dress and to himself (Colijn, 1995). Other external features play a part too.

Jana, 16, has a severe eating disorder. She is from a strict religious family. Her parents, maternal grandparents and her oldest sister are shown around in the inpatient service where Jana is to be admitted. They notice the differences in their own environment. The ward is of mixed gender, girls are wearing trousers and tight, occasionally provocative clothes, the few boys are dressed casually. Her family queries about a prayer room. They hear there is no praying at mealtimes, but Jana can pray in her own room she shares with two other girls. In this facility they clearly have different norms and values than at home. The parents are taken aback and wonder how to speak about this with their own family. The staff member who shows them around is aware of their strict religious background and takes the time to listen to what the family thinks and feels, the questions they have and how they would like to discuss all this with the family back home. The staff member can sympathise with the family's concerns. Consequently they have an open conversation, differences are acknowledged and given a place and the family feels supported. When they leave, they are a bit more confident about a positive outcome.

Before meeting a therapist, clients wonder who that person is, how old they are, how much experience they have and what they look like. An initial meeting can run smoothly when clients recognise themselves in the therapist, but this can make things more difficult too. Having a professional from a different community can feel safer for the client than someone from their own community they may not want to share everything with. Both too much difference and too many similarities could be a hindrance. Differences in clothing, background or language between practitioner and client can stimulate curiosity and exchange for the therapist and/or the client but can elicit fear or dislike if too great. External features or physical appearances can be visible or invisible and either discussed or not (Burnham, 2012). For instance a different skin colour will be visible, but could be ignored in the conversation. The exact age of the therapist isn't always apparent and could be, but not necessarily, a point of discussion.

Juliette (Dutch, 35 years old, blonde, jeans) asks Almaz (from Eritrea, 40 years of age, dark, colourful dress): 'How is it for you to see a therapist who grew up in a rural area in North Holland and never visited Africa?'

Almaz laughs and they talk about how different it is growing up in Eritrea or in North Holland. They touch on similarities too.

ALMAZ: 'I was so jealous of my sister.'
JULIETTE: 'I know the feeling.'

The meeting place

Where the first meeting takes place can have an effect on the alliance. Kim and Tony had an appointment at the GP practice they know well. However clients are often invited to an unfamiliar place such as a community-based service or a private practice. A community-based service is located in a particular neighbourhood and the building radiates a particular atmosphere: wealthy and stately, poverty and neglect or something in between homely and clinical. Clients are welcomed warmly or need to find their own way and become disoriented. The sign at the entrance often displays abstract names such as 'Challenge Trust' or more specific 'Youth and Community Work Brussels South'. The client arrives at a psychiatric hospital or a crisis centre, addiction service, parenting support centre, women's refuge or child protection service. During the trajectory of professional help, titles and names take on meaning. Initially some people can feel ashamed or hesitant because it is obvious they're seeking help for addictions, psychiatric problems, probation or child protection. It makes a difference when people can enter a building freely or when they have to ring a bell and wait for someone to open the door. What the location of the service means to the client may need to be addressed, for instance when the therapist lives and works in the same town or neighbourhood as the client and they are likely to meet on the street or in the supermarket. Clients could also recognise other clients in the waiting room. Further some discussion about the place of therapy delivery is also warranted when the practitioner works from home. To some clients this could feel very comfortable while others may become occupied with questions about the therapist's life.

> Jono's parents have an initial evening appointment with Brett. Brett's office is next to his house, and the parents can see Brett's children in the living room. During the session Brett asks them: 'Does it bother you that my practice is so close to my home?'

Home visits

Anderson (1997) wrote that a practitioner is always a guest "who participates with [clients] in a small slice of their life" (p. 99). This is literally the case when the therapist visits clients at their home. The therapist then enters the client's personal space instead of the client coming onto territory that is familiar to the therapist only. Being a guest means to be respectful and mindful of the rules and customs of the family. Perhaps it is common to take off shoes at the front door. In some religious groups a man is forbidden to shake the hand of a woman. Some families have conversations only at the kitchen table. The therapist will usually respect these rules, but attuning can be tricky. Is it appropriate to ask to see the kitchen, the children's bedrooms, the adults' rooms? Can the therapist ask to switch off the TV or turn it down or is it better to observe first how this family functions amidst background noise? What to do when the mother has prepared (sometimes on purpose) food and drink? Refusing could be perceived as rude but talking while eating could hinder a proper conversation. Other interruptions can occur such as the arrival of a neighbour, a dog who jumps on your lap, the phone ringing or the doorbell. It requires continuous attuning when the goal is to create a context for a meaningful encounter. Clients can feel judged when the therapist visits at home, but the opposite is true likewise. For example, upon arrival the professional is asked whether they're not a bit young, or five pairs of eyes are staring at them when they sit down on the sofa.

Coming into other people's lives can affect the practitioner. A social worker who regularly visits people at home said that smells tell a story: 'The air can be pregnant with the smell of fried food, animals (dogs or cats or even reptiles), dirt. After a home visit like that I need some fresh air first. In other homes I can smell the cleaning products, the house is looking very clean, or I can smell perfume.' Several studies have determined the influence of odours on emotion and behaviour (Vroon, 1997). The environment influences the therapist too and in turn their response to the environment influences the clients.

> Caren visits a solo mother with three children. When she enters the home, she immediately notices how tidy and organised everything is. Instantly she feels guilty about her own home she shares with her husband and child. She never manages to get it so tidy and organised; how does this mother do that? This brings her to her initial questions and instantly a connection is made.

Creating a therapeutic framework

In the first meeting the therapist must be mindful to create a transparent therapeutic framework. Transparency helps to establish an alliance. The practitioner makes an introduction and explains how they could work together.

> Marian greeted everybody, shook hands and walked the clients to her therapy room. 'I am Marian Kane. In here I talk with children, young people and adults and other people who have concerns in the hope reducing those worries. I've been doing this for a long time, and I love what I do. We don't always talk, sometimes we do things together. Today I'd like us to get to know each other and hear from each of you what your concerns are. It's likely that you're going to tell different stories and that's ok. You don't need to agree. I will try to understand each person and I'll ask many questions, some perhaps unexpected or even weird. You don't have to answer if you don't want to, you don't have to talk about things you don't want to talk about and please say when you don't know. Occasionally I may interrupt you. At the end of our meeting, I hope we can come up together with a plan or something else. I don't know yet what that could be.'

In the introduction Marian outlines the content of the conversation. Next, introductions are made. These can be short if she is keen to address the referral reason as soon as possible. The introductions may take more time if she likes to find out more about what is going well. Whatever Marian does, she creates interactional patterns for the duration of the therapy that influence how people speak and interact with one another and what is (un)acceptable in the sessions.

'The school has asked you to make an appointment here because of their concerns', says Marian. 'That's why the school counsellor is present for a little while to clarify the school's concerns. We would like you to hear first from the school directly, then we'll discuss what we'd like to do with that information.'

A trusting relationship is supported by a transparent therapeutic framework. Marian is transparent about why she has invited the referrer and about the purpose of the first meeting, including agreements to be made. For instance what is Marian to do when the referrer, other professionals or one of the family members contact her in between sessions? Confidentiality needs to be explained as well and additional privacy issues are discussed, such as when the therapist needs to consult with their team or that client information communicated with outsiders is shared with the clients. Arrangements are made about how clients and therapist can contact each other and when extra contact is warranted, for instance in the case of increased concerns. The therapist outlines the process when alarming information is received or a crisis occurs (Midori Hanna & Brown, 2018; Vermeire & Bracke, 2007). It is paramount to be transparent about what happens in case of risk to self or others and when the therapist is obliged to include the assistance of their team or colleagues. Such agreements can be made at the beginning or end of a session. Given that a lot of tension can be present at the start of an initial session, making practical arrangements could be better suited at the end.

Creating a therapeutic space

In systemic practice the therapist's alliance with all relevant parties implies having relationships with multiple people who have different agendas, needs, questions and problem definitions. It is not a matter of *the* working alliance but of *multiple* working alliances. It is important to create a context of polyphony wherein family members feel safe enough to discuss difficult topics or not to speak altogether. Everyone needs to feel they matter, that the therapist is interested and has listened carefully (Loots et al., 2014; Tilmans-Ostyn, 1990). Consequently the language used has to be appropriate. When children are present in the session, the therapist needs to 'play and do' amongst talking and use creative and playful methods.

There are various ways in which the therapist can create a safe therapeutic context in the first session. Minuchin (1974) stressed the importance of *joining*. He referred to the therapist 'moving with' the clients' language, attitudes and 'transactional patterns'. The therapist adapts, for instance they repeat words the clients use or speak softer or faster depending on what clients do. They take the clients' ways of behaving into account. Joining doesn't mean that the therapist always can or always has to accommodate. Each therapist has to remain alert to the possible meanings of differences in language, attitude, interactional patterns and backgrounds and how this influences the alliance (Larner, 2015). The introduction phase may require more time, for instance when language barriers need to be overcome. Families can speak a dialect unfamiliar to the therapist, who in that case can apologise for not speaking the dialect. During the therapeutic trajectory regular consideration of and attuning to significant differences is required.

Some therapists prefer to spend plenty of time with every person to hear about people's work, hobbies and particular qualities first rather than to focus right from the start on the problems (Madsen & Gillespie, 2014; Minuchin, 1974; Rober, 2017). Others (Andolfi, 2016a, 2016b) rather begin with exploring the problems and delay extensive introductions until later. They believe that clients have come because of a problem and have no need to start with non-problem-related exchanges. In this regard practitioners develop their own style and clients have different needs. Dutch people are known worldwide as being direct and assertive. In other societies introductions and speaking first about other topics bar the problems are an essential ritual to make connections. The steps taken in that 'first dance' are a co-creation of what suits the therapist and the clients.

Being curious

In the initial session the therapist will ask many questions for the purpose of understanding each person present, empathising with their stories and creating space for the multitude of voices that play a significant role for clients and therapist. Multiple examples are available of questions that initiate a dialogue; it has always been an important topic in systemic practice (Choy, 2005; de Jong & Berg, 2002; Penn, 1985; Tomm, 1987b). To create a dialogical space questions during the first meeting need to address each person's expectations.

Eddy Hudson has early-stage dementia. His wife Alison wonders whether the GP has sent the social worker Dean to take Eddy away. Their daughter Anne has commented a few times that they can't go on like this for much longer.

The alliance with Dean could be jeopardised beforehand due to Alison's fears. If Dean is mindful of this, Alison will feel heard. Daughter Anne is curious about what Dean has to offer and meets him with an open mind. The alliance with Anne is immediately focussed on collaboration. To create a working relationship with everyone and to foster dialogue, it matters that Dean's questions focus on everyone's expectations.

> Anne hopes for intervention and that her parents get help, so she can take a step back. But she doesn't want to hurt her father and is reluctant to talk about the times when her father's confusion and forgetfulness become obvious.
>
> Alison doesn't want to leave their home or be separated from Eddy. She hopes that Dean will support them to make life manageable at home. She wants to convey they are doing fine at the moment. She doesn't want to give Dean examples of when it's been difficult to cope.
>
> Eddy is anxious, he knows that something is not right in his head. Sometimes he can't remember words or suddenly utters strange words. He is very concerned and would like to discuss this, but he doesn't want to leave his home, not without Alison.
>
> Dean facilitates the initial conversation amidst this complexity. He doesn't take sides but listens carefully and explores what everyone thinks and feels.

In the event of clients being mandated to attend therapy it is very important to create space for expectations and potential reluctance so an alliance can be established and the therapy has a chance of succeeding. The practitioner who sees clients on a voluntary basis needs to avoid becoming an ally of the school, the child protection service or the partner who are adamant that professional help is necessary. When clients feel heard about the pressures and doubt they experience, professional help has a chance of being successful.

Being open for feedback

Due to the importance of the working alliance, evaluation and feedback from clients are valued. Their input is crucial for collaboration and supports the alliance from the start. When practitioners are open to clients' feedback, collaboratively they can create a foundation for the professional's input and share accountability for the therapeutic process. Various questionnaires are available to elicit written feedback from clients on a regular basis or even session by session. These questionnaires usually target the individual, but questionnaires appropriate for systemic practice with multiple clients are obtainable (Rober, 2017). Even in the absence of questionnaires the therapist can actively pursue feedback from clients and use this to tweak the therapeutic process.

In conclusion

By attending to the wider context of the request for help and the effects of the physical and material environment instead of starting immediately with 'therapy', the systemic practitioner creates a therapeutic space in which therapeutic conversations can take place. Clients and therapist collaboratively investigate factors that could have an impact on the therapy. The therapist joins in, encourages the clients to make concerns and doubts discernible and introduces a transparent therapeutic framework. Therapists are 'guests' in their clients' lives, whether they meet in the office or at the client's home. Systemic therapy starts with attending to the alliances with all parties. A good working relationship is one of the factors effecting change and therefore a major focus from that first contact onwards.

Exercise

Think of clients (a couple, a family, an individual) you met recently. After reading this chapter, is there anything you would do differently?

Chapter 6

Mapping

Introduction

> Marian is meeting with Vera, Kira and 14-year-old Ratna, Kira's daughter, for the second time. Ratna has been talking back to her teachers and can be quite aggressive verbally towards classmates. Over the last few months her grades have plummeted. At home she's getting angry too, usually at her younger brother Benny who she says is allowed everything and is always favoured. Marian suggests they explore how everybody thinks and feels about this. She suggests spending the session at mapping what is going on in their lives. 'In that way we'll know which topics we definitely need to bring up in future sessions. It will help us to decide what we'd like to address and with whom', she says.

'Mapping' is otherwise called assessment. The professional asks questions or has people fill in questionnaires to get an idea of their concerns and symptoms. It is assumed that a thorough assessment will lead to appropriate treatment. Gathering information is usually considered separate from intervention. But when people meet with a professional to address mental health or relational problems, the distinction is not so clear. In that case assessment is not just collecting information disconnected from intervention. From that first conversation people could adopt a different view of their problems and of each other or suddenly notice new things in their life because of the questions the practitioner asked. *Mapping* is an intervention (Asen et al., 2004; Reijmers, 2014c). In systemic practice mapping involves more than exploring the problem or looking for factors that contribute to the problem. Mapping, or with other words *systemic assessment*, focusses on the bigger picture, including the client's treatment history and the meaning of receiving help, the effects of the problems, their relationships and relevant contexts, the supports and resilience and the various views people hold about problems and solutions. It is about finding a shared starting point for therapeutic conversations and understanding what people are looking for (Midori Hanna & Brown, 2018; Reijmers, 2014c). To effect this there are

DOI: 10.4324/9781003272038-6

many questionnaires and lists available for the practitioner. In this chapter we discuss several areas relevant in systemic assessment. By exploring relevant and useful contexts the therapist can gradually build a picture of their clients' life, how they make sense of the world and which provisional hypotheses could be feasible or useful (Sheinberg & Brewster, 2014). Clients are involved in this process. Mapping also provides information about how people can remain connected and face the problems together.

What are the concerns?

Before people seek professional help, they have tried to find out what exactly is going on. People try to pinpoint probable causes of the problems which are not necessarily agreed on by the family, the couple or even the outside world. It is possible that the grandparents and the parents have quite different ideas about the problems. A couple's friends can have a very clear idea about what the problem is. For one partner this can feel as supportive and for the other one as threatening. Previous professionals or the referrer can have their own opinions about the difficulties which clients agree or disagree with. In the literature of the pioneer years of systemic therapy this spectrum of views of families and their networks was named *the struggle over definition of the problem* (Imber-Black, 1988). From a social constructionism perspective the term *polyphonic problem definition* could be more useful. Problems can be seen in a similar way by many or by everyone. For instance clients and significant others agree that the problem is a relationship problem, a parenting problem or an individual problem and on that basis seek help. However the meaning of the problems and their perceived severity can differ for each person. When the therapist speaks with clients, it is important to map the polyphonic view of the problem(s). After all the concerns expressed by the clients, their environment or the referrer are the reason why people ask for help (Rober, 2002).

Marian asks Ratna what she's worried about. Ratna sighs and says that her teachers irritate her greatly. Other pupils are annoyed too, but she's the only one who speaks up. When she points this out to her classmates, they get angry. Such cowards, all of them. Benny, her brother, is a lame duck too. He bothers her every time she wants to be by herself and he cries at the drop of a hat. Maybe he needs therapy, she suggests. According to Kira her daughter's problems have to do with school, she doesn't fit in well and is not receiving the right support. And Ratna struggles with the fact her father has left for Curaçao. Ratna has always been a temperamental girl, but since her father is living abroad, this has worsened. Ratna rolls her eyes, indicating she thinks this is nonsense. Vera surmises that Ratna is jealous of Benny, particularly now Benny spends more time with his donor father. She is concerned about her son as well. Ratna looks the other way and sighs. Vera also wonders whether Ratna isn't feeling so great because Kira is working so much. Vera believes it would be better for Ratna if Kira was at home more.

The practitioner explores the various views and concerns from both the people present in the session and other relevant yet absent people. Space is made for everyone's input and all those perspectives are lined up next to rather than opposite one another. It helps the therapist to connect and to get a sense of potential difficulties.

What brings you here? And what are your hesitations?

Despite everyone having an opinion about the problems, eventually one or more family members meet with a practitioner. As described in the previous chapter it can be important to explore how this came about. Did they seek help because someone took the initiative? Was it suggested by the referrer or another person? It happens that people are referred for family or couple sessions while they preferred individual sessions or vice versa. The client may be of the belief that others ought to have been invited or need help too. Ratna for instance wonders why it is her and not Benny who is seen to need professional help. Asking how people ended up in therapy implies that the therapist is aware that specialised help can have a different meaning for each person. Some people's view is coloured by previous professional input. Perhaps the person has high and unrealistic expectations or feels sceptical towards treatment. People have good reasons to seek help or may have good reasons to not-yet speak or to not attend (Rober, 2002).

> Ratna is angry at the school counsellor who referred her. She thinks that the school is making mistakes. She doesn't dislike school, so why does she need to attend a therapy session? She believes it would be better that Kira and Vera receive help without her. Her mother and Vera have been fighting quite a lot lately. Or Benny could do with some help because he cries a lot. Kira is not sure whether it's such a good idea that she and Vera attend each time. Kira thinks her daughter needs a place for herself and someone she can tell what's on her mind. Vera is at a loss. She has so much to worry about, particularly now Jaco, Benny's donor father, is making things so difficult. She is afraid that the therapy sessions will drain her energy. She wonders whether perhaps Ratna and Kira should have sessions together. They should have a good talk, she thinks.

There are various reasons that make clients hesitate to proceed with the conversation, for instance because of what others may think, believe or feel. Ratna is concerned about what her peers and Benny will say. She is convinced they'll laugh at her: 'You see, there is something wrong with Ratna.' The client may hesitate to tell their story, often expressed non-verbally (Rober, 2002), due to previous experiences with professional help or because of what the referrer relayed about the client as described in Chapter 5.

It can be related to ideas about what proper help looks like or too much is playing on the client's mind. Once the professional creates space for these hesitations, a clearer picture of each person's motivation and reasons for requesting help will emerge. It makes it easier later to consider whom to speak with and about what. Unprejudiced listening by the therapist prevents hesitations from hindering the unfolding of the therapeutic process.

What are the effects of the problems on your relationships?

The systemic practitioner focuses on relationships and contexts. Exploring the effects of the problem on how people feel and behave shifts the focus from the content of the problem to the clients' experiences and interpersonal influences.

Marian wonders what the effect is of all those troublesome events. What is the impact of the problems on their feelings? Ratna looks sullen and doesn't reply. Kira says she's feeling helpless. She wonders what she can do. Vera is feeling sad and tired and occasionally frustrated. If only Kira and Ratna would talk with each other...

'Both are stubborn', sighs Vera.

'And you, Ratna?', Marian tries again.

Ratna shrugs.

'Do you any idea what the impact is on you of those worrisome matters? How do they influence your relationship?', Marian asks while she looks at Kira and Ratna.

Kira looks at her daughter. 'I think we have become more distant', she says.

Ratna keeps quiet.

'And', Marian asks, 'what does it do between you two?' She looks at Vera and Ratna.

Vera replies: 'It destroys having fun. No one is feeling happy anymore.'

Suddenly Ratna says: 'We all fight with each other.'

Family members or partners don't have to agree or come to an agreement when the effects of the problems are outlined. Often people quarrel about what and who the problem is. Mapping the effects of the problems allows people's differing perspectives to sit alongside one another while the focus is directed to something else, namely relationships and interactions. It helps the therapist and the clients to stay away from truth battles while they're not straying too far away from the problems. It helps to find a common ground for the conversations. Exploring *interaction patterns* while mapping the effects of the problems on relationships can generate useful hypotheses. Patterns are about who responds to what or whom and how that happens. This is not to point the finger at a person as being the cause, but for everyone to understand the continuous action-reaction chains.

Marian asks for an example of a conflict at home. Vera, Kira and Ratna quickly agree this time: when they're eating at the dinner table. Do they remember the last time this happened? Yes they do. Benny was complaining he wanted more ketchup because he doesn't like his food otherwise. Ratna felt annoyed and told him to stop whinging. Benny reacted in response. Vera tried to stop the fight and urged Ratna to stop making comments. Ratna became angrier and told her to parent Benny, not her. Next Kira hit the table with the palm of her hand and sent Ratna upstairs to her room. Ratna stormed off, slamming doors. Kira then became cross with Vera and Benny. Benny was quiet and tearful and played with his food without ketchup. Vera was inwardly livid and irritated by Kira and Benny. Marian writes with capital letters PATTERN on the board. Together they discuss what that looks like. They come up with feeling annoyed with something and becoming angry, then rebuking and reproaching the other person, next the other person responds angrily and reproachfully too, leading to feeling not understood, what makes the person feeling unhappy and angry or crying, which leads to more reproaching, which elicits again a response of the others and so on. Everyone recognises this pattern. They call it 'the circle of irritation'.

Interaction chains like these can be related to a situation such as sitting at the table. When the pattern features in multiple contexts it can become entrenched and put relationships under pressure. The focus shifts when people look for patterns together and are not preoccupied anymore with who caused the conflict. It is no longer about who started it or who needs to change. Once the pattern is identified, including each person's contribution and behaviour, the therapist could comment that perhaps the pattern is the problem. The pattern then becomes an enemy they have in common and curtailing the pattern can be the aim of the sessions (White, 2007). It's not always simple to map patterns and more time can be required than available in one session. Reciprocal personal reproaches can flare up quickly and demand the practitioner to be active and alert. Marian chooses to ask about a relatively small and daily incident, because she surmises that at this point in the process her clients are able to jointly reflect on this. She decides to ignore for now the bigger, more complex escalations between Ratna, Kira and Vera.

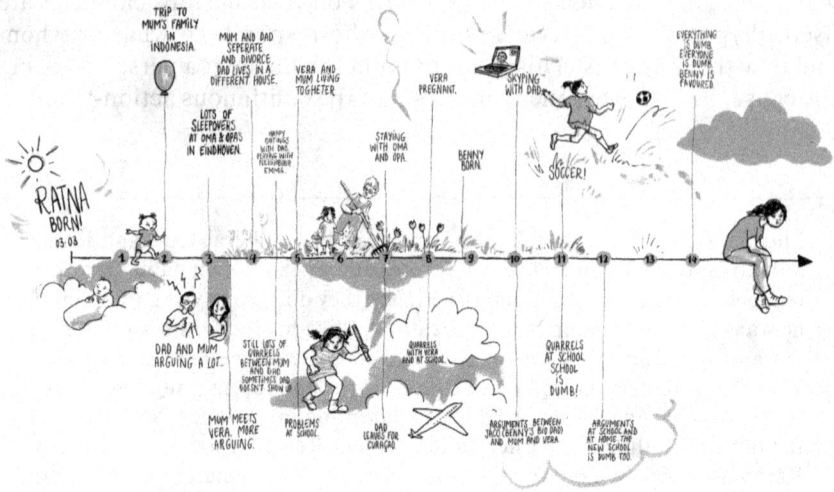

Figure 6.1 Ratna's timeline

What are the relevant relational and familial contexts?

For a systemic practitioner it is important to have a picture of the relationships between partners and family members, in the present and through time (Sheinberg & Brewster, 2014). This can be explored in a semi-structured way, for example by making a genogram or timeline together (Carter & McGoldrick, 2004; Hillewaere & Lefevere de Ten Hove, 2006; Jessurun, 2010; Jessurun & Warring, 2018). Visualising the family relationships by means of a genogram or timeline has the advantage that couples and families remain focussed and stories offering alternative or new perspectives can be exchanged. While drawing the genogram the family history and significant aspects such as *values* and *interactional routines* in families can be highlighted. A timeline can reveal meaningful *transitions*, like Kira and John's separation, John's relocation to Curaçao and the birth of Ratna and Benny.

The professional also explores themes related to *stages of life* or *stages of family* that are of significance for the family or couple. Such themes can provide insight in changes and stressors that could impact on a couple or a family (Carter & McGoldrick, 2004). A couple with a new-born baby can experience specific pressure on the relationship between each other or with their families of origin. They are not only partners now, but parents too. This can cause a shift in roles, positions and responsibilities in their families of origin, at times with unpleasant effects. By mapping these influences the therapist contextualises the presenting problems. The fights between Ratna and Benny can be understood in that regard.

While Marian is drawing the genogram she comments that Vera and Kira have to parent at two different speeds. Ratna is getting older, friends are more important to her and she wants to be more independent. This requires a different kind of parenting than Benny, who has just started primary school. Perhaps that age difference is not always easy for Ratna either, Marian suggests.

Ratna sighs deeply.

Vera responds that she and her partner expect Ratna to behave as the oldest, she should be the sensible one.

Ratna sits upright and yells: 'You always favour him. You let him do anything! It does my head in!'

Making a genogram has the effect that the practitioner can see what is missing. From this genogram it is clear there is no information about the current relationship between Kira and John. And not much is known about Kira's family and her background.

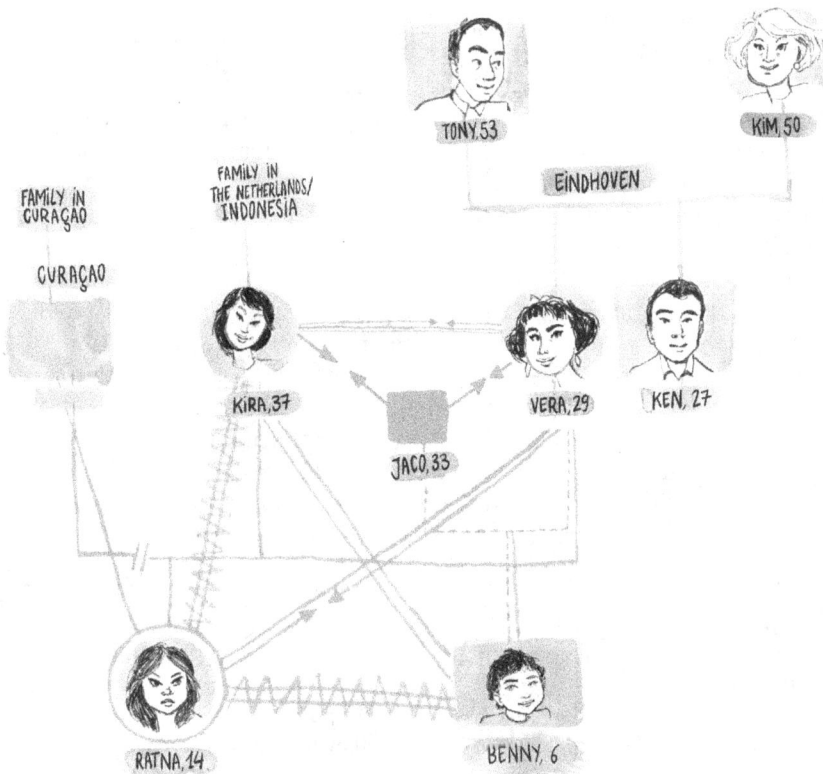

Figure 6.2 Genogram Kira and Vera

The therapist can ask questions about the nuclear and extended family's *structure and organisation* (Asen et al., 2004; Minuchin, 1974). For example: who takes which position or role? In Kira and Vera's family the parenting roles are divided. Kira and John are Ratna's biological parents, Vera is her stepmother. Vera is Benny's biological mother, Kira is his adoptive mother. Jaco is his donor father. The children too have different positions towards each other and their parents. Exploring this complexity can bring clarity. Using Duplo puppets or other objects can be helpful. The therapist, together with Kira, Vera and Ratna, can place the most significant people, represented by puppets, on the table and ask about where they live, what their position is and perhaps something about the different relationships (Diekmann, 2005).

What are potential socio-cultural influences?

Next the professional can explore cultural and societal influences. What does coming from different social backgrounds mean for a couple? What is it like to live in a family with two mothers and children by two fathers? Additionally cultural influences can be considered. Vera and Kira have a different cultural background. The Indonesian branch of Kira's family has perhaps other expectations, values and backgrounds than Vera's Dutch family. What is the ongoing effect of this in their lives and other relationships? Zooming out towards broader influences can help the practitioner and the clients to recognise social pressures and influences and what this means in terms of their beliefs and values. The practitioner can explore with couples what they believe constitutes 'good partnership'. Their responses will comprise socially and culturally supported ideas and norms, such as 'a good couple can talk about anything, they do everything together and are intimately close'. Perhaps partnership is considered intertwined with parenthood or the roles between men and women are clearly delineated. These *social discourses* about good partnership can influence how partners perceive each other and their problems (Faes, 2014; Freedman & Combs, 2015). By making the socio-cultural embedding of a couple or a family visible and exploring social discourses helps to view problems as less personal and people to feel less blamed. Additionally it sheds light on the pressures people feel on themselves and on the relationship between them and the outside world.

When Marian asks what they see as the perfect family, Kira replies: 'I believe we're not the perfect family. But nevertheless, we're proud to be different to other families.'

Everybody laughs. Marian asks about other positive sides of 'not being the perfect family'. They brainstorm together: they are more tolerant for differences, more open-minded towards each other and perhaps close-knitted too.

'And does it have a difficult side too?', Marian asks.

'You can't say much about it to other people', Vera responds. 'Usually, they don't understand and are quick to judge. You always have to weigh up what you say to whom.'

Ratna nods in agreement. In this respect she trusts only her two best friends. She doesn't want to tell her classmates, because they're not used to anything like this, she thinks.

'Does that mean that you hesitate to discuss problems with others, because you feel that people are judgemental about your family?', Marian asks.

'Yes, that's right', says Kira, 'it's really annoying.'

What is working well?

When mapping the issues, it is important to query what is or was going well. People access professional help when problems arise. And sometimes that is all they see. The 'problem-saturated story' takes centre place, becomes the dominant story and consumes everyone's efforts and attention (White & Epston, 1990). Exploring constructive connections and contexts can provide a counterbalance for the practitioner and the clients and avoid a picture that only shows to what extent the problems have infected other contexts. Instead the picture is enriched with differentiations and demarcations. For example a couple realise they are still satisfied with how they parent but have unfulfilled needs when it comes to intimacy. Or parents recognise that their son is doing well at school and has lots of friends, but the dynamics at home are not so great, particularly with his little brother. Constructive areas are also useful for identifying opportunities, supports and resilience that can help clients to face the problems. Exploring what works well is not limited to the present. Questioning what went well in the past can be particularly helpful when clients indicate that presently not much is running smoothly. Exploring non-problematic areas can be facilitated by a timeline. The therapist does not only enquire about troublesome events but specifically includes good times. Using a *context web* is another tool to visualise what has been working well.

Marian walks to the whiteboard and writes: What is going well? 'I'm going to use different colours for each of you.' Ratna picks red, Kira green and Vera black. Ratna talks about her two girlfriends she has fun with, she also likes spending time with both her grandmothers, she has no problems with her geography, biology and Dutch teachers and she relishes those evenings when they sit together downstairs when Benny is in bed or when she and Kira head into town to shop. Similarly Kira enjoys the evenings and shopping together. She has no concerns about her work or her family. Vera's list of trouble-free areas includes her work, her family, the evenings together and holidaying together. Written on the board they all see a variety of contexts in the different colours but also pleasant experiences they share.

Exploring where and when things go well is a first step towards exploring sources of support and resilience for clients. The professional can discuss how they have overcome problems in the past and which skills, strengths, events and people have been helpful. Next the therapist can explore who or what around them can be supportive now and which of those problem-solving skills they can activate. Vera and Kira for instance could notice that Ratna can be so funny and make people laugh or that Benny brags about his big sister to his friends. Kira is a great cook and the special meals she prepares are so enjoyable. And Vera she is knowledgeable about the movies they watch together.

What will change look like?

Madsen and Gillespie (2014) state that exploring what could help people move forward is often more useful and effective than focussing on the problems. They have introduced the *collaborative helping map* and start with the question where people would like to be headed in life. This is referred to as an exploration of a *preferred future*. Finding a collaborative goal or preferred future can be challenging. It requires patience and creativity to formulate a desired future agreeable to everyone. This is important because it anchors and focuses the therapy. Therefore a preferred future has to be "a mutually shared, pro-active, meaningful and sufficiently concrete vision" (Madsen & Gillespie, 2014, p. 54). In the next step the practitioner explores what could help to reach this desired future (supports) and what could be in the way (obstacles).

> Kira, Vera and Ratna would like their lives together to have less fights and more togetherness. They want to be together while able to do their own thing, without bothering anyone or being bothered by others. Like how their evenings pass occasionally. 'Supports' include making time for each other, doing things everyone enjoys, being in a good mood. 'Obstacles' include working too hard (Kira and Vera), tetchiness at school (Ratna), fighting with Benny (Ratna), stress due to a potential judicial process by donor father Jaco (Vera, Kira), the issues with Ratna's father John and exam stress (Ratna).

To highlight the preferred future even more, the professional can ask the clients about their motivations towards this goal, their values and where these come from. They can enquire who in the clients' life would support or value such future. Exploring a desired future can assist clients in developing a shared vision of therapeutic goals.

What needs to happen next?

Eventually practitioner and clients will have to arrive at an agreed starting point for the conversations. They also need to reach consensus on who to speak with. This can be facilitated by exploring the domains as discussed above. By now several issues have been attended to during the mapping process. Clients have thought about problems and hesitations. They have an idea about how everybody feels, what the effects are of the problems, how relationship patterns begin and which contexts play a role. They have thought about needs and preferences. Obviously this is not the complete or all-encompassing picture. The exploration has brought in focus differences and similarities between the clients and they have experienced what it is like to speak together. The question 'What needs to happen next?' can be considered a *decision dialogue* (Sheinberg & True, 2008), a journey in a particular direction shared by professional and clients. The decision dialogue offers the therapist an opportunity to openly discuss with the clients problematic areas and choices that came up in the exploration. For example Marian could say that Ratna was referred because of problems at school, but the exploration shows that the conflicts at home affect Ratna, Kira and Vera. The question that follows is: What direction do we take? Clients have their own ideas about what could help them. Vera is convinced that Ratna and Kira need to talk more with each other. Kira believes that Ratna needs to speak alone with a therapist. Marian too can verbalise her hypotheses, impressions and views; her voice is part of the dialogue. She may say that their stories leave her with the impression that they are struggling to talk amongst themselves or with others about the fights at home. Perhaps starting here is useful. Marian could feed back that she sees that the family is dealing with several stressors, such as the increasing pressure from donor father Jaco and the sudden relocation of John, Ratna's father. Talking about these could be helpful for everyone. The family could think together about how not to lose their connection amid the stress. But Marian can also provide several options for the family to consider. Would it be better for instance if Vera and Kira first attend sessions together to talk about their parenting and how to position themselves towards Jaco? Or would it make a difference if Kira and Ratna came together? When an agreement is reached about the direction and the setting of therapy, the compass is set for future conversations.

In conclusion

Mapping stress factors, problems and hesitations, relationships and influences, resilience, supports and the preferred future cannot be achieved in one session. It all starts at the beginning of a therapeutic process, but certain topics can be revisited later or when the conversations stall. The areas to explore as described above are like anchors. The practitioner can reassess over time which areas have not been addressed or insufficiently addressed. The sequence of the questions is not set but depends on what clients bring. Some people speak mainly about problems and are reluctant to explore their hopes and preferred future. For other people it is the other way around. Some clients will find it easier to talk when genograms or puppets are used. The work context of the professional plays a role too. Depending on their work context the therapist may have plenty of time to explore all relevant contexts over several sessions. When time is limited and immediate feedback is expected, the practitioner will need to decide which domains need exploring. In any case it is crucial to remember that mapping or systemic assessment does not equal collecting neutral information. Systemic assessment broadens the lens of the therapist and the clients and could foster immediate change. It is a gradual and shared process towards an understanding of the client's life and meanings, setting the direction for future help.

Exercise

Chronicle an ongoing therapeutic process based on the different domains described in this chapter: What is the problem according to the client? What brought them to you and what are their hesitations? What are the effects of the problems on the client's relationships? What are the relevant relational and familial contexts? What may be cultural and societal influences? What worked well or works well and what didn't or doesn't? What would the client like to happen? What are the client and you going to do next?

What is missing? What could be useful or relevant to explore further with the client?

Chapter 7

Positioning

Introduction

Mental health and social care practitioners want to help. Although it is their aim and their duty, this is easier said than done. Beginning practitioners often think of 'helping' in simple, optimistic and linear terms. For example they explain to clients how to manage their finances better, expecting them to follow that advice. This positioning can be described as a straightforward *expert position*. Unfortunately or perhaps fortunately, the practice is much more robust and recalcitrant. Within the social constructionist framework this book is based on, such position of 'simple instruction' is impossible. Both client and therapist bring a multitude of experiences, stories and backgrounds to the conversation. An issue such as 'managing finances' is never a simple question followed by a simple answer. Furthermore the practice of most professionals is very complex, and particularly for the intended readers of this book, people who work at the front line of societal problems. How do you help people with mental health problems, partners or parents who have horrible arguments, children who suffer, families that can't cope any longer with the problems and face intervention (by the state) because of serious concerns in the community?

In previous chapters we have described what a systemic perspective entails and what this could mean for practitioners. Thinking in terms of relationships and contexts, the influence of societal and social discourses, the self-evidence of polyphony, the importance of resilience and support, circular patterns of influence and how everything can be regarded as communication, provides practitioners with a compass. Guiding principles have been proposed to establish a working relationship with several people as well as frameworks to map concerns and to keep focus on significant areas. This chapter deals with how a clear positioning can be a beacon for the therapist. Reflecting about the practitioner's attitude, role and position have always been an important topic in systemic therapy. This is related to the complexity of the work: so much of what happens in conversations could benefit from further discussion. A second reason for the importance of reflecting

DOI: 10.4324/9781003272038-7

on positioning has to do with theoretical developments. In the early years of systemic therapy the therapist assumed an expert position. They steered the sessions and knew which goals to achieve (Haley, 1976; Minuchin, 1974; Minuchin & Fishman, 1981). Because of changes in the societal context and theory this shifted over the years to the therapist having to be 'neutral'. They showed understanding and compassion, but family members were none the wiser about the therapist's point of view or to what degree they (dis) agreed with different family members (Selvini et al., 1980a). Subsequently this position too came under fire due to the influence of social constructionism, where neutrality is considered impossible because the practitioner is a participant and part of a whole. Societal developments were important as well. Neutrality was considered problematic because it did not include the influence of power and dominant discourses (Gergen, 2015; Reijmers, 2014b). The notion of neutrality shifted to curiosity (Cecchin, 1987) and subsequently to not-knowing (Anderson, 1997). In this chapter we describe several positionings that correspond with a social constructionist theoretical framework.

Positioning

The term positioning, instead of position, indicates action. Positioning is an act of the practitioner who makes micro or macro choices. For instance, the therapist makes a small choice when in a family session they lean over towards the mother or turn their chair towards the mother, facing away from the father and the son. With this attitude the therapist signals an exclusive conversation with the mother while the other attendees temporarily take an observing and listening position. On a bigger scale the practitioner can be positioned by a theory or an organisation. Further professionals can position themselves in relation to the problems or with their therapeutic approach (Fredman, 2007). Whatever it is, positioning is always an action.

Overarching theoretical frameworks, such as social constructionism, describe positionings of the therapist fitting for that specific theoretical framework. This is reflected in metaphors such as *collaborative work, multipartiality, not-knowing position* or *appreciative ally*. The metaphors indicate the systemic practitioner's stance in their practice and how they could or want to relate to clients. In other words a *therapeutic stance* which entails a position, a point of view, an attitude. One could say that the practitioner positions themselves: here I stand, this is how I see things, this is how I do things. Cottyn (2021) describes the professional applying a coherent perspective as follows: "This is what I see and what I sense and feel here. This is what I will do and won't do" (p. 151). The literature refers to an attitude or a role assumed by the therapist. But positioning is more than a role. Positioning is closely related to the therapist's personal values and what they consider important in their work. In what follows we describe three positionings. All correspond with a collaborative vision where helping is regarded as a collaborative and reciprocal process between clients and therapist. In each of the three positionings the practitioner aims to attune and be sensitive to the client's culture and their way of communicating while using their feedback.

Multipartiality

"Multipartiality" (Anderson, 1997, p. 95) is a term used in systemic practice to signal that a systemic practitioner sequentially empathises with clients. The term clearly conveys the practitioner's positioning. But the term can lead to misunderstandings and be associated with the therapist alternating and purposely 'choosing sides'. However multipartiality is also connected with how the therapist's interventions (next to their intentions) affect the client. In a collaborative framework with more emphasis on the therapist's empathy and engagement, other terms such as *multilateral empathy* or *multiple (empathic) engagement* (Flaskas, 2016) could be useful. Multiple empathies reflect the empathic position of the therapist, their ability "to be in relationship" (Flaskas, 2016, p. 152) with each family member's life individually and collectively and their emotional world. Multilateral empathy emphasises the therapeutic engagement. Multipartiality or multiple empathies are described in the literature as attitudes of the practitioner. They can be regarded as skills too, but in any case the therapist positions themselves. They attend to everyone in the room (and to significant absent others) and are interested in each person. The resulting effect is that each person present feels they matter and that the therapist is genuinely interested in them and in others who are absent. In Chapter 6, 'Mapping', the following example was given.

> After Marian introduces herself she asks each person about their concerns and what they believe the problems are. If this interaction was videoed we could see for instance how Marian, when Ratna speaks, is actively listening to her; she's nodding and summarises Ratna's experiences. Perhaps she uses Ratna's own words or additional terms. Her tone of voice is one of interest. When Ratna has finished talking (but perhaps earlier, depending on how much time Ratna needs, because everyone needs to have a say) she turns to Vera. In this phase discussions are deferred until everyone had their say.

This doesn't mean that the therapist listens to each person for the same length of time, but they do check on some kind of mental map whether certain voices have not been heard yet and attend to (non-)verbal signs that can be for instance indicative of clients feeling excluded.

The not-knowing position

The not-knowing position is a far-reaching concept given it refers to a philosophical and ethical positioning of the practitioner. When the term *not-knowing position* is uttered, reference is made to being curious about the story of the family members, unrestrained by what the therapist expects to hear or what they believe needs to change based on their knowledge. The therapist as a not-knowing participant engages in a dialogue with the family or the clients. They position themselves as a guest in the clients' lives and their world of meanings. They look for ways to ask questions, to tell stories, to listen and to understand such that resonates with the clients (Anderson, 1997). The practitioner is focussed on the client as a person and on their contexts and relationships in order to respond in such a way that new perspectives are offered and more constructive stories are brought forward to make change likely (Habekotté & Reijmers, 2014; Monk et al., 1997). Their attitude reflects curiosity about what clients think, feel and experience. It implies an awareness of personal assumptions, background and societal embedding that play a role in the sessions. The term 'not-knowing' is a metaphor for a therapeutic stance that places the client in the centre. The therapist aims to understand from the client's perspective, not from their own. This is relayed through verbal reactions and non-verbal signals in the dialogue. The tone in which questions are asked and nodding support establishing contact in a respectful way.

> Lately Peter has been plagued by sudden anger outbursts. Afterwards he feels ashamed. In the therapy session Peter describes himself as an insecure, anxious worrier. The therapist asks what he would like to address first: his anger outbursts or his worrying and insecurity. Peter chooses the latter.

Thereafter, from a not-knowing position, the therapist explores with Peter the dominant story: 'I am an anxious worrier'. The therapist investigates what this could mean for Peter and tries to stay close to his story, how he tells it while abstaining from interpretations.

It is regrettable that the metaphor 'not-knowing' can lead to misunderstandings, for instance that the therapist always has to follow the client. Being directive, having expertise and being knowledgeable can be regarded as inappropriate and avoidable. As such, the position of non-knowing is associated with being passive. The dialogue seems to have disappeared (Bertrando, 2007). However not-knowing assumes an active positioning. The therapist aims to connect actively with clients and learn from them. It is described as a way of 'being with', *with-ness* (Shotter, 2011). Anderson (1997) calls it creating a *dialogical space*. The therapist is, as a matter of speech, on a journey with clients and continuously attends to the effects of what the therapist says, offers or suggests. The practitioner does use their expertise but not in a colonising way. They don't regard their knowledge as superior to the clients' and don't know better than the client what is the best way forward (Rober, 2017). The practitioner remains responsive, for example they advise clients when asked. But advice is always specific, never general or absolute.

> The therapist says somewhat hesitantly to a mother who's asking for advice about how to get her 4-year-old daughter to stay in bed and go to sleep: 'Recently, another mother told me she had come up with a bedtime ritual. She takes the time with her daughter; they run through the day together and then she reads her a story. After that she goes downstairs and sticks to the message that this has to stop now. This worked after tolerating a week of whining. Would that work for you? You could try. I'd be interested to know if it works or not.'

Many authors struggle with moulding expertise or the expert role to the concept of not-knowing (Cecchin, 1987; Cecchin et al., 1992; van Oenen et al., 2016). Questions are raised about the place of the inner conversation of the therapist, their personal experiences, feelings and ideas but not (yet) said or shown, in relation to the not-knowing position (Flaskas et al., 2005; Rober, 2002). Expertise, knowledge, theoretical framework and experience are important for many practitioners, much-needed strongholds, particularly when they work with families under tremendous pressure, when they do home visits, work in situations where safety is at risk or where various services are involved. In those situations, a third positioning may be more appropriate. Madsen and Gillespie (Madsen, 2007; Madsen & Gillespie, 2014) described this positioning as *appreciative ally*.

Appreciative ally

Madsen (Madsen, 2007; Madsen & Gillespie, 2014) stresses the importance of the therapist relationally positioning themselves when they aim to work collaboratively with families and clients. He believes that the therapist's positioning in relation to clients is the foundation of helping multi-stressed families. He concurs with what we know about the importance of a good working alliance. Madsen describes how therapists who work with families exposed to enormous pressure, encounter various relational problems. Often this results in the therapist losing the connection or unable to establish a relationship with the clients. This can make therapists feel incompetent or losing all sense of direction and hope that change is possible. The positioning of *appreciative ally* means, according to Madsen and Gillespie (2014), that therapists need to make an effort to connect with clients. Clients need to experience the therapist as someone who is on their side when they are trying to deal with or resolve problems. A relational positioning such as appreciative ally implies the practitioner assuming an attitude of respect, connectivity and curiosity. These are not personality traits but instead qualities to aim for in the relationship with the client. The therapist who is eager to obtain this positioning looks continuously for elements of competency, connection and hope in their work with individuals, couples and families. These ingredients strengthen the positioning and vice versa. Hope needs to be reasonable because unrealistic hope can lead to disappointment and frustration and exacerbate the problems (Weingarten, 2010). Being hopeful and aiming for connection doesn't mean accepting unconditionally whatever the client does or the therapist putting aside their own values and positions. But the therapist will try to find features, however small, they can appreciate and respect in clients (Madsen & Gillespie, 2014). Although it can be hard work to find something positive, it is essential. Around this grain of sand the work and collaboration can grow.

The positioning of appreciative ally implies asking questions in a respectful and curious way and attending to everyone's wellbeing. Similar to the not-knowing position the clients' life stories are at the core and their expertise is validated by attending to differences. This positioning is more powerful than the metaphor of not-knowing because the image procured by the appreciative ally is an image of the therapist asking curious questions and *doing* something. The practitioner could include other services in the treatment, is supported by a team and works in people's homes or in networks with a clearly defined role. The practitioner is firmly grounded, which is important when it comes to alarming situations.

> When Social Worker Dean, who is specialised in problems associated with dementia, talks with Eddy, his wife Alison and daughter Anne, it transpires that all three are concerned about the future. Dean refrains from taking a stance in this regard and listens carefully to everyone. At the end of the conversation he suggests they meet for a few more sessions. He acknowledges their courage in having this conversation with him about such a difficult topic. He indicates that the aim of the sessions is to have Eddy stay at home as long as possible if Alison or Anne are not too burdened and are able to carry on. With their help he wants to find out what is needed from the family and from professionals to achieve this. Dean believes this plan is a crucial starting point when they consult with other family members. They are all in agreement about this goal.

Other positionings closely related to the positioning of appreciative ally have been described. Van der Pas (1994) wrote about the positioning of practitioners who work with parents. She used the term parent coaching. This means that the practitioner in principle stands behind or next to the parents, or to be more exact alongside their parenting. Turnell and Essex (2006) *Signs of Safety* model shares similar ideas regarding positioning.

Pressure on the positioning

Various factors could interfere with the systemic practitioner holding on to the aim for positioning. These include the clients' expectations, the severity of the problems or personal values and norms. The therapist can be tempted to take an expert position or to come up swiftly with solutions, when for instance protocols, such as Attachment Focused Family Therapy, have to be followed. Pressure can be exerted by an organisation or the society. The therapist can be expected to check safety in the family or there is massive pressure because the problems are seen as individual pathology. It also happens that with most (and particularly complex) problems several professional networks are involved who feel responsible for a specific aspect. This informs what they expect of the systemic practitioner. This could undermine a positioning of appreciative ally or not-knowing attitude. It is not easy to hold on to multi-lateral empathy, curiosity and interest, to delay judgement or to stand consequently next to clients in their battle against the problems. This is certainly the case when the problems are serious or very complex or when intense emotions are at play; the therapist will notice they strayed from their preferred positioning. They may notice for instance they moralise, use their personal judgement as norm, are stuck in their own emotions or feel they don't know what they are doing.

What helps

Triadic positioning, formulating *goals* collaboratively and *focussing on what supports the clients* can help the practitioner to maintain their positioning and to determine the direction of therapy.

Triadic positioning

"Triadic positioning facilitates the expansion of the lens by adding a third party. The formed triangle places disagreements between two people in a wider context and reconnects them" (Cottyn, 2021, p. 156). Specific to triadic positioning is that the third party does not necessarily have to be a person. It can be a dominant discourse, a perspective, a problem, the neighbourhood, a network or a legal framework the client has to relate to. Client and therapist discuss the effects, pressures and expectations of this third party.

When the systemic therapist aims to assume a triadic position they and the clients explore together for example the societal ideas that play a part in the problems, how arguments affect their relationship or what the effects of stressors such as illness are. This can happen through externalising conversations or by other means. White introduced and developed the technique of externalising conversations (White, 2007; White & Epston, 1990). In externalising conversations the therapist aims to position themselves in such manner they can in conjunction with the client look at the problem's influence. A problem is separated from the person, and therapist and client explore how the problem influences or has influenced the client's life, relationships and family. Consequently the problem and the client or family are no longer one and the same. Externalising can be applied to other influences too, such as the strengths of a family. Externalising makes space for reflection. It creates a setting where therapist and client can connect and explore if opportunities for change are present.

In Chapter 6 we saw how Kira, Vera and Ratna described the problems between them as problems with 'the circle of irritation'. They came up with the metaphor 'the circle of irritation that bothers everyone'.

Externalisation creates space for the professional as well. Cottyn (2012) describes how the therapist can link problems in the alliance with pressures from society. The professional can achieve this by taking a meta position or in other words a macro-triadic positioning. Cottyn applies this to parent coaches, but it can be utilised in other situations. It helps therapists to develop a more connected view and feel more empathy for clients, even when they display unacceptable behaviours (Neyens, 2017). Madsen and Gillespie (2014) state that externalising is more a conceptual attitude than a technique.

There are other ways to maintain a triadic positioning. It can be useful to spread different tasks amongst several professionals and wise to not have one professional fulfil different roles in the face of huge pressure from clients, the organisation or society. This pressure can relate to the expert role, to claims about 'what is happening here' (van Oenen et al., 2012) or to safety (De Cock, 2008; Hurst, 2011). One therapist for example could verbalise the societal pressure on safety while another can support the clients from an empathic stance. This in turn can result in triadic processes (or possibly in complicated discussions as we will see in Chapter 10).

A shared goal

Formulating a goal everyone agrees on can help the therapist to maintain their positioning and the direction of the therapy. What is it the clients, the family or the couple want to achieve (Madsen, 2007)? The most significant conversation is not about 'how did this happen and why' (nevertheless important elements in the client's story) but rather 'where do you want to go'? McAdam (2002) described what a collaborative goal could be in families where safety is at risk such as '120% safety and how children and parents can be protected while achieving this' (Ekholdt, 2016). Formulating a goal in conjunction with the clients helps the therapist to maintain a positioning of *appreciative ally*. They too are poised for the clients to reach their goal.

Buffering processes

Another way for systemic practitioners to maintain their positioning is to identify buffers: who or what can support the jointly formulated goal? They could focus on networks and how networks could become buffering agents. In the context of intercultural work with families and migrants Tjin A Djie calls this 'protective coats' (Tjin A Djie & Zwaan, 2007). Omer endeavours to enlist acquaintances, neighbours and friends (Omer, 2011; Omer et. al., 2013; Omer & Wiebenga, 2015) and Van der Pas (2014) suggests thinking in terms of buffering processes when it comes to parenting and refers to the importance of social networks and societal support. Widening the field with buffering processes results in broader support.

In conclusion

In conversations practitioners position themselves but are not always aware of this. Conversations do not evolve automatically but are guided by the practitioner's responses and actions, in other words by how they position themselves. Positionings are embedded in theoretical frameworks.

In this chapter we described three positionings that correspond with systemic work. Discussions within the systemic framework about these positionings are ongoing. Nevertheless, the premise is that positioning and being transparent about this are paramount. The positioning chosen by the practitioner is informed by their systemic lens, their task assigned by society, the organisation they work for, their experience and their person. The positioning of appreciative ally could suit a practitioner better than the positioning of not-knowing and vice versa. It is important to reflect about systemic positioning and how choices in this respect are made. Being transparent about positioning is like a steady anchor for the practitioner in an often confusing and chaotic field. It is a common thread in the work with complex relational problems. When the therapist is aware of their positioning, they will notice when they stray away from it, when the alliance deteriorates, polyphony disappears, when they feel constrained and their inner dialogue gets stuck (Rober, 2005). The therapist needs to take the time and the space then to reflect, involve colleagues and make considered decisions about bringing these reflections into the conversation with the clients (Cottyn, 2012, 2021). Positioning is dynamic, a process of trial and error and requires effort. Positioning is hard work and feedback oriented, an action that always requires reflection.

Exercise

The motivation to attend therapy can differ greatly between the people involved (in session and in the outside world). For instance one partner of a couple is highly motivated for relationship counselling while the other partner thinks it's a waste of time but agrees to attend this once. Or parents ask help for their adolescent child who is not interested in the slightest. You could take another example from your practice.

Consider the different positions you could take. Write down a few sentences for each.

Expert position. Think of three different angles for interventions from this position (such as providing psychoeducation, research shows that...).

Multiple empathy. What kind of questions do you ask? What interventions can you do when you strive to empathise with everyone? You could ask about the partners, but don't forget to consider the children, grandparents, family, the outside world, the referrer.

The not-knowing position. When you position yourself in the not-knowing position, which questions and comments come up for you?

Appreciative ally. What would be an indication that you are positioning yourself as an appreciative ally? Which questions and interventions would be relevant here?

Reflect on the possible effects of each positioning.

You could role-play this with colleagues.

Chapter 8

Settings matter

Introduction

Except when they have to follow set procedures, systemic practitioners need to decide whom they are going to speak with: whom to work with therapeutically, and about what? Meet with the same people each time or can this change? In an individual setting when parents or a close friend accompany the client to support the change process, what does the therapist take into account? What does it mean when the setting is changed and, for example, relationship sessions are transposed in family sessions? Settings can change spontaneously, for instance when in an individual therapy suddenly the partner joins because of unhappiness about the relationship. Or when during family therapy the mother stayed home because she had a terrible fight with the father. The literature usually portrays one particular setting. Each setting (individual, couples, parents, families and groups) comes with a theory of practice characteristic of that setting. Consequently practitioners tend to stay within the same setting (Alblas, 2005). Though setting changes are common in some contexts such as in the day-to-day practice of family caseworkers in care and protection (Bolt, 2017), where they are taken for granted and not given much attention. Who to speak with is a question repeatedly considered in the work with the Dufour family. After a family session with Vera, Kira and Ratna, therapist Marian asks them to consider whether it is best to have the next appointment with Vera and Kira as parents, with Kira and Ratna as mother and daughter or with the family; three different conversational settings. A change of setting was implied when the suggestion was put to Kim to bring Tony for the second session. This is an example of how a deliberate change in setting can be used as a therapeutic tool. A conversation with Kim and Tony would be a totally different conversation than only with Kim. Settings create a context and have specific consequences.

This chapter deals with the various settings systemic practitioners are faced with. We will discuss sessions with an individual, with couples, parents, families and group and network settings. Within systemic practice each setting has its own history and is connected with specific dominant

DOI: 10.4324/9781003272038-8

social discourses that influence therapists and clients. We briefly describe what the reasons might be for choosing a particular setting. Each choice influences the therapeutic relationship and we will discuss relevant focal points. The chapter finishes with a reflection on setting changes. The systemic framework including all systemic skills and techniques as described so far forms the common thread. In this respect both choice and change of setting are important.

Speaking with individuals

History

Systemic practice is often believed to imply working with several people. From the early years some systems therapists have been interested in the position of the individual in systemic therapy. Ackerman (1966) considered family therapy as complementary to individual conversations with young people. In 1983 Weakland described "working with families or couples through one person" (p. 46). And Haley (1971) regarded individual therapy as a way to intervene in a family. There was a time when systemic work with individuals disappeared in the background because of the belief that change in families automatically resulted in change in individual family members. This has since changed because of theoretical developments focussing more on individuals within the system, on individual differences between family members and on their differing perspectives. Individual therapy based on systemic principles and interventions has a firm place now (Boscolo & Bertrando, 1996; Hedges, 2005; Reijmers, 2014a).

Dominant beliefs

Individual therapy is influenced by how society views individuals and what is expected of them. In our Western society important qualities include independence, self-actualisation, personal responsibility and making personal choices (de Regt, 2014; Peters, 1999). Both success and failure are seen as personal. Happiness is another common term, and not being happy or 'being out of sorts' is increasingly considered as problematic; you need to do something about it. Even in circumstances where it is normal to feel unhappy, for instance when grieving or in case of illness, the unhappiness is assumed to be temporary because it is important 'to process it' or 'to give it a place'. There is also huge focus on autonomy and boundaries. Adolescents have to become independent from their family, mainly from their parents, and as an adult you are not expected to live with your parents. An elderly parent prefers to not live with their children because 'they have their own life'. These are socio-culturally determined beliefs and therefore changeable and valued differently by people. Different beliefs circulate in non-Western families and other social reference groups (Davolo & Fruggeri, 2016; Jessurun, 2010; Jessurun & Warring, 2018).

Why individual therapy

People usually experience and define their problems as personal. Adults seek individual help for their issues. Adolescents and young people often prefer to speak to a therapist alone. Parents wish for their child to speak with a professional about their problems. This can be a useful entry point for the therapist depending on the kind of problems and the minimal impact on relationships. There could be valid reasons to not invite family members: the client prefers not to, family members aren't keen or the kind of relationship requires careful exploration first. Individual therapy can be the choice of setting even when relationship problems are obvious, for instance with high conflict after separation (Cottyn, 2009, 2021) or when teenagers terrorise their parents (Vermeire, 2017). There could be organisational reasons to provide individual therapy. Many organisations and mental health and social care practices are organised around individual questions and problems. Financial and legal frameworks too focus on individuals. It is important to keep in mind that speaking with one person is an option. Is this a setting that offers hope and opportunities for change?

The therapeutic relationship

The exclusive intimacy of the therapeutic relationship is not paramount in systemic practice. So in conversations with individuals the systemic practitioner looks for relevant contexts and relationships and brings others in. However the relationship between the therapist and the client is dyadic. The client describes problems, situations and patterns from their personal perspective and experiences. This colours their emotions and their stories. The therapist can be surprised when meeting other people the client has been talking about. They had formed quite a different image of the person based on the conversations with the client. In this dyadic relationship the systemic practitioner needs to ensure that the child, the adolescent or the adult with whom they speak feels listened to and understood. It requires careful attuning to connect to individual meanings and feelings and 'bring in' others.

Rose, Agnes and Dirk's middle child, has decided to seek help.

In the session Rose describes herself as insecure and not very confident. Steven, the therapist, asks her whether she's always thought of herself like this. That doesn't appear to be the case. She's not anxious or insecure in every situation. And people don't regard her as such. During the session Rose suddenly comments that all those questions make her feel stupid about thinking and feeling like that about herself. Others have been saying the same.

This is important information for the therapist. It indicates that the timing was off: Rose cannot hear the comments by others as constructive. The therapist's questions apparently give Rose the same feeling as the reactions from her friends and family. This created distance because the questions aligned with and strengthened the voice inside Rose that says she's stupid because she feels insecure.

> Steven thanks Rose for her valuable feedback. Is it correct that when family members or friends say similar things to her, she feels worse? That's correct. And is it correct that his questions make her feel she shouldn't be so 'dramatic'? Rose agrees: 'A little bit, yes.' But she thinks that is stupid too because she knows that's not how he meant it. Steven confirms this was not his intention, but perhaps it shows the importance of mapping how feeling insecure and lack of confidence influence her life. This seems a good starting point. He asks Rose to let him know when she gets this feeling again and praises her for bringing this up.

The therapist looks through the lens of the individual client and is at the same time the person who has to make a difference. This requires careful balancing between distance and proximity.

Focal points

Self and emotions

In individual therapy the focus is mainly on *I: I want* or *I feel* and about *yourself: what do you want* or *what do you feel.* The (usually underlying) belief is that everyone has a robust, unchangeable core, your *I* or *self,* that remains the same irrespective of the circumstances. In systemic and other approaches (Verhaeghe, 2014) it is assumed that our self is formed in diverse contexts and that how we feel and behave depends on the context. That we are Dutch or Flemish and one-eighth Portuguese, female, LGBTQ or doctor can be more or less prominent in different contexts (Savenije, 2014a). Everyone has multiple identities and emotions are often the focus in individual therapy. Emotions are regarded as individual and very personal. But emotions are related to societal and cultural norms. We learn about emotions, what is appropriate or inappropriate and how to express emotions in our family and in society. How we express emotions depends on age: children and adolescents express their emotions differently than from adults (Wilson, 2007). And emotions are messages, verbal and non-verbal expressions in relationship that have effects and can be (mis)understood. Emotions can be viewed through a relational lens (Fredman, 2004; Hedges, 2005). This can be a challenge for practitioners used to empathically interpret emotions for clients, such as naming an emotion that seems appropriate for the situation the client describes: 'That must have made you feel angry.' This could resonate with the client or the therapist's personal interpretation. The systemic practitioner will explore the context in which the emotions occur. How the emotions are expressed, what is their meaning and their effect? They align with how the clients verbalise their emotions.

Contexts

In systemic individual therapy the practitioner looks for those contexts relevant to the client's problems and perceived by the client as significant. When working with individual clients therapists tend to venture not further than the family context. Instead it can be helpful to draw on the white board all relevant contexts the client connects with in that moment (Pearce as cited in Hedges, 2005). This can include non-problematic contexts.

We introduced Zeynep in Chapter 3.

> As an aide for Zeynep and herself Maria first draws a circle in the middle of the board, representing Zeynep. Around the circle she draws various important contexts: once circle is Zeynep's family, one circle is her work, one circle are her girlfriends who support her. Another circle has a question mark: her wish to have a boyfriend. In subsequent sessions more circles key words and symbols can be added.

The silencing of polyphony

Depending on the situation, the problem or the client, when the therapist overidentifies with the client's perspective, it leaves no space to play with differences. The therapist empathises with the client and blames the person causing the client's suffering. But the opposite can happen too: the therapist feels more empathy for the reactions of people in the client's life and less for the client. The therapist's inner dialogue (Rober, 2005), careful considerations about what to focus on and what to say, has stalled. It is then that the therapist needs to reflect by for instance reframing the client's actions, imagining how colleagues would respond and permitting 'a dissident voice'. They can consult colleagues to help move along the inner dialogue. The therapist could then introduce the regained polyphony in the conversation with the client, for instance through verbalising different ideas, citing a colleague's comments or feeding back a team discussion. The colleague or the team form a virtual reflecting team to reintroduce multiple perspectives.

Talking with couples

History

The history of couples counselling does not run quite parallel with the history of systemic practice. Couples counselling started in the 1950s with informal, strongly educational *marriage counselling* without a theoretical foundation. In the 1960s individual therapists, mainly analysts, started with *conjoint therapy*: meetings with partners who each had their own individual therapist. Next the field was overwhelmed for a while by turbulent theoretical developments in systemic therapy. Initially therapists focussed on what was believed then as couples aiming to control the relationship. Haley (1963) regarded relationship problems as related to an indistinct hierarchy in the relationship, lack of flexibility in roles and rigid symmetrical or complementary conflicts. Jackson (1965) spoke about the *marital quid pro quo*, an implicit marriage contract. In a relationship partners behave according to predictable patterns of which they themselves are not aware. These patterns can be verbal or non-verbal and function to maintain the balance in the relationship. This concept was influential for a long time. Nowadays parallel with developments in systemic therapy, more attention goes to attachment, cultural differences, power and gender differences. The therapist is no longer seen as a neutral observer who has a script about what constitutes a good relationship. Influences from individual therapies, like psychoanalytic therapy and behaviour therapy, have retained and regained their importance (Gurman, 2015).

Dominant beliefs

A variety of ideas and images about relationships exist in every society. They influence therapist and clients in what is considered problematic and the desired solution. Currently in Western societies love and the romantic ideal take centre stage. We expect intimacy, support, fellowship and facilitation of personal development. We are each personally responsible to make the relationship successful (Faes, 2014; Perel, 2006, 2017) and a high degree of emotional competency is expected (Rober, 2017). Partner relationships are considered essential. Not having or not wanting an intimate relationship is regarded as a shortcoming or a deficiency. Regardless of the variety in partner relationships, a monogamic, heterosexual relationship remains the dominant model. This comes with beliefs about gender (being a man or a woman), sex (exciting and spontaneous), falling in love with others (adultery), age (can women be older than men?), ethnicity (usually people are in a relationship with a partner of similar ethnic background and couples with multi-ethnical backgrounds experience specific problems), religion, education, work and money. There are also societal ideas about how to solve relationship problems: 'you have to talk about it'. All couples, including couples from other cultures or different from the monogamic heterosexual model (perhaps even more than others), feel the pressure of these dominant beliefs (Faes, 2014; Perel, 2006, 2017). Various ideas about partner relationships also circulate in mental health and social care services and amongst practitioners (Bongaerts, 2014, 2017). Therapists who aren't used to working with alternative forms of relationships or with culturally different relationships can feel out of sorts with couples who don't fit the dominant model.

Why speak with couples?

Partner relationships are important relationships. The breaking up of a partner relationship due to separation is one of the most stressful times for partners and families. Partners usually hope for a long-term relationship enabling them to raise their children safely and lovingly (if they want children) and grow old together. Taking into consideration the multiple influences that can affect a relationship over time, these are high expectations. Just think of the 'normal' stages of a family influencing the partner relationship, such as becoming a couple, having one or more children, raising children in the different stages of their lives and eventually being a couple again when the children have fled the nest. Carter and McGoldrick (2004) identify all these stages as significant tasks. How these evolve is influenced by socio-economic factors, illness, relocation, migration, individual problems of family members, demands of ageing parents and so on. Currently many young adults live longer with their parents for economic reasons and because of lack of affordable housing. Partners bring along their own history and background. Their families and social networks also play a role in the partner relationship. When the relationship is not going well, it is not surprising that partners worry about the longevity of the relationship and seek professional help, sometimes following advice from others to go and talk with someone. Couple counselling is one of the fastest-growing modes of systemic therapy (Gurman, 2015). Sexuality and a third party in the relationship are topics that are particular to helping partners, with many publications to date (Emmelkamp-Keizer & Aptroot, 2014; Luyens & van Steenwegen, 2014; Perel, 2006).

The therapeutic relationship

The therapeutic relationship with a couple is a triadic relationship. For the couple this means that the therapist looks in as an outsider. This can elicit concerns such as: how does the therapist see me? What do they think about our relationship and our problems? Or the clients entertain thoughts such as: 'surely, the therapist will succeed in changing my partner'. A triadic relationship implies instability: coalitions can change frequently. Although couples usually want to improve their relationship against a backdrop of intense relationship dynamics, they often have different ideas about how this ought to happen. It requires the therapist to balance this tension actively to preserve the couple's relationship and to make space for different views and new interaction patterns. To keep focus the therapist needs to make decisions continuously about what to address and how.

Focal points

Multipartiality can be a challenge

In conversations with couples it can be challenging to retain an attitude of multiple empathy. Often it is easier for the therapist to empathise with one of the partners or they find one partner nicer, more sensitive or more intelligent than the other partner.

> Myrna and Paul, two young doctors who have been living together for a little while, reveal in the session that they have terrible arguments about the expiry date of food. When Paul has the time, he checks the cupboards and throws away all the tin cans and packets that have expired. Myrna thinks that's complete nonsense. She never pays attention to the dates. Recently she finished a piece of pizza with a bit of mould on it that had been in the fridge for a while. She wasn't concerned, she trusted her body to indicate if it wasn't good for her. It made Paul furious. Henk, the therapist, doesn't understand Myrna either. His mother has similar weird ideas.

In couples therapy the conversation is often about this type of small, ordinary events. Everyday differences, for instance about domestic matters and who does what at home, can erode the partner relationship because they keep occurring and each partner believes the other person could easily solve the problem. How difficult can it be to screw the top on the toothpaste or not make an issue of it (Kaufmann, 2009)! In our example Henk could choose a number of interventions. He could leave Myrna and Paul to discuss the issue together and watch over the theme, the structure and the safety in the conversation. Or he can explore the pattern of the conflict first with Myrna, then with Paul to avoid escalation of the conflict. Rather than focussing on the content Henk could explore with each how the conflict affects the relationship. These are just some of the possibilities. Whatever Henk chooses to do, he is part of the triad.

> Henk invites Myrna to say a bit more. While he is talking with Myrna, Paul is listening. This may generate new thoughts and feelings in Paul. Although these can be addressed later, Henk is keeping an eye on Paul. Is Paul listening calmly or is he sighing and shifting in his chair?

Henk is paying extra attention to Myrna because he doesn't have much sympathy for her point of view. He would like to understand better why she thinks this way so he can be more empathic. He is making an extra effort for the therapeutic relationship.

Bringing forward positive stories: A counterbalance

When working with couples, the therapist not only focuses on concerns and problems but also on more positive aspects of the relationship. This can change the atmosphere of the conversation and increase the chance that partners feel safe. This can happen in the introductory session. The therapist could ask the couple, before they divulge their problems, to talk more about each person's strengths and qualities (Chasin & Roth, 1990). After making an inventory of the problems and concerns, the therapist could ask what made them feel attracted to one another. It is common that what was so attractive in the beginning is now so annoying: 'She was so calm, I really liked that because I was always so busy' or 'He knew so well what he wanted, I was more a doubter'. When partners have been together for a long time, the therapist can ask what made them decide to live together. People usually take factors into consideration that facilitate living together, such as the partner's reliability, the stage of life, wanting to have children. Compliments the couple exchange and what is working well are often snowed under by criticism and could be given deliberate and repeated attention in support of the relationship (Gottman & Silver, 2015; Vansteenwegen, 2014).

Managing high conflict

Although the saying goes that 'arguments clear the air', this is not the best starting point for relationship counselling. It could end up being a case of 'my word against yours' and a barrage of hurtful statements that exacerbate the problems. The therapist needs to be able to manage the intensity of conversations and escalations without being swept away themselves, while keeping an eye on the alliance. This requires an active attitude, transparent positioning, clear goals and skills such as adding structure, clarification or slowing down of the conversation. Sometimes agreements have to be made. For instance in case of a violent relationship the main theme in the sessions becomes how the spirals of violence can be broken and more safety created (Groen & van Lawick, 2009). This can be achieved by using safety maps (Faes, 2016a), which are illustrated in Chapter 10.

Vulnerabilities

Intense conflict in partner relationships is often related to specific individual vulnerabilities. For instance someone who was often left alone as a child may have developed a sensitivity in this area. People develop ways to manage this, survival strategies. Someone who has felt abandoned may have developed withdrawal as survival strategy ('I'll do it myself') or is clingy ('Don't leave me'). Keeping this in mind can help the practitioner and the partners to reframe and understand better its related interaction patterns, the so-called *vulnerability cycle* (Scheinkman & DeKoven Fishbane, 2004).

Focus on other contexts

It is almost unavoidable that during partner relationship sessions the therapist gets sucked into the reciprocal interactions. The focus contracts more and more to what plays between the couple. The practitioner can lose sight of the many other pressuring and supportive contexts of significance. Zooming out can help. One partner's job can provide safety while potential redundancy or financial problems can put a relationship under tremendous pressure. Parenting that is going well can make a couple stay together, despite being unhappy about their relationship. But when they start arguing as parents too, this can be the straw breaking the camel's back. Family relationships and friendships too can support or undermine the partner relationship.

Separation

Every society has rules about partner separation. In Western societies separation is common and the number of divorces is on the increase. Separation can be a joint or a one-party decision. It may have been on the cards for a while, or one of the partners made the decision to the surprise of the other partner. A third party can be involved. The decision to separate is an enormous change in context. When the decision is reached during relationship therapy, a change in setting is usually indicated. It is no longer advisable to continue therapy with both partners together. A few systemic treatment modalities have been developed for high conflict separation and when children are involved. The setting can become only one of the partners (Cottyn, 2009, 2021) or expanding the setting to a group (Visser & van Lawick, 2021). Systemic mediation for ex-partners in high conflict after separation who have children is also available (Decraemer & Cottyn, 2017; Parkinson, 2019).

Speaking with parents

History

Parenting coaching existed long before the introduction of systemic therapy and came from the USA in the context of the *child guidance movement*. Its practice was developed by social workers mainly who had plenty of practical yet undocumented experience (van der Pas, 1994). That practical experience disappeared because of, amongst other things, the rise of systemic therapy. Initially a link between the children's problems and the dysfunction of the family was the main focus in systemic therapy. The whole family had to be present to resolve the problems. In addition there was the belief that problematic parenting was related to problems in the partner relationship. The focus shifted from talking with parents to the couple relationship. Parent coaching was still offered, but mainly to support individual help for the child and often in a pedagogic framework. This has changed. In systemic therapy in The Netherlands and in Belgium attention is more directed at the specific position of parents and some systemic approaches focus on parents. The aim of parenting coaching now is to support parents in their parenting (van der Pas, 2003; Omer & Wiebenga, 2015).

Dominant beliefs

Parenting is in the societal limelight. While forming a family is considered a private affair, parenting evokes societal interference and control (Perel, 2006; van der Pas, 2003). An abundance of advice circulates about bringing up children and parenthood: courses, supports, protocols, books and TV-programmes. Raising children is simplified to implementing – sometimes supported by scientific research – parenting advice. The language used is often borrowed from developmental psychology, neurology or neurobiology. Concepts such as developmental stages and attachment are often the starting point and are presented as universal and timeless (Van den Berge, 2011). The dominant belief is that the basis for children's problems is the way parents interact with their children. It is a discourse of parent blaming, mothers usually more than fathers (Alan, 2004; Jakob, 2018; Van Reybrouck, 2012).

Why parent coaching?

Parent coaching is always connected with problems of children. And there is a huge variety in children and in problems. Parenthood is vulnerable and is in the case of problems with children acknowledged by attending to the parents. This may be the parents' need, what practitioners believe is necessary or society's worry about the parenting. The last usually represents concerns about safety, authority problems or neglect (Carr, 2012). However parents can struggle with normal child behaviour, for instance when their new-born baby is difficult to console or their complacent child is now a rebellious and irreverent adolescent. Depending on the age of the child, parents have to respond to different demands. In general parents become involved with professional help because their children have serious problems they can't manage or they are embroiled in interactions that no longer effect change and include siblings, family members and the wider context. The parents have become isolated because responses from bystanders are unhelpful (Van Reybrouck, 2012). The goal of parenting coaching is to support the parenting. Although this sounds self-evident, this is not easy. Parents often feel judged or blamed by professionals who try to establish what went wrong in the parenting to explain the child's problems.

The therapeutic relationship

Parent coaches can experience considerable pressure from other professionals who work with children, colleagues, teachers, other experts or society with its principal focus on children's safety, care and protection. Consequently parent coaches need to position themselves clearly. van der Pas (1994, 2003) developed the now well-established concept of *the positioning of the parent coach*. In principle the parenting coach tries to place themselves in the parents' shoes. Even when parents behave irresponsibly, the parent coach presumes that parents have an *awareness of responsibility,* in principle unconditionally and ever present; it is not a choice. This awareness is not exclusive to biological parents and extends to parents who do not raise their own children (van der Pas, 2003). Omer has stated that an awareness of responsibility can include an active position of non-violent resistance. For instance when parents communicate to their problematic children: 'We are present in your life, even when times are tough. You can't fire us, you can't divorce us and you can't silence us. We'll always be there for you and are not giving up (on you)' (Bom & Wiebenga, 2017; Jakob, 2006, 2018; Omer, 2011; Omer & Wiebenga, 2015).

Focal points

A dilemma for the practitioner

Parenting coaches can feel stuck when parents act irresponsibly or make things very difficult for the children. The parents and the therapist can sense the pressure from the environment in their alliance. The practitioner can create space by reflecting with parents about expectations and demands regarding parenting. As such the tension felt in the therapeutic relationship can be connected with the societal pressure: this is not about something between professional and parents, but the effect of societal expectations about parenting on parents and the professional. The position of the parenting coach resumes its triadic form and frees up space to take up its positioning as parenting coach again (Cottyn, 2005, 2012; Wilson, 2007).

Who to invite?

Parents are often invited first, prior to any kind of intervention. This highlights that it is the parents who refer: this is about *their* child. But this doesn't make it clear who shall or ought to be invited. When the parental system consists of a father and a mother, they need to be consulted about who is attending the sessions. Can Mum come by herself while Dad attends every so often? Or is it important that both parents attend? They could consider how the parents see their roles and the practicalities associated with having both parents attend at the same time. Despite separated parents having a parental agreement, this doesn't necessarily mean they can attend together without friction or that they agree that conversations are held with one parent only. When the children live mainly with one parent and see the other parent occasionally, sometimes the therapist speaks with the parent where the child resides or where the problems occur (Jakob, 2018). This begs the question whether this is a well-considered option and inclusive of the other parent. Legal contexts too play a role in choosing whom to invite and whom to inform.

> Tom (13) is referred because of depressive symptoms. His parents are separated. He lives with his Mum, but Dad has visitation rights. This is working reasonably well but is not great. Both parents are legal guardians.
>
> When it comes to Tom, the contact between the parents isn't the best. At the initial meeting only Mum is present. She says she prefers not to come with her ex-husband. For Tom it doesn't matter one way or the other. In a phone conversation with Dad it transpires that he is keen to meet with the therapist. They make an appointment. If and how the parents are to be involved in Tom's therapy is the agenda for discussion and consideration.

Attend to what is supportive

Systemic practitioners pay attention to what goes well in relationships, to exceptions and to supportive contexts. In parenting coaching the concept of *buffering factors* comes to mind, a term introduced by van der Pas and now well established. Buffering factors for parenting can include a satisfying division of tasks between parents, the ability to take a meta-position (for instance the ability to reflect: 'what do I think is happening?'), 'good-parent experiences' (when your child thanks you, 'Mum, thanks' or when as a parent you get the feeling you've done something good) (van der Pas, 1994). Support from the environment is another important buffering process. When parents can lean on others, they can carry risks (Cottyn, 2005; Jakob, 2018; van der Pas, 2014). Particularly when professionals feel increasingly anxious or concerned about the parenting or about how children are treated, it can be helpful to identify buffering factors. Support from the environment should not be taken for granted. Grandparents, friends and neighbours often believe that there are problems because of the parents (Baert, 1990) and parents are overwhelmed by advice: 'give more love', 'set boundaries', 'learn to let go of your child'. To feel supported parents need to have regular conversations with family and friends about what they perceive as supportive and what isn't (Van Reybrouck, 2012; Visser & van Lawick, 2021).

A common thread

In high conflict situations it can be helpful to support parents in their daily interactions with their children by finding something they can hold onto. Something that prevents them from reacting in the heat of an argument but instead helps them to wait 'to strike the iron when it's cold', as Omer describes (Omer & Lebowitz, 2016; Omer & Wiebenga, 2015).

Connection with the context

When parents fight about the children and escalations are likely, it is advisable to consider the context. Perhaps the family is transitioning, and new forms of parenthood need to be developed because the old ones don't suffice any longer. For example in developmental stages such as children growing up, separation, step-parenthood or illness. The idea that *parenting reorganisation* is needed can be a helpful framework for the professional. It helps parenting coaches to not be swept away by lack of clarity or patterns of conflict (Cottyn, 2021).

Talking with families

Instead of starting with a historical overview, we begin with 'Why family sessions' as we covered perspectives about *the* family in Chapter 1, and in Chapter 2 how systemic therapy has evolved in theory and in practice.

Why family sessions?

One of the core ideas of systemic therapy is that families are the context *and* the solution for problems. Initially this was reflected in practice: the family member with the problem had to be seen with the whole family (Breunlin & Jacobsen, 2014). Over time family sessions have become one of many options rather than the preferred setting. Often the therapist works with a subsystem: only with the parents or only with the child who has the problems and its parents. This can happen because of the type of problems or because of organisational and financial barriers.

What could be the reasons to hold family therapy sessions? An important reason remains that each family member has a unique place in the family and is part of a connective family pattern. This is immediately visible when all the family members are present: the eye contact between a son and his mother; the sister who doesn't present with problems but is obstructive during the session; the way the family deals with Dad who lost his job and is visibly depressed (Minuchin, 1998). A second important reason is that in family sessions more and other sources of support can be accessed. Perhaps the father who appears to be on the outside is clearly worried about his daughter and has ideas about how he can support her. Or older siblings can provide valuable support. A third reason for conversations with the whole family is that some problems affect everyone in the family. A fourth reason, connected to individual resilience and how family members deal with problems, relates to how the family over time has interpreted and responded to the outside world. How this happens and who is instrumental becomes clearer when all family members are in attendance (Breunlin & Jacobsen, 2014; Rober, 2002; Wilson, 2007). Finally the practitioner can immediately intervene in family sessions, perhaps to motivate change or to normalise experiences that are part of the functioning of families and relationships, of stages of family life or of other things. The therapist can intervene in patterns that intensify the problems. Maladaptive interaction patterns can be cut short and immediately talked about and positive interactions and connecting patterns can be practised in session (Gurman & Burton, 2014). While the idea that families are part of the solution for serious family problems may sound romantic, it transpires that in general significant others in someone's life, like the other family members, have the will to form a supportive community (Madsen, 2007).

The therapeutic relationship

The alliance in family therapy is defined as multiple empathic. In Chapter 5 we described the essence of a good therapeutic relationship with all family members.

Being multiple empathic and remaining so requires effort. It is often easier for practitioners to speak with the person who took the initiative than with the person who is quiet and it can be easier to talk with adults than with children (Wilson, 2007). It is important to respect and explicitly acknowledge the not talking, hesitations about therapy or reluctance to attend (Rober, 2017). Children of all ages can participate actively in family sessions with drawings or other non-verbal activities. Although the therapist is not responsible for the content of the family session, they are responsible for the process. They ensure safety and space for everybody and when needed intervene to stop negative escalations. They clarify expectations, structure and goal of the sessions. Because cultural and socio-economical differences between practitioner and the family could be substantial and influence the alliance, perhaps family sessions can be regarded as multicultural meetings. Both microcultures can be on the same wavelength but this won't always be the case (Boeckhorst, 2014; Jessurun, 2010; Jessurun & Warring, 2018; McGoldrick & Hardy, 2008). It is important that the therapist remains vigilant whether all family members still feel part of the conversation. If not this points to a rupture in the therapeutic alliance and needs to be addressed and repaired.

Focal points

Sessions with whom

Family sessions don't need to commence with inviting the whole family. Some therapists prefer to start family sessions with a conversation with the parents. They can consider collaboratively who and how to invite other family members. Other therapists invite the whole family from the start, including children, to get a feel for the family dynamics and to avoid being influenced by the parents' view of the problems (Rober, 2014; Wilson, 2007). Some therapists decide who to invite, others leave this decision to the clients. Where the sessions take place can vary: at the service, the practice or the family's home. Working with a family means the practitioner aims to have regular conversations with everyone present. This won't be always feasible but the family remains the main setting and this has consequences. In principle information will be shared with everyone. When family members can't attend, somehow, they need to stay in the loop. Attention needs to go to the absentees and what their opinions may be. In the context of family sessions, it can be useful to speak separately with a son and his father about a specific topic, in line with the agreed goal of the family sessions. However such change in setting is only temporary.

Several generations

When working with families, including adults and children, the therapist needs to connect with the various generations present. The age of the children can vary from baby to adolescent to young adult. And presently sessions occur with elderly parents and their adult children. Working with adults, children and young people requires the therapist to adjust their language and systemic interventions. Systemic practitioners who work mostly with children and young people report how to make space for them in the session: toys for the younger children, paper and crayons for drawing, perhaps some smaller chairs. The use of words and language matters too.

> Bella and Hayden attend with their 4-year-old son Otto. The parents sit down. Otto walks to the toy kitchen in a corner of the room and is curious. The social worker, Monique, shows him some kitchen utensils and asks whether he likes to cook. Otto nods.
> 'What is your favourite food?', Monique asks.
> 'Pizza', Otto replies.
> Next follows an animated introduction with Otto and his parents about the foods they each like and dislike. In the meantime Otto is 'cooking' in the kitchen and is walking backwards and forwards to offer everyone snacks.

When the therapist is talking with the parents, certain concepts may need to be 'translated' in age-appropriate language for the children to understand. Questions need to be simple, about behaviour instead of feelings and children find it easier to answer multiple choice questions than open questions (Wilson, 2007). Most children find it difficult to talk about feelings. So do adolescents. They prefer a degree of down-to-earth-ness and shy away from talking too much about how they are feeling. This can be respected. Feelings can also be expressed non-verbally (with clay for instance) or given a workable name (Fredman, 1997). Children can be asked to draw during the session and subsequently talk about the drawing, in a bid to hear from them what they made, not to interpret it (Rober, 2014). When working with children it is important to create space for playfulness and creativity: playing is talking (Reijmers et al., 2005). These are vital adjustments because it has transpired children want to be included in family sessions, even when they are not the focus of the conversations (Rober, 2014). Adolescents too, when present, want to be taken seriously and partake in the sessions as fully-fledged participants (Savenije, 2014b; Wilson, 2007).

Framing the problems

It doesn't take much in family sessions for the therapist to feel overwhelmed. Carter and McGoldrick (2004) offer their family stage model, a framework that can help the therapist to focus their view, thoughts and actions. This has been referred to in previous chapters. The authors state that families, because of their children growing up, develop continually. They identify a number of developmental stages and each stage is characterised by specific tasks. The stage of young parents with a baby places other demands on a family than the stage of a family with teenagers or than the stage of family reorganisation because the parents are separating. In the transition between two stages families are extra vulnerable. Family development is further influenced by what they call stressors: events such as relocation, changes in socio-economic circumstances or illnesses in the family. Although the reality is more complex than this model can represent, it offers a framework to contextualise and normalise problems. In the next two examples the referral reason is similar, but the problems are contextually embedded differently.

> Gemma (15) has been referred because things are not going well at school. At home she has become argumentative, particularly with Mum. In the first session it transpires that the family is going through a hectic time. Last year Mum unexpectedly fell pregnant and gave birth to a baby brother. Gemma and her brother David (13) are not impressed. The parents are unsure how to fit everything in.
>
>   Marley (15) has been referred because things are not going well at school. There is a lot of fighting at home, mainly about 'rules' and 'agreements'. Marley shouts that she's 'hit puberty': her parents need to leave her alone and let her do her thing. Although her parents agree that Marley is a teenager now, they feel out of their depth. Marley is the eldest and was always such an easy child. The parents now argue with each other about what to allow Marley.

In the family developmental model Gemma's problems appear to relate to a transition stage in the family with the addition of a new baby. In Marley's case the transition is a different one, the stage of adolescence. This can provide a different angle.

Noticing change

Talking about problems rather than about what is going well or what has worked well in the past can be a pitfall for the therapist. This is common in working with families because family members too are often preoccupied with what has not been or is not going well. To remain focussed or bring to the fore success stories, what has improved a bit, fights that didn't escalate for a change et cetera are important skills of the systemic professional. The same is true for the ability to zoom away from the specific family context to other contexts such as school, work, friends, neighbourhood or extended family relationships.

Groups and networks

Therapy can occur with family groups, parent groups, partner relationship groups and groups that work with individuals from a systemic foundation.

Groups

Multiple Family Therapy (MFT) dates from the 1960s, founded by Laqueur, LaBurt and Morong (1964). They started involving the families of young people diagnosed with schizophrenia. Laqueur organised family groups with four or five patients and their families. The variety of perspectives in the groups provided instantly new information, leading to changes in interactions and bringing in the outside world and society (Asen & Scholz, 2010; Lemmens et al., 2007). Since then several models of family group interventions have been developed, often pertaining families with one family member who is experiencing psychiatric problems (Seikkula & Olson, 2003). Experiments with family groups dealing with physical illness have occurred too and family group therapy for multi-problem families has grown out of therapeutic community work (Asen & Scholz, 2010). Often the groups are run in inpatient wards but increasingly more in outpatient mental health services (Lemmens et al., 2007). An example is the *No Kids in the Middle* intervention group programme for parents caught in an acrimonious separation and their children (Visser & van Lawick, 2021). Other parent groups are run based on systemic principles, for instance for parents whose child has serious problems such as addiction. The groups are meant to support parents and not necessarily part of an individual therapy (Van Reybrouck, 2012). Couples counselling can also be offered in group format, which began in the 1960s, with a similar focus as relationship therapy, namely improvement of the partner relationship. Other partner groups deal with specific problems such as sexual problems, violence or complex separation (Neeleman & Bout, 2014; Visser & van Lawick, 2021). The format of groups varies widely: open, closed, limited in time or long term, one or more facilitators, with or without observers. Selection, intake and preparation differ too. Currently its application is rather limited, possibly because of lack of training or competency amongst professionals, or a lack of finances and support. There may also be barriers for family members; often it is not easy to find motivated participants.

Why a group?

The presence of other families, several parents or partners provides an immediate shift towards a relational position. Problems are framed as a problem the couple or family is struggling with (Lemmens et al., 2007; Neeleman & Bout, 2014). This commonality can make people feel less alone and less isolated with the problems. People recognise their problems in others, exchange experiences and can advise each other as peers. Further non-problematic stories spontaneously take up space in groups. For this to happen it is important that group members are not too diverse: they need to be able to recognise themselves in the other participants.

The therapeutic relationship

In groups run on systemic principles the families, parents and couples are considered experts of their own lives and principal advisors for each other

(Cooklin et al., 1983). The facilitator stays on the periphery while the context of the group renders possibilities and changes. The facilitator facilitates interchange, initiates themes and notices opportunities where families can help each other. It is important that space for various perspectives is created.

Networking

Networking is another example of systemic help in a group setting. Often it relates to complex family problems where significant others are invited to think together about the professional help. Examples are provided in Chapters 9 and 10. Consultation with networks can be helpful when several organisations and professionals are involved with one family. Consultation amongst all professionals involved, preferably with the clients present, can clarify each person's roles and responsibilities in the therapeutic trajectory. Professionals in a network are caring outsiders who cannot provide immediate solutions but within the network can look for ways to improve the situation.

Choice of setting

Choosing the setting is an important consideration because it influences the therapeutic process and what may be revealed. Talking with only the parents is a different kind of conversation than in the presence of their child or children. Talking with a client individually about their relationship is very different to speaking with a couple. Each setting elicits other aspects; choice of setting has an effect. Individual sessions with a child can feel supportive to parents but have the potential for parents feeling excluded or deprived of their influence. When the therapist chooses to speak with an adult individually, it is possible that the influence of the problems on others is not fully seen or understood. Alternatively the family can feel reassured that help is underway. Each choice of setting brings its own complexities. It is vital to be transparent about the choice of setting, the considerations made and the consequences.

Changes in setting

During the helping trajectory the setting may remain as it is, but changes can occur. It is feasible that once one trajectory is finished a new one starts. The change in setting can be requested by the professional, the clients or in consultation. It can happen spontaneously or deliberately. When the setting is altered, other aspects of family members come to the fore and interactions can be quite different. A mother may be forthcoming in a family setting or when she attends with her husband but is very quiet when her own mother comes along (Van Daele, 2014).

The practitioner can feel overwhelmed by spontaneous changes in setting.

Jeremy (43) has been seeing psychologist Michael for a while, but lately with reasonably big gaps between sessions. The main topic is Jeremy's feeling that people are too demanding: his mother, his disabled brother who needs care, his work. Jeremy married two years ago. He doesn't say much about his relationship, but Michael was under the impression that Jeremy was feeling better and supported by his wife. Three months ago, their baby daughter was born. Jeremy doesn't mention her often, but he complains of tiredness and low mood.

Jeremy and Josie, his wife, are sitting in the waiting room. In the session Josie gets straight to the point: she doesn't feel supported by Jeremy, he doesn't engage with their daughter, withdraws more and more, sits in his chair for hours and plays the victim. Josie is furious. Jeremy drinks too much and she doesn't want an alcoholic as a father for their daughter. Just like Jeremy Michael feels overwhelmed and unprepared.

This spontaneous change in setting leads the couple to agree to have some joint sessions about the problems. A change in setting could have been considered much earlier, for instance when Jeremy got married, when they realised Josie was pregnant or when the baby was born. To mark these transitions and associated changes considerations could be made regarding a change in setting or inviting the partner along. Collaboratively a decision could have been reached about changing the setting (Alblas, 2005).

Changes in setting happen when people, who are not the current or future client, are asked to attend. This could be a one-off, for instance when a partner, a close friend or another professional is invited to an individual session. But the setting can change frequently, for example when in family sessions the parents are occasionally seen separately for feedback (van der Pas, 2014). Or when parents are included at appropriate times in the individual therapy of their children. During the course of therapy the practitioner can reflect regularly about which setting is likely to effect change the most. Some circumstances make it ideal for the practitioner to change the setting temporarily or permanently, such as when severe problems are affecting everyone significantly. This could be the case with serious (possibly chronic) physical illness, psychiatric problems with one of the partners or the children such as depression, compulsion or anxiety or in the case of acute family crises (Asen et al., 2004; Meerdinkveldboom et al., 2019).

Well-considered changes in setting require careful orchestrating and preparation: why are people invited, what is the focus of the session, are family members invited by the therapist or by the clients? Consensus is needed about what and what not to discuss. When the setting changes the role of the therapist changes. The practitioner needs to be aware of this because they too will find themselves in a different context (Van Daele, 2014).

In conclusion

Changes in setting are important in therapy. Each setting brings different meanings to the fore and relates to specific societal expectations and perspectives about professional help. Usually professionals work steadfastly in one setting because it is familiar and comfortable. However, changes in setting can be instrumental to align with clients and support change processes. This always has consequences, for instance for the therapeutic relationship, and needs to be carefully considered, preferably in consultation with the clients.

Exercise

Think of an individual client. Draw a big flower in the shape of a daisy. Place the client in the centre of the heart (disk). The leaves represent the different contexts relevant to the client: family, extended family, work, religion, friends, neighbourhood, hobbies, professional help. During therapy, which contexts are in the foreground? Which contexts remain in the background? What could be the effect of bringing those contexts to the fore? Does paying attention to the different contexts prompt inviting others?

Chapter 9

Individual vulnerability in context

Introduction

There are many people who struggle with mental health problems, typically regarded as 'disorders' and in need of individual treatment. In a bid to utilise less medical or psychopathological terminology, instead of 'disorder' the term *individual vulnerability* is often suggested (Bak et al., 2017; Timimi, 2014). This is our preference as well. Individual vulnerability indicates it is something to be reckoned with. 'Having an individual vulnerability' is as description not as charged as 'having a disorder'. From a systemic perspective individual vulnerability can be influenced positively or negatively by the contexts in which the client lives and the client's relationships (Friedli, 2009).

The client's environment and the reciprocal influence between an individual vulnerability and the context are significant focal points for systemic practitioners. In this chapter we describe what to focus on, which dynamics frequently occur and how the therapist can hold onto systemic perspectives when individual vulnerability is present.

Individual diagnoses

The intake team is discussing Yannick who was referred after another panic attack, this time lasting for half a day. Yannick is 27 years old. He lives alone, occasionally temps and states he is struggling with a gaming addiction. His symptoms started after he abandoned his study and have worsened in the last two years. At the moment he's not very motivated, sits for hours behind the computer, his house is 'a dump' and he's not paying his bills. Yannick feels constantly tense. Now and then he meets with friends from high school and scouts; he values seeing them. He has a girlfriend but sees her infrequently. They know each other from the gaming world. Yannick is of a sturdy build and dresses casually. He thinks himself ugly and lazy because he can't achieve much. He wants to work on his self-image and his 'anxiety syndrome'.

DOI: 10.4324/9781003272038-9

> After this introduction by Ben, the therapist who did the intake, the psychi-
> atrist says that she has the impression that Yannick suffers from a generalised
> anxiety disorder. She believes it appropriate to have a conversation with him
> to confirm this diagnosis and talk about taking medication. The psychologist
> is thinking more about an avoidant personality and suggests extending the
> assessment phase to include some personality tests. Ben comments that he
> made a good connection with Yannick who was articulate and appeared at
> ease during the intake. The team decides to book an appointment for Yannick
> with the psychiatrist. In the meantime Ben continues seeing Yannick to work
> on improving his self-image.

Psychiatric diagnoses are common usage in everyday language. 'I have an
anxiety disorder', 'he is autistic', 'I am borderline', 'my child is aggressive',
'my mother is depressed' and 'she is psychotic' have become labels people
use to describe their own or others' problems. The diversity in psychiatric and mental health issues is immense. Diagnoses have some things in
common: the symptoms are considered an illness or disorder, medication
is prescribed and treatment is usually focused on stabilising or improving
symptoms. This individual perspective is similarly present in how professional help is organised. Files are made per person, in the name of the
referred client. The intervention is focused mainly on one person and usually starts after a diagnosis has been made.

Models used to explain individual vulnerabilities are generally of the linear kind. They try to pinpoint the cause of the disorder such as genetic vulnerability, problems with brain functioning, personality problems, factors
such as past or current traumatic events or heightened stress level arising
from significant changes in living circumstances. In Yannick's case the team
considered impeding personality factors, a probable anxiety disorder and
lack of self-esteem. An individual focus obscures the many interconnected
influences present. The environment in which the client lives, their relationships and sources of support and resilience are at risk of fading in the background, whereas these take centre stage in a systemic perspective. There
is always an association between an individual vulnerability and context
(Beach & Whisman, 2012; van Os, 2003). Therefore it is important to attend
to the client's whole life situation and its many contextual and relational
influences.

The interaction between individual vulnerability
and context

People's strengths and vulnerabilities differ. But individual vulnerabilities too are influenced by contextual factors and in turn individual vulnerabilities influence the environment. Some contextual factors generate

a supportive effect, others are a burden. Research shows that a low level of conflict and supportive relationships have a stabilising and de-escalating influence on symptoms (Gerlsma et al., 2012; Ilfeld, 1977; Varese et al., 2012). Other helpful factors include meaningful activities matching people's capabilities, rest and routine and support provided by school or work (Rowe, 2012). It is also known that too much stress and too high emotionality in families can reinforce psychotic symptoms in clients (Hooley, 2007). Individual problems or vulnerabilities can have an impact on the environment as well. From research we know that physical or mental symptoms of children or adults contribute to significant changes in the family environment or the partner relationship (Enzlin & Pazmany, 2006; Kiecolt-Glaser & Newton, 2001; Lange, 2014). Whether environmental factors are supportive or burdening depends on the person, the couple, the family, the situation, the history and the social and cultural backgrounds. It is not straightforward to predict what the effect of an individual vulnerability on the environment might be. A quiet, withdrawn child can cause concerns for its parents, while other parents don't see this as a problem.

> Ruth (23) has been admitted to an inpatient psychiatric ward because of severe depressive symptoms. In this context she is regarded as someone with a depressive disorder. It is an ordering that fits a medical-psychiatric perspective. But her friends view the symptoms as an expression of her sensitive nature. They know her as a woman who is deeply concerned about the suffering of others and the world and can be deeply moved by what other people say and do.

Not only the *meaning* of an individual vulnerability can change with the context but how the individual problems are *experienced* can also be influenced by contextual factors, in other words, by characteristics of and changes in people's lives. Receiving a diagnosis is an example of a context factor (Fondelli, 2007). A diagnosis given to someone in the family can be a different experience for each family member and change the relationships.

> The parents of 14-year-old Tim are relieved when they hear he has been diagnosed with 'autism'. Now they know what it is, they can take the right actions to help their son. Tim disagrees, the diagnosis makes him feel 'abnormal'.

Other context factors can include values, interactional habits, stage of the family, stage of life, migration, relocation and so on.

> Mohamud Mohamed Aayan and his wife fled Somalia eight years ago and settled in Belgium. Mohamud suffers terrible headaches and pain in his feet that cannot be medically explained. He spends his days in the dark lying on the couch and reacts furiously to what he views as his wife's lax and adulterous behaviour. She doesn't dress properly; she meets people outside their religious community and neglects him and the household. He is also worried that he can't find a job but his wife can.

> The Baxter family moved six months ago from the country to an apartment in the city. In their previous place of residence they knew everybody and the children had plenty of space to romp around. The change makes the mother feel more anxious and emotionally pressured. It doesn't take much to provoke an irritable reaction and her husband regards her now as 'a real borderliner'.

In a systemic framework the practitioner directs the focus towards how the individual vulnerability influences the person and their environment and which context factors are at play. These interactions generate tension in relationships and harbour opportunities for change. We describe in what follows how this can guide the therapist's interventions.

A guideline for contextualising

Systemic practitioners broaden the lens to explore contextual influences. They pose questions to understand how the client's problems are embedded in their lives and what they mean. They are curious around what explanations the client and others offer for the difficulties and what situations and events they associate with the problems.

> In the conversations between Ben and Yannick it transpires that Yannick's life became problematic when he stopped studying at 21 and decided to live on his own. He wasn't interested in the course at all and hoped that 'real life' would suit him better. Yannick finds working as a temp hard. He finds it stressful to have to adjust time and again to new colleagues, tasks and customs. Yannick believes that without a proper diploma he's only good for jobs he doesn't like. Consequently it makes him take on a job only once in a while. Gaming is costing him more money than he has. He plays at a high level and would like to go to other countries for special competitions but can't afford it.

He has barely enough money to pay the regular bills. He is very nervous about his financial situation. Yannick's anxiety and financial problems put pressure on the relationship with his girlfriend and his parents. All his friends own a house and have a steady job, while he's not achieving much. He sees himself as a 'loser', someone who can't keep up with society. He feels that his father judges him similarly. Yannick believes he has made the wrong choices in the last few years and feels stuck in many areas. This makes him even more tense and anxious.

In the event of individual vulnerabilities various contexts play a part and the systemic practitioner explores what the relevant contexts are and maps potential burdens and stressors.

Seven-year-old Luka's behavioural problems worsened when he started primary school. In class he has to sit on his chair the whole day and pay attention. He can't play and romp whenever and is unable to expend his physical energy.

Marlise's low mood and intense feelings are related to the separation of her parents. She now lives in a blended family, in a new house and a different place. She misses her comfortable space and doesn't see her friends anymore. She can't get used to the new rules and the new people she has to live with. And she has lost her position as Dad's favourite.

Jonathan (42) suffers from delusions, associated with the poor condition of his apartment. His mood gets disrupted by the trouble caused by the neighbours, their frequent fighting that disrupts his sleep and safe space, the dripping taps, the mould on the walls and the vine that's creeping uninvited into his house from under the garage door.

In addition to stressors, the practitioner also explores supportive contextual factors or in other words sources of support and resilience.

Yannick's anxiety symptoms are not always as severe. He rarely feels anxious when he is with his friends in a pub or when he does enjoyable things with his girlfriend. Gaming relaxes him too. He is good at it and it gives him a sense of competence.

A wide lens helps the practitioner to elicit the histories, circumstances and experiences that relate to the individual vulnerability. These are stories and buffering factors related to a specific person in a specific context, with their own relationships and unique biography.

Relational effects

When someone is vulnerable and responds to stress or adversity with low mood, panic attacks or psychosis, the family relationships or partner relationship are influenced (Baars & Van Meekeren, 2013; Berg-Nielsen et al., 2002; Bongaerts, 2014; Enzlin & Pazmany, 2006). For example children and young people will react to their parents' or siblings' limitations. Responses can differ widely: one family member can become rebellious and argumentative, another more withdrawn or particularly caring and helpful. Parents will wonder how to respond best to the needs of their child with a vulnerability. It is a journey that can bring them closer together but may also cause conflict. One or both partners with a vulnerability can find a way forward together, or partners feel alienated and lonely and become emotionally withdrawn. Their individual vulnerability can affect children if they have any. Children can feel embarrassed, seek support outside the family or protect their parent(s).

When a child, young person or adult with an individual vulnerability ends up in therapy, it is likely that relationships are under pressure and the client is experiencing a loss of connection.

> When girlfriend Vicky starts 'to whinge' about living together, Yannick doesn't visit her as much. He doesn't know what Vicky thinks of this. Yannick believes that his father sees him as a dilly-dallier, a bit like an uncle on mum's side whose philosophy is: 'why make it difficult when you can have it easy?'. His mother is worried. One of Yannick's friends committed suicide when Yannick was 17 years old. Yannick suspects that his mother fears he might do the same. Out of concern she comes and cleans his apartment occasionally. Yannick detests their 'meddling' and he doesn't visit his parents as often. When he does, he keeps the visits very short, often leaving frustrated and angry. Once back at his apartment, he games. This helps to keep his emotions at bay.

The systemic practitioner listens with a twofold focus (White, 2007). They pay attention to both the individual and to the interactions, relational patterns and what happens outside and inside the sessions. Ben hears in Yannick's story how difficult it is for him to connect and how he experiences relationships. At the same time he tries to understand what this could mean for his parents, sister and girlfriend and imagine potential effects of Yannick's anxiety and insecurity on these relationships. Do his parents or girlfriend worry, do they feel helpless or have they become impatient? What do they think is happening and what solutions have they perhaps tried?

Explorations like these can help to consider, in consultation with the client, who to include in future sessions. As discussed in Chapter 8 the systemic practitioner introduces polyphony, even when they work with one client. They take note of the concern from families and couples and how this affects everyone. The systemic therapist is also aware of the potential polarisation between the person who is 'sick' and the other, 'healthy' family members. Finally they explore the potentially troubled relationships with the outside world as an effect or a trigger of the individual vulnerability.

Involvement under pressure

Generally by now clients and their families or partners have been on quite a journey. When problems persist, difficult topics may no longer be discussed. People stay quiet to protect one another, physical and emotional distance grows. Some form of under-involvement occurs or the opposite happens where people become over-involved. There is often conflict resulting in frustration and helplessness. The focus in the sessions narrows to the person with the individual vulnerability and what has happened *this* time. The problems are all-consuming, the atmosphere is charged. The immense involvement between people influences everyone in the family and their network.

> Although initially Tim's parents feel relieved about Tim's diagnosis, they often fight about what is the best strategy. The paternal grandparents put their two cents in when they comment that the parents talk too much and act too little; when Tim is at their place, everything is fine. Tim's brother is sick and tired of the whole thing and retreats to his room.

A person with an individual vulnerability often leans on the immediate environment such as the partner, children, parents or siblings. When the therapist regards the over-involvement or under-involvement as relational effects of the individual vulnerability, with its own influence, it helps to remain non-judgemental about the family members' reactions, identify patterns and discuss effects. It is a common effect that when care and effort don't seem to pay off people become suspicious towards the person with the individual problems. Is this because the person doesn't want to or can't?

> Tim's parents often wonder whether Tim's nagging and feeling inferior to his brother has to do with his autism or is he using his diagnosis to get his own way.

When concern and involvement are under pressure, stereotypical patterns can emerge such as one person is caring and the other one is strict and increases discipline. Or one person is clingy and wants to solve problems, while the other one avoids action. Or the people involved keep changing positions. When such patterns become established Boeckhorst (2003) labels these as *devilish spirals*.

> The Bosh family is made up of Dad, Mum and their son Max (9). The school requested Max to be tested for ADHD. He now takes medication for this. But since he has been on medication, his parents don't recognise their son anymore. Where has that lively, funny and creative boy gone? There are no problems at home. The parents want the medication to cease. Mum's parents totally agree, but Dad's parents think this irresponsible. Heated discussions occur within and between both families and the parents feel increasingly irritated. They're angry with the school because Max' teachers can't manage his behaviour.

The parents disagree with each other, their respective families react similarly and rejection spirals between the parents and school emerge as well. Devilish spirals are circular interaction patterns of criticism, rejection or negation on different levels. They influence everyone involved and the relationships.

Polarisation between sickness and health

Thinking in terms of individual disorders can have the relational effect of a divide between who is sick and who is healthy. The person with the problems is 'the sick one' who needs help and the other family members without disorders or problems are 'the healthy ones' (Decraemer & Reijmers, 2017; Smeltzer, 2007). Such statements touch the relational level of communication. In fact this dynamic is always present but not necessarily problematic, for instance, when everyone accepts the distinction and a balance is found in managing the vulnerability. Regardless it remains important to keep this in mind. The person who has the problems may struggle with the distinction sick-healthy and believe they are fully responsible for getting better. On the other hand family members or partners could feel a huge attachment and responsibility for the wellbeing of the 'sick' person.

> Richard and Lilian have been married for 15 years. Seven years ago Richard was diagnosed with bipolar disorder. He has been taking medication and his mental health has stabilised. But lately there has been increased tension between the couple. Lilian finds the atmosphere in the house terrible and thinks that Richard has been unpredictable and gets angry quickly. She fears a repeat of the crisis of seven years ago. For that reason she contacted the GP without Richard's knowledge. When the doctor made a house call, Richard was furious. He slammed the door and now threatens divorce. He is convinced that many of the current tensions are related to difficulties in their relationship and not to his illness.

When the difference between the 'sick' person and the 'healthy' person is accentuated, the person who has the problems and others around regard that person as 'the problem'. The client's pathology becomes the focal point. In other words the problem story becomes dominant. The 'sick' person's behaviours and interactions are automatically associated with the 'illness'. The 'healthy' people could feel they have to be strong; they are not to burden others or to have problems themselves. This is often the case for partners but can happen to brothers and sisters too. This could result in little to no conversation about personal experiences to spare others. However the polarisation can also lead to a battle of truths about who is to blame, what is the cause, who is sick and who is healthy: 'You are a classic borderliner.' 'Take a look at yourself. You're autistic.'

> The doctor once told Richard that denial of the illness is part of the manic phase. So Richard believes that everything he brings up as to why he and his wife are having difficulties won't be taken seriously by the doctor. He has a sense that everything he says will be explained that way. As if there's nothing wrong with Lilian! He finds it increasingly hard to listen to Lilian minimising her contribution to the strain in their relationship and hopes that a professional who sees them together will recognise the relationship problems he's experiencing.

When a shared goal for therapy sessions is established, the sick-healthy dynamic usually fades in the background. This may require a bit of translation.

> Tim, who disagrees with his diagnosis, doesn't want to talk about 'living with his autism'. And certainly not in the presence of his parents who have a different view. The therapist 'translates' the diagnosis in a conversation with Tim and his parents. She talks about his high level of sensitivity and how this affects people. It is an angle Tim and his parents agree with and understand.

When everyone accepts a reframe of the diagnosis, it paves the way to discuss differences.

> The therapist notices that Richard and Lilian both want to do something about the problems. But Lilian focusses mainly on her husband and hopes he'll feel better, while Richard hopes the relationship will improve.

It is expected that tension between shared goals and different solutions will recur in the sessions and need to be addressed regularly.

Difficulties with the outside world

When problems are severe, relationships with the outside world are usually strained or broken. Friends disappear, social circles become smaller, neighbours complain or ring the police. The client loses their job and consequently their income. They struggle to find meaningful activities. Pressure could come from the school, the social housing corporation, social services and so on. As a direct or indirect consequence, the client and their loved ones can find themselves isolated.

> Yannick is no longer inviting his friends to his home because he is embarrassed about his 'pigsty'. He sees them less and less and only in the pub. But he doesn't really have money to spend. Consequently he spends more time alone and that is not doing him any good. He is also being bothered by several agencies. Every time he receives a letter in the mail, he braces himself... no doubt it's another reprimand! He puts it on the pile of other such letters, out of sight.

Pressure from social services increases the tendency to protect oneself or hide away from the outside world. When clients close themselves off from the external world, agencies often intensify their interference, for example someone makes a house call, letters take on a threatening tone.

It is important that the therapist explores the client's relationships with the outside world and how these can be managed.

> Jacob's parents are having counselling because they don't know how to deal with their son who lives independently. Jacob suffers regularly from psychotic episodes. When he's not doing well, he ceases all contact. He lives at the top floor of an apartment building. The caretaker rang his parents to say that Jacob bothers his neighbours by shouting at them, sending them weird emails and knocking on their door in the middle of the night. If this doesn't stop the caretaker is going to inform the police. His parents and the therapist discuss ways of reinstating contact with Jacob and reassuring the neighbours. The parents suggest they talk with the caretaker and compose a mail to the neighbours explaining what's happening with a plan of action.

The systemic practitioner could initiate including the outside world where appropriate and if the client agrees. They could invite the neighbours or ring the social housing office, consult with financial services or speak with a teacher.

Even in the absence of increasing demands made by agencies, family members, partners or clients can close themselves off from the outside world. Children who live in violent families or with a parent with an addiction problem, depression or some other serious problem, don't tell other people much (Östman, 2008). They stop inviting friends into their home out of shame and to protect their family. Fear of being judged often plays a big role.

> The eldest daughter of the Harker family has been placed in care because she told concerning stories about her stepfather's boundary crossing behaviour and alcohol abuse. Her mother and stepfather feel the eyes of the neighbours burn. They believe everyone is gossiping about them. They hardly venture outside and do their grocery shopping in another town. During the day they close the curtains. They feel increasingly paranoid towards each other and towards the outside world.

The systemic professional will consider the potential judgement from the outside world, including from professionals, and the associated anxiety and shame. It is important to focus on how the client can break through that isolation.

Including family members and partners

Presently many modalities of professional help emphasise the importance of family members and partners in the therapeutic process and take the client's context as the starting point. There are MST (Multi System Therapy) and MFT (Multi Family Therapy) teams, FACT (Flexible Assertive Community Treatment) teams in The Netherlands and mobile teams in Belgium. Services collaborate more with people with lived experience and families of clients, network meetings are organised and so on. These modalities don't necessarily apply a systemic perspective, but the developments are nevertheless encouraging and important. Including significant others is not a luxury but a necessity; their presence is vital. In joint sessions clients, family members and partners can discuss issues important to them and experience how emotional connectedness can shield them against the problems. Joint conversations can contribute to finding alternative ways to interact with each other, to better function as parents, a family or a couple and to find collectively supported solutions (Baars & Van Meekeren, 2013; Baucom et al., 2014; Cornelis et al., 2014; Decraemer & Reijmers, 2017; Enzlin & Pazmany, 2006).

Searching for common ground

Speaking with clients together with their significant others is not always easy. Family members or partners can have strong feelings about the person with the problems, such as sadness, shame, anger or helplessness. They may hesitate to attend sessions out of fear of escalations or being judged by professionals (Cornelis et al., 2014). Clients have doubts too. Yannick for instance is not keen on his girlfriend or parents attending the session. He is worried that they want him to take medication and that the conversation will be solely about him. When an individual vulnerability is present, the challenge is to find a collective platform for managing the problems. The polarisation sickness-health could intensify when practitioners invite family members in their role of support people, the healthy ones who are helping their sick family member. When roles are polarised as such, the problems other family members may have are pushed to the background. The therapist can ignore the fact that not only the client who was referred but also the partner or other family members struggle with symptoms that fit a diagnosis (Jones & Asen, 2000). In any case inviting family members in their role as informant or support person leaves the existing orderings or punctuations and related conflicts unchanged.

> Lilian comes along to Richard's session because she thinks that otherwise Richard wouldn't ask for or receive help. She is doing this for him. Richard wants to talk about their relationship, not about himself or his bipolar disorder.

When someone presents with an individual vulnerability, the latter and all its troublesome effects take quickly centre stage. It makes it harder to attend to what is going well, the areas in which people experience connection and common ground.

> The therapist discusses with Tim and his parents some of the unpleasant effects of being 'highly sensitive', such as Tim absconding, the tension at home and the parents feeling they are walking on eggshells. They discuss how it affects each person individually and the family relationships. By using the term 'high sensitivity' the therapist can identify constructive elements and similarities between family members that facilitate connection. Such as Tim's care for others and sensitivity he shares with his mother and grandmother and his sense for order and aesthetics like his father's.

Keeping the focus sharp

It is important that the focus of the systemic therapeutic conversation is clear in order to work towards connection, even in the face of intense emotions and big differences. The therapist can explain explicitly that the conversations are not focussed on individual problems but more on their effects on people and their relationships, including their lives, their experiences, their hopes and what is feasible. In times of crisis or acute situations it can be helpful when the client and significant others can reflect together about possible solutions or ways out. Specific systemic frameworks can be of support here. Cornelis et al. (2014) use the method of Consensus Oriented Systemic Interviewing and Intervention (CSII) in the first session. The session is guided by three questions (the three Ws): *What is happening? What has been tried in terms of solutions? What needs to happen now?* based on the principle of consensus. The Open Dialogue approach (Seikkula & Olson, 2003) is another model with a clear focus. This approach structures how people can reflect together about problems and how such polyphony can result in breaking through helplessness and finding a collective foundation for professional help. Although these models have been developed for adults, they can be applied to young people and their parents such as with youth who have complex problems in several areas in their lives and are unable to find the way to mainstream help (den Otter et al., 2009).

Providing psychoeducation in a systemic way

Often family members or partners are invited to receive psychoeducation. They are given information about the disorder, the prognosis, its course and what to look out for, for instance, that research shows that in case of psychosis it is best to avoid expressing negative or intense emotions; or that a predictable day structure and clear communication can help someone with autism. However information about a diagnosis can be 'heard' differently and mean different things to different people. The systemic practitioner who keeps this in mind while providing psychoeducation will avoid positioning themselves as an expert, as someone who knows from the outside what the disorder is like. They will consider the various meanings and effects a diagnosis can have and carefully select words that resonate with the family (Andersson, 2016; De Vos, 2012). The professional speaks about what can be expected overall, the different phases, the course of the disorder and how other clients have managed. They can inquire about the client's and family members' knowledge and ideas. Such informative stories can create a framework in which clients and the family can position themselves while retaining the focus on effects, contexts and reciprocal relationships.

> Myriam (19) was admitted when she developed a psychotic episode after using cannabis. In a conversation with Myriam and her mother, the therapist talks about 'the psychosis'. She says she knows a number of people who have had similar experiences, how they saw it and dealt with it. She gives some examples. Is there something in these stories they recognise or is it totally different for them? The stories about other people's experiences help Myriam and her mother to reflect about how to live with 'psychosis'.

Psychoeducation can be used as a form of externalising problems. Systemic practitioners position themselves in such a way that they are not talking about the person but about 'the illness'. It is 'the illness' that afflicts all parties and people have to relate to it one way or another.

A pitfall

Sometimes significant others are invited because the professional suspects that the client's problems are related to problems in the partner relationship or family relationships. In the past this belief was endorsed theoretically. There was for instance the theory that symptoms functioned as a circuit breaker of underlying family problems or an attempt to restore the family balance (Haley, 1979; Satir, 1983). It was assumed that once the family or relationship pathology was addressed, the individual problems would dissolve.

Parents or partners are often invited based on the belief that their responses intensify or even cause the problems. When parents or partners are regarded as 'overconcerned', it is often assumed this could prevent their vulnerable child or partner becoming independent. Professionals advise those parents or partners 'to let go' of their child or partner. Such orderings have a strong appeal, particularly when emotions run high and the burden is heavy. Perspectives like these can make parents or partners feel they are to blame and contribute to practitioners losing sight of *connections* and many other influences beyond family relationships. The systemic practitioner aims to avoid such cause-consequence thinking by taking the angle of connections and interactions and their effects.

Patterns in professional help

The relational effects of an individual vulnerability are not limited to the client and their nearest and dearest. They are also felt by professionals and elicit specific patterns (van Oenen et al., 2007). Frequently occurring patterns include the suction power of symptoms, excessive attention for resilience and parallel processes (isomorphism).

The suction power of symptoms

To maintain a systemic approach and positioning and consistently keep in mind connections when working with psychopathology is a challenge for the systemic practitioner. The seriousness of the symptoms and the extent of the dysfunction in relationships can be thrust forward to such an extent that it obscures seeing other aspects of the person or the relationship. This is considered *contextual blindness*. The disorder and dysfunctional relationships become the focal point. This happens when the therapist feels helpless or frustrated or when the behaviour is all encompassing, incomprehensible or bizarre. The practitioner may feel pressured to come up with solutions and take action or may believe that nothing can be done. Their aim to position themselves as multi-empathic, to be curious about the clients' lives and experiences, and their flexibility and creativity in seeking alternative perspectives could be at stake. A client who is rigid and principled becomes 'a true autistic man', the child bouncing off the walls 'a typical ADHD case', closely connected family members a clear case of 'a symbiotic family'. Such labels reduce the professional's broad perspective. Applying the methods described in Chapter 7 such as working triadically, paying attention to buffering processes and systemic positioning can be helpful here. Further consultation with colleagues and supervision can support maintaining a systemic positioning.

Only eye for resilience

The opposite can happen as well: the therapist protects themselves against the strong appeal and limitations of a diagnosis. A pattern emerges of only focussing on resilience, sources of support and opportunities while limitations of clients and their lives are ignored. To avoid this pattern it is useful to keep in mind that a constructive view of people and relationships is not a goal but a means to discuss people's problems, limitations and dilemmas (Bongaerts, 2016). The practitioner can reframe a woman who ignores her own boundaries as a very caring woman who is considerate of others. From that point of view they can explore how this affects the woman and others around her positively and negatively. In another example the therapist acknowledges a client's parenting role which makes the client feel supported and able to reflect on how their bipolar disorder affects their children.

When the professional attends to problems and possibilities equally, it implies, how paradoxical this may sound, that they remain hopeful. However being hopeful and creating hope is not simple when the margins for change are small. A term such as *reasonable hope* can help here (Weingarten, 2010). It refers to formulating feasible and concrete goals, protects against illusions and incorporates despair and doubt.

Ben is finally having a conversation with Yannick and his girlfriend Vicky. Yannick feels supported by Vicky but their relationship is strained. Vicky has her own vulnerabilities. She often feels down and stays in bed. She feels good when she is with Yannick. She dreams of having her own house and children which will make the problems go away. Yannick is keen but is aware this will be for him difficult to achieve. So many responsibilities and restrictions, the idea itself makes him feel anxious. Ben can empathise with Vicky's dreams and Yannick's anxieties. He decides to explore other scenarios and asks Vicky what she hopes for if living together doesn't work out.

> Vicky replies: 'Doing more together.'
>
> 'And if that isn't possible?'
>
> Eventually Vicky resolves to do things together at set times and dare to think together about their future. Perhaps about having a Living Apart Together-relationship, even having a child one day that lives with her. Yannick replies that this kind of future puts him under less pressure and makes him feel less anxious. He likes to think a bit out of the box.

Ben explores what are feasible or fitting expectations for this couple at this point in time. Introducing reasonable hope requires the therapist to reflect constantly on personal beliefs and preferences. For instance the ideal picture of a successful life or a great relationship influences the practitioner too. This could be a barrier to a conversation about an achievable future. In our example this could happen when Ben believes that living together is the best option which renders him unable to discuss other relationship forms with Vicky and Yannick. Or he may avoid the topic when he believes that this couple won't ever be able to live together. In addition the practitioner needs to be aware that what constitutes a feasible future now is not set in concrete. The future is uncertain and new opportunities can present themselves. What seems achievable and appropriate now can change in the future.

Parallel processes or isomorphism

When practitioners, just like family members, have different opinions about what the problem is or the best approach, parallel processes can eventuate (Nieweg & De Rooy, 1992; Rynes et al., 2014). In the General System Theory this is called isomorphism (Boeckhorst, 2014; Von Bertalanffy, 1968). Isomorphism refers to the phenomenon of the occurrence of structurally similar patterns in different systems, for instance when stereotypical family patterns are repeated in teams or between organisations. As an example one therapist always tries to be understanding (like the father), while the other therapist always wants to undertake action (like the mother). Or one practitioner wants to do more and more while the other one argues for more distance. Practitioners and teams can, just like families, get caught in devilish spirals (Boeckhorst, 2003).

> Max's parents are angry with the school. They suspect the school is not with the times and too concerned with order and tidiness. They believe that the teacher is incapable of managing her class. The parents want to stop Max's medication. The school disagrees: Max is unmanageable without medication. The teacher and the school counsellor wonder if it would be better if Max

changed schools. When the parents hear this, they consider filing a complaint. Max's psychiatrist is frustrated. He thinks the parents are irresponsible, they deny Max the best medical care. He pressures the parenting coach to discuss this with the parents. The parent coach isn't happy with everyone criticising the parents. But the team is of the opinion that it is her task to address this with the parents. They don't understand her reluctance. The atmosphere at the team meeting turns sour.

In her team the parenting coach starts to feel what the parents feel in their encounters with professionals. And her team makes similar statements as the school's. It can be helpful to recognise and label these parallel patterns in both client and professional system, the so-called isomorphism patterns (Boeckhorst, 2003, 2014; Trip, 1995).

Managing differences in teams

It is common that different views on individual vulnerability exist in teams. Boeckhorst (2014) mentions the frames of the professional. Those professional frames are formed through the practitioner's training, professional body, role and work experiences; all these can be quite diverse. This can lead to confusion, particularly when it is no longer recognised that these are views rather than truths, diverse and perhaps complementary perceptions (Lebow, 1997; Reijmers, 1999, 2007). In those circumstances team members see the different opinions as useless rather than useful, conflicts about the truth occur, team members give orders or believe that a colleague with a different view is not providing the right intervention.

Ben hears from a colleague that he's too naïve. His colleague thinks that all this attention for context and resilience negates the seriousness of the problems. Ben should work with Yannick's avoidance behaviour, the rest is superfluous.

When severe problems are present, it is necessary to collaborate with others. The intense involvement and efforts by many and the urgency of the problems can lead to one or more members to claiming a monopoly on truth. Reaching a level of consensus or understanding about what is the matter can be thwarted by such truth claims and battles supported by hierarchical differences and by theoretical frameworks not shared by all team members.

Working in a team that harbours different points of view can be enriching when colleagues respect each other's expertise, recognise the existence of different perspectives and accept there is no sole solution. Similarly when rivalry and power in terms of 'who's got the upper hand' don't dominate, team members accept not only differences but also similarities in the team, for instance that everyone is making an effort to provide the best help possible. This reciprocal attuning usually happens on a practical level. Reflecting on the effects of interventions with a focus on what is helpful for clients and their families instead on how team members differ in theoretical perspective, can increase the quality of the professional help (Castelijns, 2016).

After the team meeting about Max and his family, the parenting coach wonders what she could have done differently instead of advocating for the parents and intensifying the battle around views. Once she has distanced herself from the battleground, she surmises she could have asked her team how to discuss the value of medication when parents are against it. She could have asked her colleagues what the effect of this could have been and if it could have de-escalated the conflict.

In conclusion

In our society individual vulnerability is primarily addressed and treated individually. The focus is on the person, the diagnosis and the appropriate treatment. Intervention is directed at learning new skills, insight into the illness, managing the illness, medication and so on. Within a systemic view of individual vulnerability, the focus shifts from the illness to its influences and meanings. The systemic practitioner works with the interchange between individual vulnerability and context and pays attention to the relational effects of an individual vulnerability. This is a challenge. However given the multiple meanings and complexity of this issue, it could give clients, significant others and teams much in return. Psychiatric problems are seldom simple. It is an illusion to believe that individual vulnerabilities can be approached with a 'one size fits all' way of thinking and intervening. A systemic approach is one of many approaches that can be of use.

Exercise

Think of three cases where an individual vulnerability is present, such as depression, borderline problems or ADHD. Reflect on these individual vulnerabilities from three perspectives (Dickerson & Zimmerman, 1995):

Individual perspective: how is each vulnerability perceived from this perspective (for instance as a (neurological) disorder, a skill deficit, a behavioural problem, a developmental problem)?

Family perspective: how do you view each individual vulnerability when you understand it as influencing the family dynamics?

Sociological perspective: what is presently expected in Western society and subsequently what are the pressures experienced by individuals with vulnerabilities, their family members and the wider environment?

On a piece of paper draw three columns: one for the individual perspective, one for the family perspective and one for the sociological perspective. For each case write down a few sentences in each column. Next consider the following questions:

What differences did you notice between the different perspectives?
What perspective would you use with these clients and why?
What would your professional stance be in each perspective?

Chapter 10

Multiple and complex problems

Introduction

Systemic therapists have always attended to families with multiple and complex problems. Minuchin worked with families in poor neighbourhoods of New York, mainly with solo mothers and their children. *Families of the Slums* (Minuchin et al., 1967) is the result of this work. McCarthy (1995) wrote about helping poor families in Ireland from the point of view that these families have the capacity to retain their dignity in difficult living circumstances. Turnell and Essex (1999, 2006) developed a systemic approach for families where child (sexual) abuse is suspected. Finally Madsen (2007) introduced a treatment model for what he called *multi-stressed families*.

Families who are dealing with multiple and complex problems used to be called *multi-problem families*. The negative connotation of this term is that the problems are assumed to be part of the family's identity. Madsen's term 'multi-stressed' may do those families more justice: it is about families who deal with and respond to multiple stresses and pressures (Madsen, 2007). Several services and professionals are usually involved and there are concerns about important areas such as addiction, financial hardship or parenting abilities. People may suspect neglect, violence in the relationship, escalating spirals of conflict or physical, emotional or sexual transgression. These problems are often part of a wider problem such as poverty and exclusion. In this chapter we look at how a systemic framework can provide guidance in working with complex presentations.

Professionals under pressure

Working with families with complex problems often means practitioners have to deal with crises or acute demands and experience huge time pressure. The problems are usually long-standing and the efforts and interventions of various services and professionals involved have not resulted in fewer concerns. The files are getting bigger but hardly contain new information. New professionals who read the files are easily sucked into the same repetitive

DOI: 10.4324/9781003272038-10

spirals of helplessness. Colapinto (1995) describes those spirals of helplessness in which the family and the professionals can find themselves. When the concerns, in spite of various interventions, don't abate, professionals tend to seek other, usually tougher interventions with yet other professionals. The family is left with the impression they can't deal with the problems and feel and behave increasingly powerless. And this brings about further intervention. The spirals continue to escalate. Everyone is trying hard but there is no positive effect.

Safety is an important topic when families experience multiple or complex problems. How safe is the situation for the children, adults and elderly? How likely is it that children, elderly or other family members are neglected, physically or sexually abused? Are family members living in fear? Do children look after their parents at the expense of playing? What do parents, caregivers and children disclose to the professionals and what do they keep to themselves?

> The Drayton family is referred by the GP. Bert (45) hardly leaves his bed since he's receiving a sickness benefit due to back problems the medical profession can't explain. The benefit is insufficient, debts are growing and eviction is looming. His wife Trudy (43) is desperate. She was working temporarily as a check-out operator in a supermarket but made so many mistakes they dismissed her. Trudy reproaches Bert daily and complains constantly. Their son Rhys (17) feels for his mother and is terribly annoyed by his father. He lives at home and is enrolled in a course for financial support worker but skips the lessons regularly. He talks a lot with his mother. He tries to motivate his father to get out of bed but they have been physically fighting over this at least three times. Their daughter Lara (15) has a boyfriend and spends a lot of time with him. When the atmosphere at home is tense, she leaves. Trudy is worried that Lara might move in with her boyfriend which makes her feel more desperate and angrier. Bert claims more and more they would be better off without him and that he will end his life. He has requested the GP to assist with euthanasia. After another physical fight between father and son, Trudy rang the police. At that point professional help stepped in.
>
> Practitioner Marc hears about the father's suicidal ideation, the fights between father and son, the looming eviction and the spiral of powerlessness keeping everyone in its grip. He feels responsible for the safety of this family and feels that he has to make sure that the father doesn't commit suicide and that the financial debts and looming eviction are prevented.

In cases of domestic violence serious concerns about a family, bystanders worrying about the safety of young children, a mother drinking too much or adolescents terrorising their parents and creating unrest in the neighbourhood, professionals are expected to provide solutions and put things in order. When a child or adult has been abused or neglected, people want to know immediately which professional services have been involved. Professionals are made responsible and could be legally liable.

The effect is an increase of fear in mental health and social care services and practitioners. Control becomes the focus. Policies to reduce family violence are leading to more protocols, duty to report, risk assessments and other procedures. So far it is unclear whether all that extra work results in increased safety in families or partner relationships (Bartelink, 2018). The focus on control can be a threat to collaborative work with families. It leaves little space to explore with family members what is needed to have a safer and less stressed life. The pressure on professionals to ensure safety is huge. Simons (2017) posits we live in a 'risk averse' society. Professionals and organisations try to protect themselves by sticking to the rules. This can make parents or partners feel threatened and judged. This also impacts the safety in a relationship or a family: "Safety is found in how people interact with each other; it is a relational event" (Simons, 2017, p. 233).

The pressure increases when children are involved. Cottyn (2021) comments that safety of children is a topical and compelling theme in youth care. Having to judge safety and good or bad parenting has an effect on practitioners. They may take a moralising stance to feel less powerless or an expert position to feel competent (Gupta & Blumhardt, 2016). Professionals feel they have to rescue children and removing them from their home can be seen as a solution (Matt & Weeda, 2008). It is a pitfall for practitioners when they position themselves as the better, protective parent, the better partner or the protective friend. Cottyn (2005) claims that parenting and growing up safely are idealised in our society and 'failing parenting' is taboo. When parents speak about losing control or not enjoying being a parent, the professional feels the tension from the pressing societal norms about parenting. However talking with parents about the things that go wrong and thinking together about support or buffering factors that can prop up their parenting can improve the situation for children and their parents (van der Pas, 2014). The starting point is that children and adults need safety and security to develop well and that families and professionals need to work together to make this happen.

To avoid being sucked into the spiral of fear and powerlessness and to continue to see opportunities for change, the professional can ask some key questions. The following four questions provide an ordering and a guideline for the systemic practitioner: How do I position myself? How do I assess and ensure safety? Who do I involve in the therapeutic process? How do I maintain a reflective stance?

The first question refers to the desired positioning. In the case of multiple problems and concerns practitioners need to be firm in their positioning to avoid being overwhelmed by so many requests for help. From this positioning the problem areas and concerns are mapped and questions about safety are addressed. Next they consider what contexts and which people can contribute to the alleviation of the concerns. The final question relates to how the practitioner self can remain upright and retain competency in such demanding therapeutic contexts.

How do I position myself?

A clear positioning is important when multiple or complex problems feature in a family. Through stance and words the practitioner clarifies that behaviour harmful to children and adults is unacceptable but relays at the same time their commitment to work with the family members. The therapist is on the side of the clients and works collaboratively to reduce stress and risk of harm and improve their situation. Examples include the position of *appreciative ally* (Madsen, 2007) as described in Chapter 7 and the positioning developed by Turnell and colleagues in working with families where (suspected) abuse or sexual abuse of children is happening (Turnell & Essex, 1999). When dealing with complex or multiple problems the practitioner needs to balance between being alert to and realistic about potential risk situations and working collaboratively as much as possible with the families and their network to improve safety. To achieve this the practitioner can formulate the disapproval of destructive behaviour as a common goal rather than something the professional demands from the family. Practitioners and family members together can seek a better future for everybody, without violence and neglect.

When Marc visits the Drayton family at their home for the first time, he would like to explore with the family and others around them, whether it is possible to work on alleviating their concerns and reducing the violence and suicidal ideation. He wants to avoid being put in the expert position and having to solve the problems. He wants to share the responsibility with the family members and involved others. He would like to make an inventory with the family of their wishes and goals. Bert, Trudy, Rhys and Lara agree that the fighting and chiding has to stop.

The result of this method of working is collaboration and support and not judging or controlling the clients. Professionals are present in a powerful and facilitating way and start from the belief that most relationships and families have their own ideas and capabilities to improve their situation.

Before the practitioner can explore these, space needs to be made for verbalising concerns.

> Bert is lying on the couch and doesn't want to talk: 'It's no use.' Trudy wants to talk and launches into what has been going wrong because of Bert's defeatist and reluctant attitude. She wants Marc to make sure they won't be evicted. Bert needs to be given something that makes him more active and he needs a plan with his employer, perhaps about different work.
>
> Rhys is sitting next to his mother and nods a lot: 'Yes, that's how it is.'
>
> Marc feels the pressure mounting and interrupts Trudy: 'I understand how desperate and powerless you're feeling and that you'd like to talk more about that. Today however, I would like to hear everybody's concerns and find out with you all what you'd like to achieve in the next little while and who or what could help to achieve that.' Marc addresses Rhys next: 'Rhys, what would you like to see changed?'
>
> RHYS: 'Dad has to act normal again, everything will be better then.'
> LARA IS ABSENT: Marc asks what Lara would say.
> TRUDY: 'Lara prefers to be with her boyfriend. I fear that I have already lost her.' She has tears in her eyes.
>
> Bert joins in and says that he has spoiled everything. It would be better if he wasn't here so they would be able to carry on with each other. He doesn't see any light anymore; his back stops him from working and that is not going to improve.

Even when there is huge pressure, the client's preferred future guides the collaborative process. This is especially important in families with multiple stressors because if too much attention is paid to the problems, a spiral of blaming, defensiveness and powerlessness is set in motion, leading to more blaming and sadness. The professional input is organised around four questions relating to the preferred situation: "Where would [the family] like to be headed in [their] life? What gets in the way? What helps [the family] get there? What needs to happen next?" (Madsen & Gillespie, 2014, p. 51).

> First Marc explores the well-functioning areas. The family talks about Trudy's culinary skills, Bert's dry wit that comes out occasionally now but has always been his trademark, Rhys's willingness to help at home and with friends, Lara's determination. Marc asks each time for concrete examples and positive memories as these facilitate connection and support. Then Marc asks them what they would like to achieve in the near and far future. Trudy would like more cosiness at home and less picking on each other. Bert wants to have less back pain so he can do more. He wants Rhys to complete his study and

live his own life. Rhys wants to have his own life, but this means that his father has to take more responsibility.

Bert responds irritated and says to Marc: 'See, he doesn't have any respect for me, he wants to tell me how to live my life and Trudy allows that to happen.' Marc: 'Bert, you say that you miss being respected. When you talked about the good years, you all interacted respectfully. Is treating each other with respect something you'd like to move towards? Can I write that down?' In this way Marc summarises the preferred situation.

Marc reframes Trudy's complaints as her wish for everyone to trust and support each other again and for more cosiness in the house. This turns out to be a shared hope, just like their wish for the fights to cease and for Rhys to finish his education. Formulating a preferred future they all share makes them feel connected.

Afterwards they map what the obstacles are on the road to their preferred futures. They externalise and formulate the barriers on an individual, relational and socio-cultural level. All this is done carefully. The financial problems and looming eviction are included in the conversation. Marc is empathic and instrumental in finding words together for their frustrations and feelings. Marc asks Rhys about what stops him completing his course.

Rhys says that he struggles to deal with his frustration about his father and his disappointment with his sister who stays away. He feels abandoned and feels so much pressure to keep everything going. It makes him 'boil over' and very angry, also physically, with his father. He is no longer interested in school and feels like a failure.

After making an inventory of everyone's obstacles, Marc asks which sources of support could help in dealing with the barriers. Who are involved around them, who could help? Again Marc takes the initiative and focuses on identifying sources of support: relevant contexts such as family, friends, neighbours, sports clubs, hobby clubs and church communities, including contact with the debt collector service and the social housing corporation.

Rhys names his study friends, his desire to finish his course and the contact with his Uncle Sam who did the same course. He'd like to play sports again; he has neglected that lately. And he'd like to find a part-time job so he can earn some money and can go out. Rhys has great memories of many good years with his parents and sister; especially his memories of playing soccer and swimming with his father make him feel happy.

Finally the family develops a joint plan with agreements about who does what with whom. Rhys for example will contact Uncle Sam to make a study plan for next year. Often having sessions frequently in the beginning helps to stop the spirals of powerlessness. With new steps taken it can be beneficial to underline the family's competency by decreasing the frequency of the sessions; this is however a joint decision.

How do I assess and ensure safety?

Given the shocking statistics of domestic violence against children, partners, parents and elderly (Alink et al., 2012; Barnett et al., 2005; Hamels & Nichols, 2007; van der Veen & Bogaerts, 2010) the government implements measures to curb domestic violence. In The Netherlands and Belgium hotlines operate for domestic violence and child abuse and there are guidelines and trainings for police officers, doctors and mental health and social care practitioners. In both countries Family Justice Centres (FJC's) provide centralised medical-forensic, judicial, psychological and financial support for clients. And specific Victim Support services are operational in many countries.

Violence and safety are complex topics. Each story is unique, but when professionals are able to connect with family members and the contexts they live in, it is possible to work together to increase safety (Stith et al., 2012; van Lawick, 2014). The helping profession makes use of standardised risk assessments, hoping to detect and address risk of harm and violence (de Vogel et al., 2013; Hamels & Nichols, 2007). Such tools help to identify problem areas and provide support for the practitioner. However when questionnaires are considered a reliable account of real life in families separate from the practitioner and the working relationship with the clients, problems can be underestimated or overestimated. It is preferable to stay in dialogue and seek collaboration with families and their network (Bolt, 2017; De Sterck, 2017; Hamels & Nichols, 2007). Hurst (2011) stated that a personal decision of the (experienced) systemic professional together with family members can be a better way to achieve more peace and safety in a family than relying on risk assessment lists.

The systemic practitioner has several methods at their disposal to identify risks with the family and make a plan to achieve more calm and safety. This is illustrated with the following three examples: describing image by image what has happened to slow down escalations; drawing maps of safety with clients and 'signs of safety' which aim to work with family and others on a safety plan.

Describing image by image what happens when conflict threatens to escalate into violence offers the therapist and the family members an overview of the relational complexity when conflicts spiral out of control, of each person's needs and worries and of the action-reaction pattern of behaviour.

As such safety can be discussed without reverting to a reductionistic perpetrator-victim discourse.

Things got completely out of hand at Steve and Carrie's place. Steve manhandled Grandma out of the house in the presence of five-month-old baby Carol. The police were called and Carrie said she can't continue with Steve. When after introductions therapist Sally enquires about their fights, Carrie and Steve tumble over each other in mutual recriminations and defences. Sally raises her hand to stop the conversation. She says she notices how involved they are, how it affects them and how desperate they each are to tell their story, but she can't keep up with their tempo. She explains she'd like to hear about the last time things got out of control, but in slow motion, moment by moment. This can help clarify what is at play and opportunities to prevent further escalation. Sally invites Steve and Carrie to tell her exactly image by image what they each did, thought and felt. In this slowdown Steve and Carrie give Sally and each other information about what they believe is happening.

The practitioner can ask questions that provide information about people's inner dialogues and the relational meaning of actions. The 'speedy' attack-counterattack type of conversation characteristic for these situations can become a slower conversation where clients are invited to step in each other's shoes. Carrie may say that she feels as if Steve is only interested in himself and not in her or his daughter. Steve may explain that he feels excluded and is annoyed with the frequent visits from his mother-in-law. Thus all voices are heard. Through circular questions Grandma's voice can be added: What do Carrie and Steve think she was thinking and feeling? Or baby Carol's voice: What is her experience? Carrie could be asked whether she knew Steve felt so excluded and Steve could be asked whether he knew that Carrie felt invisible to Steve. The elicited information clarifies for the family members what happened at the time of the escalation and what contributed. They can discuss if there were moments where an alternative route could have been chosen. The family is the experts here. They are best placed to think about what they could have done differently and what could have de-escalated the situation and by doing so they formulate their own safety plan.

Steve is thinking that next time before he comes home, he could ring Carrie to see how her day has been and to let her know he is on his way. Carrie plans to greet Steve when he arrives home instead of ignoring him. Both want to speak with Carrie's mother and make better arrangements about her visits. They want to let her know how grateful they are for her help. Steve wants to pay more attention to his non-verbal behaviour. When he notices he's wound up, he'll go out for a walk. Carrie agrees.

They discuss further in detail their safety plan and how they will evaluate it. The care for baby Carol is another concern for the therapist who will work with the parents towards their shared goal of optimal and safe development of their child.

Another systemic technique to map safety derives from *safety maps* developed by Faes (2016a) for therapy with couples where conflicts get out of hand. Faes draws big 'maps of safety' on a flip-over including what clients prefer to see more of, such as peace, safety, togetherness and fun. These goals are written in the middle of the map. Then routes towards those goals are drawn; more can be added in subsequent sessions. Some routes prevent escalation, such as calling a friend, being aware of physical responses when one feels angry and being able to calm down beforehand, diversion, doing something such as 'I'd better hang out the washing, fix a bicycle, go for a walk or cook'. The relational effects of each suggested action are explored and whether the partner or family members experience it as a positive action or as abandonment. Together they seek the best and most appropriate routes towards more peace and safety. The map also includes what they've succeeded in and when things went well.

A third method to promote safety builds on *signs of safety* (Sillevis, 2011; Turnell & Essex, 1999). It is a method developed in youth work when there are concerns about violence or sexual abuse of children but is perfectly applicable to other situations that give cause for concern about safety, for instance relationship abuse or elder abuse. The therapist starts to map the situation together with the family members and involved professionals. A genogram identifies the significant family members and other people. Next the family is asked what is working well. This can create space to talk about the concerns: what do warning signs look like? The aim is not to uncover the truth but to identify concrete concerns about the dangers. People don't need to agree. Family and professionals can verbalise what would happen if the situation doesn't change and how more unsafe it could become. Everything is documented (Wiggerink & Vogel, 2017). All involved are then asked to score safety for the children in the family on a scale from 0 to 10. Based on this short-term goals are formulated and practical steps to reach those goals. This could mean that a child needs to live elsewhere temporarily. First the parents work with professionals towards safety before their child can return home. It is possible though to increase safety when the child or children remain living at home. After the exploration the family members network members and professionals make a safety plan. This includes well-defined goals and concrete, detailed agreements about the steps needed to reach the goals. The plan is reviewed regularly and adjusted when necessary.

There are concerns about Theo's (15) sexualised behaviour towards his sister Lenny (11). Theo denies it all. In a joint session the focus is not on whether the abuse took place, but what steps can be taken to alleviate these concerns. Practical steps include that Lenny is never alone with Theo and that her sister Carla (13) is sharing a room with her for the time being.

When young people are violent towards their parents, it is advised to apply *non-violent resistance in families*. Parents are supported to reposition themselves as present parents with *connecting authority* (Bom & Wiebenga, 2017; Omer, 2021).

All these methods have in common that in collaboration with a couple or a family a safety plan is developed detailing who needs to do what to improve safety and how to evaluate the actions.

The different methods can be combined in conversations with clients.

Olga (24) is a solo mother who came to The Netherlands at the age of 20. She is exhausted from many sleepless nights. Her daughter Anya, 18 months old, keeps her up almost every night. Olga is in panic. She worries that she won't cope and won't be able to look after Anya. Financial troubles are adding pressure. A few times Olga has put Anya forcefully back in her cot and slapped her. She yelled and Anya screamed. The neighbours rang the national child abuse hotline and now a counsellor is about to visit. Olga is petrified that they will take Anya off her. Therapist Fenna is a woman in her 40s with a friendly demeanour, that is reassuring. Anya is awake and is sitting on Olga's lap. Fenna's open questions invite Olga to tell a lot about her life, her failed relationship, her love for Anya and her desperation and guilt when she gets angry. Fenna asks Olga to describe image by image the last time it went wrong. Olga's inner dialogue and its effect become apparent. Subsequently Fenna and Olga make a map of safety showing what goes well and the routes leading to more safety. Fenna and Olga think together who could support her. Olga replies that she doesn't have family here, but she has friends, some from the Polish club, and they live nearby. She can ring those friends any time, that makes her calm. When she feels tense, she wants to calm down first before attending to Anya. She is going to speak with the GP about her problems and exhaustion and see whether someone can provide guidance regarding Anya's sleep issues. Olga wants to invite her girlfriend to come along to the next session to see how she can support Olga, like looking after Anya occasionally so Olga can have a sleep. Fenna is to visit again next week. Olga is relieved when she says goodbye to Fenna.

This method of working is often applied in mandated help for youth or adults. When safety plans don't appear to be working (or not sufficiently), other interventions can be indicated such as the temporary removal of a child, a temporary protection order of an adult or a temporary stay in a safe house. Such radical interventions are never the therapist's decision alone but well considered by the team and subject to legal endorsement.

Who do I involve in the therapy?

Due to the complexity of family relationships and legal frameworks the question of who to involve in therapy when it comes to families with multiple problems is a complex issue. An example is the legal protection of the privacy and self-determination of adults. Working with the wider network is only possible when clients recognise the benefits and are motivated to invite significant others. When the request for help includes concerns about children, the question can be asked: who are the parents? This is a substantive and a legal question. Some children grow up with a parent and a stepparent while the other biological parent is not on the scene. But that parent can still be a legal guardian. In Chapter 6 questions about the legal position of Jaco, Benny's donor father, could be posed. Does he have legal guardianship? That doesn't appear to be the case. From a legal point of view, Jaco does not need to give permission for Benny to receive therapy. But perhaps John, Ratna's father who lives in Curaçao, does. It is important to have knowledge of the legal frameworks, particularly when family members are sensitive to feeling included or excluded.

Who do we invite?

Regardless of the legal context the question of who to involve in the therapy is relevant. The professional needs to remember their work is not with individuals, but with people embedded in a context featuring important others, people who support them and people they are bothered by, family, friends, school, colleagues. It is essential to work with the social network around families with multiple or complex problems because the influence of the network is often bigger than the influence of the professional (Imber-Black, 1988). When the practitioner works together with people the client trusts, the helping process is more likely to be successful (Beckers, 2017; Hydén et al., 2016). In adult care the practitioner and the adult client discuss who is involved, who knows about the concerns, who could reflect with them and who could do what. Even after some initial reluctance most clients can be motivated for this. In youth care the same can happen for the child or young person together with their parents. School is an important environment for children and help is sometimes requested by the school. In that case inclusion of school, teachers or mentors is appropriate in the therapeutic process with children and their families. In consultation with the parents and preferably with the child too, it is decided how for each situation the involvement will look like. Engaging support figures can be a crucial step in the helping process.

Olga is prepared to bring her girlfriend to do some reflecting with her. She also wants to cooperate in a conversation with the neighbours who made the notification. Olga's mother is visiting around Christmas for a month, and she wants her mother to know what's been happening and help her. Her mother doesn't speak Dutch, but Olga and her friend can help with that.

It can get complicated when the people involved disagree about who to invite.

Hanno and Isha are young parents. They are struggling with multiple problems, amongst those a considerable debt due to excessive on-line purchasing. Because they both work Hanno's mother babysits regularly. Grandma blames her daughter-in-law for the stress and debts because she did most of the purchasing. Grandma is quite vocal about this and critical of Isha. Isha doesn't want to involve her mother-in-law. 'I hate her, she's never accepted me, she's even hit me once', she says. Her husband Hanno comments that the children adore his mother and therefore it is important to invite her along. It drives him crazy that his mother and his wife are always complaining about each other.

Over time the individual focus on perpetrators and victims in violent family relationships, evidenced in for instance assertiveness training for victims and anger management for offenders, has shifted to establishing a network of people who are going to be around long-term (Hydén et al., 2016). An example comprises organised family network meetings (based on the model of Family Group Conferences and restorative justice) that take place in The Netherlands and Belgium with a focus on empowering families and their support to voice and find their own solutions for their problems. When there are concerns about children for instance, people from the social circle of the parents, family or friends establish a protective network with the aim to guarantee the basic requirements for children's development and that parents and caregivers are able to function (Nuyts, 2012; Schuurman & Mulder, 2011). This particular conference model is also applicable in adult care (Bredewold & Tonkens, 2021).

The question of who to involve is not always a neutral question. In cases of domestic violence the person who referred themselves often prohibits the professional from making contact with the partner. Realising that violence in relationships is often more closely connected to destructive relational dynamics than to individual problems can guide the practitioner towards finding a cautious way to involve the partner. When young people are aggressive and a cause of concern and their parents are feeling powerless, it can be helpful to ask the young person, who is usually not motivated for therapy, to bring along a person they trust and can be involved in the intervention. The therapy doesn't start until the young person brings their YIM (Your Identified Mentor) (van Dam et al., 2021).

Professional systems

Generally several organisations and professionals are involved in families with multiple and complex problems. Every professional endeavours to provide the best help from their position. Aligning the many professionals can be problematic (Imber-Black, 1988) because of organisational differences in terms of procedures, perspectives and frameworks (Boeckhorst, 2014).

Corine and Frank divorced three years ago. They have three children: Lea (11), Janie (9) and Beau (6). Corine has a new partner, Monty, who has two sons of 17 and 15. Frank is suspicious about the new family situation and suspects that Monty's sons are interfering with his daughters. Frank wants to apply for solo legal guardianship. He is losing sleep over the concerns about his daughters and sought help. Frank has made multiple contacts with a hotline for domestic violence. His mother and sister share his concerns. Lea, Janie and Beau appear stressed at school. School is mainly concerned about Lea who is very quiet lately and is looking very tired. School contacted a family support service. The family therapist is visiting both parents at home to assess safety and what can be done for the children and the parents. Lea has her own counsellor because of concerns about her functioning. Whether there is inappropriate behaviour by Monty's sons plays a role in this. The family therapist refers the parents and the children to a group programme for parents and their children caught in conflict after separation. Getting the professionals on the same page is complex. Frank's therapist is, in agreement with Frank, concerned about the situation at Corine and Monty's home and rings the family therapist and the group programme facilitators. He stresses the importance of investigating Lea being abused. The family therapist concluded, based on her risk assessment and her experience, that both families are doing reasonably well, in spite of many differences between them. The group programme facilitators request that the other professionals tow the same line, otherwise they won't be able to work with both parents and the children. It seems vital that calm is created in the professional network.

Collaboration, consultation and alignment are an essential part of the helping process for families with multiple or complex problems. Because the involved professionals all have different tasks and work from different perspectives alignment takes time. It is not inconceivable that the professionals find themselves stuck in isomorphic processes, for example in a battle about who is providing the best care similar to the parents fighting about who is the best parent. Given the professionals' workload and pressure to be efficient, connecting with colleagues can be challenging. If alignment is not considered a priority, there is the risk that the different interventions have zero results.

Based on the need and necessity to integrate professional help, to align interventions and clarify responsibilities, a guideline for youth care and child protection was developed in The Netherlands with the motto: 'One family, one plan, one manager' (Bolt & van der Zijden, 2015). The case manager is typically the practitioner who is connected the closest with the family, usually a systemic practitioner. They coordinate the help and support the family members and the people in their social and professional networks in developing a plan. In Flanders the coordination happens via youth care support teams. Often plans are made during *round table conferences*, attended by family members, their social network and professionals. They explore what help was offered before, what worked and what didn't, the changes the family members and the others would like to see happening and what steps to take and by whom. Coordinating the services and maintaining a clear direction ensures that clients know who does what and why. This is not only important in youth care and child psychiatry but also in adult and elderly care.

How do I maintain a reflective stance?

In this era of protocols bureaucracy and market forces in mental health and social care it would be fair to state that professionals experience multiple stresses. As a result they too can feel powerless, frustrated and a victim of the increased pressures of work and regulations. The question is how to access space for reflection, remain creative in the work and keep seeing opportunities. Stress can be high in situations of multiple problems and crises. The effect is that all involved will struggle to reflect properly. Actions and reactions are emotionally charged, leading to domineering interaction patterns of blaming and defending or doing nothing at all. In crisis people find themselves at a stalemate and only see danger and problems. To remain reflective and creative in times of crises it is thus important in the conversations with clients to make space for slowing down, reflection and delaying responses.

Dena receives a phone call from a grandmother, the mother of a client she's been working with for a while.

Grandmother screams in the phone: 'When is something going to happen? It can't go on like this! My daughter has so much on her mind that she drove into a crash barrier. Her car has been written off. I had the children when this happened.'

Dena says she can imagine how shocked Grandmother is and that calling her was a good idea. Dena asks whether the daughter knows that her mother is contacting her. This is not the case. Dena requests Grandmother to tell her daughter, otherwise they can't speak further with each other. Dena states that she would like to consult with her team and will ring the grandmother or her daughter back as soon as possible.

By validating the grandmother's panic Dena is feeling less stressed. By not responding immediately and instead planning to consult with team members, the therapist creates some personal reflective space.

It can be advisable to see families in conjunction with a colleague, especially when the practitioner feels so threatened that it precludes reflection. When two therapists prepare, facilitate and review the sessions, panic decreases and efficiency of the intervention increases because they can stay in dialogue and are not overwhelmed by spirals of helplessness (Nieuwpoort, 2006).

Methods such as working with safety maps, Madsen and Gillespie's (2014) directive questions, Omer's method of non-violent resistance (Omer, 2021) or the group method *No Kids in the Middle* (Visser & van Lawick, 2021) help to order the influx of information and stressors and to work purposefully. That too provides space for reflection.

According to Wilson (2017) remaining creative is not an individual skill or a magic trick but the result of great teamwork, of *co-creativity*. Working together in a team where the day-to-day practice is a priority is motivating for professionals. The day-to-day face to face work with families and talking with the team about that work and its constraints and opportunities keeps professionals going. Providing help to multi-stressed families and couples is difficult and intense. Team meetings in which the team members discuss their families can be a source of support for the practitioner. However team processes can end up in similar spirals of feeling powerless, for example when colleagues offer several pieces of advice which make the therapist feel they have failed. Such isomorphic processes, as described in Chapter 9, always linger in the case of complex situations. Similar to how families are viewed in collaborative interventions as capable themselves of improving the situation, when the practitioner is regarded by their multidisciplinary team as having sufficient resources available to recognise opportunities for change, team discussions will benefit the professional. Making space for the therapist's and team members' inner dialogue can also be useful.

AYSHA: 'The only thing that mother does, is complaining. She says she can't enjoy anything anymore. To me she appears so down. Sometimes I think, is she going to commit suicide? And I wonder whether she is neglecting her children.'

The team asks Aysha the four questions of Madsen's collaborative helping process: What do you hope to achieve? What barriers do you see? What sources of support and strengths do you see? What needs to happen now and what are the first steps?

Aysha responds that she hopes to have a good contact with the mother so they can work together to the point that the mother is confident again that she can cope with her children. One of the barriers is that the mother often cancels appointments. When she does attend, she leaves such an exhausted and sombre impression that Aysha feels hopeless and doesn't quite know what to do. Aysha identifies as sources of support that the mother always looks well dressed and has no debts. And by wearing a hijab she portrays herself as Muslima. Perhaps her faith is a source of support? While Aysha talks, she is feeling relieved. 'If this mother takes her faith seriously, perhaps the risk of suicide is small.' After all this Aysha can talk about what needs to happen next. Aysha would like to see the children and decides to do a home visit when the children are home. She also wants to talk with the mother about who is important to her and who could be invited to do some reflecting with her.

Aysha is keen to discuss the family again in the team sometime in the future.

Helpful multidisciplinary team meetings as intervention can prevent burn-out. Particularly in the case of complex problems, when the pressure is high and frantic, working together is a *must*.

In conclusion

We discussed a number of options and pitfalls when working with families with multiple or complex problems. Stressors in such situations are diverse: debts, looming eviction, suicidal ideation, relational problems, violence. They all need to be attended to by the practitioner. Some stressors are unique to a family, other problems are common. When dealing with multiple problems, it is important to focus on protective factors around a family, such as friends, work and societal organisations and on positive experiences. Using specific methods when working systemically with families with complex problems can help to structure the sessions, elicit particular questions and themes and provide guidance for the next steps. In this way practitioners can order the chaos generated by complex problems and concerns about the safety of children and adults.

Any method needs to respect a family's uniqueness and their requests for help. Four questions can be used as guiding principles: How do I position myself? How do I assess and ensure safety? Who do I involve? How do I remain reflective? The starting point is a robust and present positioning of the practitioner, who does not minimise the concerns, but is not paralysed by them either. They are capable of dealing with pressure from clients, services and society. They seek collaboration with family members and their social networks. They work actively and collaboratively within a team and create, together with team members, space for reflection and creativity.

Exercise

When working systemically with families facing multiple problems and stressors, often several professionals are involved. If you know such a family, map everyone who is involved and with whom. Map for each family member which professionals are involved. Are these professionals connected or do they work independently?

Once you have finished the mapping, reflect, preferably with a colleague, on the effects of all the professional help. What messages are (implicitly) given to the parents and to the children? Are these messages supportive and strengthening, or not? If you could have your way, what would you change?

Chapter II

The systemic practitioner in action

Introduction

In previous chapters we have seen how the practitioner acts, intervenes and applies techniques. The therapist aims to establish a working relationship, map the problems, assume a positioning and facilitate change. As illustrated previously the practitioner's work consists of connecting with clients, listening to multiple voices, reflecting, formulating hypotheses, posing systemic questions, intervening and continuously attuning based on the client's feedback. Throughout this process the therapist orders the abundance of information into hypotheses. A hypothesis represents the presumptions about the connections between the client's problems or concerns and the contexts they live in, their relationships, their history and their personal strengths and limits. A helpful hypothesis is not necessarily correct, but a hypothesis that projects a desired process of change. Hypotheses can help the practitioner to order information and can be shared with the clients and prompt a dialogue about what is happening and what needs to be done. Hypotheses can provide a direction but are never fixed; during the course of therapy, they can be adjusted or supplemented as required.

Hypotheses help to orientate which questions could be relevant. These are *systemic skills* and include the therapist taking into consideration the phase of the therapeutic trajectory. For example asking a father the systemic question, 'Who is, according to you, the most burdened by your remarrying Ella within the year?' can, at the start of the therapy, be perceived by the client as a judgement from the professional with the effect that the father responds defensively or doesn't return. In a different scenario when the working relationship has been established and the father trusts the therapist, the same question can be perceived as informative and lead to reflection.

In this chapter we highlight a number of techniques and skills that are part and parcel of the systemic practitioner's toolbox (Midori Hanna & Brown, 2018; Savenije & van Lawick, 2014). We note that it is difficult to

DOI: 10.4324/9781003272038-11

separate interventions and the categories below are thereby our choice. For instance all verbal interventions have non-verbal components and each non-verbal intervention comes with the verbalising of experiences. Further, visualisations such as drawing a genogram can slow down or focus the conversation and we could have opted for discussing these as separate interventions.

Systemic questions and relational listening

All therapists ask questions. They ask questions to make introductions. They ask about work, hobbies and relationships. They ask about concerns and problems people are seeking help for, when the problems started and in which situations they occur. They ask why people seek help now. They ask questions to explore the client's goals and opportunities for change. Systemic practitioners are interested in how problems affect relationships and how in a continuous circular process relationships influence the problems. They listen with a 'relational ear'. Therapists develop *relational listening* by being curious about what may be relevant contexts and the relational effects of the problems (Mason, 2019). Those reflections result in systemic questions. In turn the therapist will listen with a relational ear to the responses, subsequent questions will follow et cetera.

> Nick says that his headaches started after the birth of daughter Lena, their first child. The therapist asks more about the headaches: when do they occur and how are they related to Nick's life and history? And she asks what the effect is on the relationship between Nick and Lena and between Nick and his wife, as parents and as partners. And what is the effect on the relationship with the grandparents, the family and the outside world?

A therapist always has to consider how and why to formulate certain questions. In the beginning of the therapeutic process the main aim of questions is to map and clarify the problems. The therapist tries to understand how all people involved experience the problems, what their concerns are about, what the relational effects are of their concerns and what their hopes for change are. Later in the process systemic questions can be intended to encourage reflection and enable change (Tomm, 1988). The therapist's intention and its impact on the therapeutic process are not necessarily one and the same. A systemic question intended to understand something better can instigate change; a question intended to encourage someone to behave differently can generate more information. Systemic questions surface more easily when the therapist is interested in the relational space and prompt clients too to relationally listen to one another.

In what follows we detail three types of systemic questions: circular questions, questions about resilience and positive exceptions and questions aimed at contextualising the problems and concerns.

Circular questions

Circular questions are questions about relationships and what happens in these relationships. This includes interactions and the meanings attributed to those interactions by the people involved. This type of questions provides insight into relational patterns and into the connection between the clients' concerns and problems and the relational space they live in. Circular questions invite the clients to verbalise what they think is happening in the other person or in the relationship or what they think the other person is about to do. Tomm (1987a, 1987b, 1988) wrote three articles about interventive questioning in which he differentiates between types of circular questions and between the therapist's intentions, such as aiming at collecting information or aiming at change. It is possible that people view their problems differently as an effect of circular questions. Circular questions help to slow down a conversation and provide structure because each person is approached separately. This brings calm. Circular questions can be directed at various relational aspects.

We consider the following four types of circular questions essential: directed at behaviour, at orderings, at the effect of the problems on relationships and on the future.

Circular questions about behaviour and its relational effects

This type of questions probes the behavioural responses of family members, partners or other people involved and what behaviour this elicits in turn.

In the conversation with Tony and Kim Milan asks Kim: 'What does Tony do when you are on the phone with your mother for half an hour?'

KIM: 'He leaves, and I have to deal with it.'
MILAN (ADDRESSING TONY): 'You go away?'
TONY: 'Yes, I do. There is no end to those conversations. It's always the same complaints about nothing and Kim always gets cranky. I don't want to be sucked into that, I prefer to do something else then.'
MILAN: 'How does Kim react to that?'
TONY: 'I go for a long run and when I return home she looks at me reproachfully. I'd rather leave again straight away.'
KIM IS CRYING: 'I don't know what to do.'

Behavioural sequences and their relational effects are mapped out.

Circular questions that bring order

These are circular questions that introduce an ordering by categorising: more or less, before or after, smaller or bigger.

> Dean, a therapist specialised in problems related to dementia, visits Alison and Evan Hudson for the second time at home. Again their daughter Anne is present. At some point he asks Anne: 'Who in the family is the most concerned about your father?' Then he asks who is the least concerned, followed by the same questions but now pertaining Alison. Family members who are not present can be included.

In the family session with Ratna her mother and Vera, Marian asks: 'Who is best placed to calm Ratna down when she is so angry and upset? Who is not so good at it?'

Circular questions about the influence of the problems on relationships

In Chapter 6 Marian asked questions about the problems' influence on the relationships.

> 'Do you have any idea how the troubles affect you? What influence do they have on your relationship?', Marian asks while looking at Kira and Ratna.
>   Kira looks at her daughter: 'I believe that it creates distance between us', she says.

Marian then names the recurring pattern. She could have chosen however to continue with circular questions. For example by asking Kira: 'What do you think Ratna would say if I asked her how the fighting affects you all?'

Alternatively Marian could introduce a time dimension and ask about the difference between *the present and the past*.

> MARIAN: 'Who can tell me when there was no fighting yet?'
> VERA: 'When Benny was little, we were cheerful and happy. Ratna too, she always wanted to help with Benny. John came once in a while but Jaco not as much.'

Whoever answers or whatever the response, it always leads to further relational questions that shed more light on the context in which the problems occur.

Circular questions directed at the future

Penn (1985) developed future-directed questions and provided several examples of questions that can be asked about the future.

> MARIAN ASKS VERA: 'Suppose that John, Ratna's father, came to live in The Netherlands again, what could that mean for Ratna? What would you notice? How would this affect your relationships?'

Or about the desired future:

> MILAN ASKS KIM AND TONY: 'Suppose you go away together for a long weekend and I would ask your son Keiran what he thinks you'd do together, what would he say?'

By asking the question in this way, Kim and Tony look at themselves from the perspective of Keiran (who is absent). This can help to see possibilities again that were slumbering in the background.

> TONY: 'I think he'd say that he hopes we'll laugh a lot together because that's what we used to do.'
> KIM: 'I think he'd say that he thinks we'll go for walks together, we've always enjoyed that.'
>
> 'But the children never did', Tony adds. They both laugh.

Turnell and Essex (2006) use circular, future-oriented questions when safety is at risk. Suppose that Jaco, Benny's biological father, had made a notification because of concerns about Benny's safety. Turnell and Essex describe how in such situations future directed questions about safety could be part of the conversation with involved others, including Jaco.

> MARIAN ASKS JACO: 'Suppose that Benny is totally safe with Kira, Vera and Ratna, how would we know this? What would you notice? How would Vera and Kira know this? And the school?'
> MARIAN ASKS KIRA: Vera and Ratna the same questions.

As such the therapist introduces a projected safe situation in the future and explores what that would look like, how people would know the situation is safe and how this would influence the relationships. This gives insight into what may need to change.

Questions about resilience and positive exceptions

Focussing on strengths and enquiring about what is going well now and in the past has always been important in family therapy (Walsh, 2006).

> Anita has been working for a while with an Irani family because of the father's sombre mood and the mother and daughter's anxieties. In the course of therapy the symptoms have lessened. When things don't go well, the father tends to feel depressed again. Anita decides to focus on resilience. She asks which problems the family have conquered previously. And what did they do in Iran to help someone with low mood. The father says that his own father used to help people by telling them beautiful stories or doing something with them. Once he and the neighbour painted a fence sky blue; it made everyone happy.

With these questions Anita aims to reconnect the family with their resilience rather than feeling consumed by feeling powerless and hopeless. If this is successful, Anita can ask how the family could notice resilience currently, perhaps in small exceptions.

> The mother talks about how the father managed to find his daughter a bicycle so she could attend school. Anita asks the father how he got that idea, how he knew where to find a bicycle, how he managed to choose a good bike, how he knew how big the bicycle needed to be, whether he checked the bike for safety and so on. Later they can talk about cycling lessons, how the parents are teaching their child to navigate the traffic and so on.

Connecting with day-to-day subjects or details can make it easier to find positive exceptions. Talking about divvying up chores, grocery shopping, sleeping patterns, transporting and collecting children, playing, sports and cooking can provide a treasure trove of information about things that go well or in other words positive exceptions. By highlighting constructive exceptions, the therapist helps the family members to focus on stories in which the problems don't feature or are less prominent. Often positive stories have been 'pushed away' by the problem story. By bringing those stories to the fore, people can see possibilities again (White & Epston, 1990).

> 'Brent (13) never takes initiative', his mother says. 'All he does is gaming. He doesn't meet his friends, he doesn't want to sit at the table for dinner, he doesn't do any schoolwork and when I make a comment, he talks back to me.'
>
> 'Don't be such a bore', Brent says.
>
> Julia, the therapist, asks him what game he likes to play. Brent enthusiastically tells her about Counter-Strike where he and his team defeat terrorists. Julia asks more details about his approach and his role in the team. His mother is surprised to learn about her son's initiatives and leader position in the team. Next they talk about when Brent uses his initiatives and when he doesn't and how much initiative he took as a little boy.

Moving from the problem story to a story infused with possibilities is another important skill of the systemic practitioner.

Questions aimed at contextualising the concerns

Another important skill is asking questions about the contexts that may play a role in the concerns and problems and with potential to present a different perspective of the problems.

> Neal and Tara are worried about their fighting and lack of intimacy. After the birth of their second child a year ago, their relationship deteriorated. Liz, their therapist, asks whether they've talked with friends about this. Do they think that things have changed too for friends who have been parents for a few years? Tara says she knows of a friend with similar problems. She and her friend believe their husbands are jealous of the children and the attention the children are getting. Neal disagrees; he never talks with his mates about it. He is actually very happy with his children but believes he and Tara have to make time for each other. Liz asks how his parents managed this. Neal thinks for a bit and responds that his parents struggled too. The conversation shifts to how almost all couples struggle with the transition from partnership to parenthood.

This range of questions takes the focus away from the individual and gives centre place to the societal context, family stage, stage of life or significant events. When the systemic therapist explores contextual influences, they take note of which connections appear helpful or useful for the clients. They consider the contexts that can help the clients and others to see, feel and act differently. They aim to avoid seeing one specific connection as the one and only truth. Some parents can find it enlightening to see the connection with a particular stage of life while for other parents this feels as minimising their problems. One couple appreciates recognising the connection between their conflicts and the values in their families of origin while this form of *contextualising* is unhelpful for another couple. To the contrary by connecting the conflict with interaction habits in their families of origin, they feel even more hopeless about their situation. A useful angle for a client may not mean much for the other people involved. Time and again the therapist has to reckon with the effects of *contextualising* on the clients and their environment, because effects are polyphonic and not set in concrete.

Reframing and positive connotations

The pioneers of systemic therapy have always aimed to define behaviour, interactions and problems in a way that creates space for change.

> Mr and Mrs Young referred themselves because of their heated arguments. Mrs Young is finding it difficult that her husband is so quiet, never says a word and withdraws himself. She feels abandoned and excluded by him. Mr Young thinks that his wife always has a go at him and can't leave him in peace.

The practitioner who would like to reframe Mr Young's behaviour could describe it as 'he prefers to stay in the background', 'he is thoughtful' or 'he is someone who gives others space'. Mrs Young's behaviour could be reframed as 'caring'. However positive connotations need to be the right fit for the conversation. If Mrs Young is angry, such reframe could be perceived as 'excuses' and 'justifications'. The therapist could then reframe Mrs Young's anger as 'being sensitive' and her complaints as 'her wish to have a closer relationship with her husband'. In the latter the therapist names the hope aspect of emotions: Mrs Young wants to achieve something with her anger. Often the intentions, hopes and needs behind behaviour are positive: the hope to reach each other, to be heard, to make sure that the children grow up well. By zooming into good intentions partners and family members can have a different experience of each other. Such positive connotations could shift interactions significantly. They also have a positive effect on the therapist's experience of the interaction. For example they now perceive Mrs Young as someone who feels she is missing out and consequently have more empathy for her.

Not only behaviour but relationship patterns too can be positively relabelled.

> Marian is using systemic questions when enquiring about Ratna's angry behaviour.
> At some point she asks Vera: 'What do you think would have happened if Ratna had not run away?'
> Vera: 'It probably would have gotten worse.'
> Marian reframes that by running away Ratna prevented the situation from further escalating while her brother Benny was present.

Ratna is implicitly labelled as someone who cares for the home situation and Benny. Searching for positive connotations can assist the therapist when they notice their own irritation or feel stuck.

> Once Milan knew that Kim and Tony had not talked with each other about the first session and attending therapy together, he felt disapproval. 'How is it possible that you don't talk with each other about that.' He decided to leave his irritation for what it was. When he thought about it later, he realised this was about him too. He is the one who always wants to discuss things like this. He reflected that perhaps Kim and Tony didn't discuss it to avoid hurting each other as their way of caring for one another. It was a reframe that created space for Milan to explore carefully how this worked for the couple.

When behaviour and events are given overwhelmingly negative labels, a reframe can soften the connotations and result in the spirals of conflict being less powerful in interactions. Instead space is available for meanings that reconnect and enable change.

Slowing down and amplifying

In conversations with families or multiple people professionals can become easily overwhelmed by the inpouring of information. The conversations usually happen at high speed: one word leads to another, the clients know each other's point of view, they react, defend and attack. They are familiar with everyone's behaviour and interpretations and the conversations can quickly be emotionally charged. This process can be slowed down by posing questions, making a joint inventory of the concerns and the problems, suggesting a reframe and pausing around specific interactions.

The therapist stops the conversation temporarily and focusses on specific information, a particular situation or interaction. Ample time is taken to discuss situations in more detail; in a way they are amplified. For instance in the case of escalations: What was the fight about? What exactly happened?

A moment-by-moment analysis follows, helpful with families where conflict is out of control as discussed in Chapter 10. The family members alternate in taking the floor, and each person can say what they thought, felt and did. This structure of pausing the interactions for a while allows information lost in the heat of the argument to surface.

Externalising and de-blaming

Externalising has been covered in several previous chapters. Externalising conversations is a technique developed by White and Epston (White, 2007; White & Epston, 1990) and applied and further refined by the authors and others. Externalising disconnects the problem from the person. The problem is the problem, not the person. Often the problem is given a name. Next how the problem influences the client's life, relationships or the family is explored, in other words the relationship between the clients and the problem and the influence of the problem on the relationships. A well-known example is working with children with encopresis (Freeman et al., 1997).

> Isaac (7) names his problem 'the brown danger'. He came up with the idea that his mother can alert him when she thinks he needs to go to the toilet, but with a code, like: 'Could you check whether we need to buy toilet paper?' His Dad thinks that teaching Isaac some judo moves can make him stronger; they could practice for ten minutes before dinner. His Mum suggests making a calendar and using stickers to indicate how strong Isaac has been that day and how big 'the brown danger'.

Externalising can be useful in many problem areas. When arguments recur in a relationship, the escalating struggle can be named 'the destroyer of love', an intruder who is bothering everyone and corrodes the identity of both partners and their relationship. The therapist explores with the partners when the fights entered their relationship, what their relationship would look like when 'the destroyer of love' has been defeated and what actions could disempower the intruder. Externalising as technique can also be used with individual diagnoses. The diagnosis can feature in a systemic conversation as follows: 'Which form of ADHD has joined your family? When? What does it do with your relationships?'. Subsequently the practitioner can enquire about exceptions: 'On what days or moments is ADHD not present or barely noticeable?'

Visualising

Systemic practitioners utilise visual representations regularly. Well-known examples are genograms, timelines such as a lifeline or a tree of life, family drawings, network drawings, interaction drawings or puppets. In the chapter

'Mapping' Marian drew a context web with the clients. Visualisations help to slow down conversations and interrupt escalations. Drawing together, looking at the drawing and talking about it creates distance from the problem story and allows a more reflecting position for clients and therapist alike. Below we discuss genograms, timelines, network drawings, drawings of interaction patterns, family drawings and working with puppets or other objects.

Genograms

A genogram is a visual representation of a family throughout a number of generations. Standard symbols used include squares for males and circles for females, but genograms change with time: we have squares and circles with a triangle inside for gays and lesbians, a dotted triangle for bi-sexuals, a circle in a square or square in a circle for transgenders or both same size for people who define themselves as non-binaries. Ages and dates of death are added. Horizontal lines represent relationships within the same generation, vertical lines represent intergenerational connections. This gives a wide variety of possibilities. In Chapter 1 we saw an example of a genogram covering three generations. Although simple it could be extended with Dirk and Agnes' parents and siblings to have a better insight in their background. Or it could be spruced up with other symbols and images such as photos, colours, drawings of animals or objects (Buurma, 1999; Hillewaere & LeFevere de Ten Hove, 2006; Lewis, 1989). Genograms are usually composed with the family and depicted by the therapist or the family. Making a genogram provides a clear focus: everyone's attention is directed to the genogram.

In the early days genograms were mainly used to elicit information about personal details of each family member, relationships, relationship ruptures and the quality of relationships (McGoldrick & Gerson, 1985). This way, a genogram can be used during the introduction phase. It quickly gives an idea about the family composition, who the most important members are, their intergenerational embedding and significant events.

Currently genograms are applied in a variety of ways (Hillewaere, 2006; McGoldrick et al., 1999; Mumford & Weeks, 2003; Wiggins Frame, 2001). Genograms can help to zoom in on stories connected with the relationships in a family, with specific events, new or broken relationships, births and deaths. In addition to focusing on the problems while the genogram is further explored, sources of support and strengths can be added. Traits across generations could be identified such as musical talent or recurring problems such as addiction. The therapist can ask how previous generations overcame similar problems. Or the family can be asked about important traditions and rituals, joyful moments, friendships, heroes, spiritual or religious values, favourite books and stories and positive qualities. Jessurun

(Jessurun, 2010; Jessurun & Warring, 2018) uses genograms with migrants to help them talk about where they come from and about their family and cultural traditions, rituals and strengths. They tell stories about their current situation and the connections with and in the country they now live in. Stories emerge relating to their travels, differences, identity, what they miss and what is going well now. When questions come from a curious and open stance, a genogram can be a tool that connects and creates space to speak about emotionally charged topics. Talking and drawing often has a de-escalating and normalising effect.

Making a genogram can be a one-off activity or the genogram can be revisited during the course of therapy as an aide memoire, to add new information or to delve into particular topics.

Timeline

A timeline or a lifeline is a visual representation of the client's life history and can be used with individuals, relationships, families and organisations. We gave an example in Chapter 6. Mostly the therapist draws a line from left to right. For individuals the line starts with their birth and finishes in the present. A timeline can be extended beyond that to have people reflect about the future and which events could take place, for instance by using future oriented circular questions. In case of relationships or families a starting point needs to be agreed on, for example when granddad and grandma married or when partners met. It can be valuable to pay attention to the individual lifelines of both partners before they met and to the future they expect or hope for. Significant events of the client's life, their relationship or the family can be symbolised with the year, words or colours. Symbols can be sketched such as flowers and rocks to mark the meaning of an event. Positive events that have reinforced the resilience and problematic or painful events are noted. Births, relationships, illnesses, deaths, relocations or other significant life events can be marked on the timeline (Suddaby & Landau, 1998).

When the client has been through a lot that is likely to be difficult to talk about, for instance for refugees or families with complex problems, the making of a timeline can offer a structured way to tell (parts of) their story. A timeline categorises information and helps clients to speak about significant events in their lives and their meaning now and in the past. A timeline can evoke memories and stories that can be added later. The diversity of information a timeline can hold is huge but ultimately it is the representation of a process with a past, present and future with positive and negative sides.

Tree of life

Clients could draw their own tree of life. The roots represent what they have learnt in their lives and from whom and their deeply rooted survival powers.

The soil represents what and who nurtures them, what and who allows them to take root in the present. The trunk represents what makes them strong, what their qualities are. The branches represent dreams and hopes, the leaves who is important for them now. The fruit represents what they have been given in life and from whom. The flowers represent what they have given to others. This method has been developed in the work with traumatised children in South Africa and Australia but can be applied to adults, multiple family members and groups (Denborough, 2008).

Drawing a genogram, timeline, lifeline or tree of life is a process. Elements can be added throughout, and the meaning of events may even change over time.

Drawing as dialogue

Many systemic practitioners utilise drawings in sessions with families and couples. Minuchin (1974), Rober (2017) and others make space for children, encourage them to draw and talk with the child and its family about the drawings. Drawing provides a starting point to establish contact and an opportunity for children and adults to express what otherwise may be difficult to talk about.

> Barbara comes with her two children, Finn (4) and Aïda (8), to the session. She is embroiled in an acrimonious separation. Her ex-husband, the children's father, left the home after a violent escalation. Barbara does not know where he is staying and is afraid he may abduct the children. Barbara talks in a hard and reproachful way and sounds panicky. Finn and Aïda are unsettled. Therapist Eveline asks them whether they would like to draw, perhaps about something fun they did together. She hopes to alleviate the emotional level of the conversation and make the session more collaborative. She suggests that Mum could help. Finn immediately starts to scratch and colour in. He draws a number of balloons he saw at the fair. Aïda draws her mother, brother and herself under a tree. A little man is standing behind the tree. At Eveline's request to elaborate about her drawing, Aïda says that she, her brother and her mother are having a picnic at the park. Their Dad is standing behind the tree; he's hiding, but so wants to be part of the picnic, she says.

Systemic professionals utilise drawing as a creative method to engage in conversations with a family about important topics. They can ask parents and children to collaboratively make a drawing of their family, for instance by drawing family members as animals or by drawing a ship or their house with details about what happens in there, or by other means (Gil, 2015; Klijn, 1991; Van Ramshorst, 2004). Adults may find this childish or difficult because they claim they can't draw or they don't have the best memories of drawing at school. Mostly clients can be convinced that whatever they draw is ok, it is more about communication and experience than about performance. Apart from drawing and painting, clay or other materials can be used, illustrated by Scheller-Dikkers (1998) and Klijn (2006). Drawing has its place in couples therapy too. The couple can draw their relationship and each person is represented by a character, animal or object (Rober, 2009). The drawing facilitates a conversation about important relational themes.

Using puppets and objects

Puppets, wooden forms, blocks and other objects can be used to represent family members, the deceased, relationships and contexts (Gil, 2015; Rober, 2017). Coloured blocks can symbolise what supports and what burdens people and their relationships (Yücel, 2013). Multiple voices within one person can be visualised, for instance the angry and the caring mother or the strong mother and the vulnerable child within (Diekmann, 2005). Simple objects spread out on the table such as cups, spoons and sugar cubes can represent relationships and events (Vermeire, 2015).

Network drawings

A network drawing is a visualisation of the personal and professional networks involved with a family. A personal network represents the family's social embedding: friends, church, work, colleagues, clubs and other relationships. Sports clubs and friends are frequently important support systems, like the theatre club for Dirk and the choir for Agnes. The same applies to the children. A network drawing can bring stressful and supportive influences in focus. A church community can be a connection of support or burden, work and colleagues can be felt as a support or a burden. The differences can be marked with different colours.

It can be relevant to map the professional network. A professional network drawing identifies which services are involved with a family and in case of many professionals provides clarity. All these organisations and professionals and who they are involved with are drawn around the client or the family, sometimes including the different goals of the different professionals. Family members can indicate how big the influence is of the different professionals, for instance by adjusting their size on the drawing.

Mrs Tenek, who is depressed, is having sessions with her own therapist. An organisational social worker is in contact with the father who is at home sick. An appointed child guardian is involved due to an earlier investigation regarding concerns about the safety of the children. The eldest child, who has the diagnosis of autism spectrum disorder, sees a therapist and another child diagnosed with conduct disorder has a therapist too. The family is also receiving help at home from a parenting support person which was organised by Child Protection. And they are dealing with a mentor to address financial problems. The family is now referred for community-based family support because the concerns haven't abated. The overview of all the organisations and professionals involved shows clearly how busy the parents and the children are with keeping so many appointments and that they continuously receive the message that something is wrong, that their failings are many.

A drawing of the professional network results in a much clearer view of the entire professional care system and of the effects of the various helping trajectories. In consultation with the family discussions take place about what help is needed and what steps they can take themselves or with support from people in their personal network. The effect is usually a decrease in the number of professionals and the family regaining control.

Drawing interaction patterns

In Chapter 6 Marian drew a graphic representation of a repetitive interaction pattern on the board: one of the children makes a comment, someone else gets involved to prevent an argument, the conflict escalates regardless and everyone is feeling awful and isolated. The family named it *the circle of irritation*. Such interaction drawing externalises the destructive pattern and is recognised as a burden to all family members. This can help to decrease escalations and demonisation of others (Visser & van Lawick, 2021). Scheinkman and DeKoven Fishbane (2004) draw a vulnerability cycle for couples. It shows each partner's vulnerabilities and the survival strategies they have developed. Often the survival strategy of one partner touches on the vulnerability of the other partner and vice versa.

Stan often felt left alone as a child and is afraid of abandonment. When Shirley is away a lot, he feels irritated and angry and starts to control her. Shirley is the only daughter of a solo mother who surrounded her with much care but was also anxious about the dangers of the outside world. Shirley has always felt tightly controlled by her mother and had to break away from her. Control is therefore her vulnerability. When Shirley feels controlled, she distances herself and withdraws. The more Shirley withdraws, the more anxious Stan becomes. The more he controls Shirley, the more she creates distance. This process continues to escalate.

By drawing such interaction cycles on the board or paper, partners can see they are trapped by a destructive pattern. This can then be externalised: not the other partner but the pattern is 'the enemy of love'.

Non-verbal interventions and movement

All communication is verbal and non-verbal. Body language, sound and volume of voice, remaining silent, it all speaks volumes. Systemic practitioners frequently use non-verbal interventions when mapping the problems and in processes of change. Words are still spoken with non-verbal interventions, but the angle differs. Experiential exercises and roleplaying situations provide immediate physical experiences that can be the impetus to change. This can happen simply by placing chairs for absent family members and asking the attendees what those people would feel, think or say (Mous, 2014). Or family members can be requested to sit on the chair of an absent person, for example a parent is asked to sit on a little chair of an absent child to undergo what the child's experiences may be. Below we describe in more detail two specific forms of getting moving: enactment and sculpting.

Enactment

Enactment is a method developed by Minuchin (1974). He used situations that occurred during family sessions. He asked family members to reposition themselves to experience a new, more preferred situation. For example he asked parents to work together in a way that allowed their child to play alone for five minutes. He wanted the parents to have an experience of good parenting and authority in the hope this would become a physical memory and accessible in the future. In relationship sessions using enactment is common, for instance by Johnson (2004): the partners are invited to say something to each other they no longer say at home.

> Milan asked Tony, when it became evident how much he cares about Kim and how much he wants to help her, to say to her: 'I hate to see you so sad because I love you and I want to help you so badly, but I don't know how.'

A context of direct interaction is created by the client not talking with the therapist *about* what's bothering them but saying it directly *to* their partner. The effect of this directness needs to be assessed. It can create positive tension and facilitate further progress or too much tension that ends up being a barrier.

Sculpting

With sculpting family members or partners are asked to make a sculpture of their family and the family interrelationships. These can be symbolised through distance, some are close to one another or further removed, or with a specific body posture or facial expression (Faes, 2016b; Papp et al., 2013; Satir, 1972, 1988; Savenije & van Lawick, 2014).

> The therapist asks Ivan to present how he experiences his relationship. He places Milena at the door, with her back to him and her hand on the door handle. He is standing further away, looking at her with his arms extended to her and a desperate look on his face.
>
> Milena's image is totally different. She sits hunched over on a chair, her head in her hands and Ivan hanging heavily on her back.
>
> Both have to make an image of how they would like it to be.
>
> Ivan asks Milena to look at him and wants to stand next to her holding her hand.
>
> Milena wants Ivan to stand on his own two feet. She wants to stand next to him yet at some distance. Both are looking forward, their hands can touch or let go.
>
> The configurations bring up many questions and clarify a whole raft of things. The conversation changes.

The sculpting image can include children and grandparents or stepparents and stepsiblings in the case of blended families.

The practitioner needs to feel confident and comfortable with every systemic intervention but particularly with non-verbal interventions. Some therapists use enactment and sculpting frequently, others never.

Feedback and adjusting

As mentioned in several previous chapters being open for feedback from clients and continuously adjusting the therapeutic process are important skills of the systemic practitioner. This does not mean that the therapist gives in blindly to all of the client's requests. In the process of feedback their own evaluation of the therapeutic process plays a role too.

> When Marian wants to invite Jaco, this is too soon for Vera. She's not ready yet. Marian takes this feedback seriously and prioritises the working relationship with Vera. At the same time she keeps the option open to include Jaco in future sessions.

Repeatedly asking for feedback from clients also guides the therapeutic direction. Clients seek help because of concerns and problems and are hopeful of a better situation. By regularly eliciting feedback about the clients' experiences of the therapy and its effects, the practitioner is able to continue to attune and keep course.

In conclusion

The systemic practitioner listens with a relational ear and asks questions on that basis. Listening and asking questions like this results in reframing and de-individualising. The attention is focused, and the conversation is slowed down. Specific situations and interactions are magnified and externalised. Systemic therapy is supported by the many ways that processes can be visualised, by non-verbal means and by continuous feedback.

Using a particular intervention is related to the problems for which help was sought, the phase of the therapy, the working relationship with the clients, the location (at a service or at the client's home) and the personal preferences of the therapist. There are many options and interventions possible. New playful online interventions have been developed in the time of the pandemic (Vermeire & Van de Berge, 2021). Systemic interventions are all linked and part of a connective therapeutic process. This requires on the one hand the practitioner to be steadfast in keeping course amidst a polyphony of voices and possibilities and on the other hand to be creative and improvise to find methods that fit ever-changing situations.

Exercise

Take an example from your own practice.

Think of a situation featuring different values. The mother for instance believes that parents have to listen to their children while the father is adamant that children have to learn to listen to their parents. The maternal grandmother supports the father while the paternal grandmother supports the mother. List some of the circular questions you could ask to whom and what the effect could be. The questions could relate to relationships, contexts or cultural values.

Next write down a few questions about positive exceptions. For example: when did the parents manage to listen to the children and simultaneously maintain the structure to retain a positive atmosphere? What can they say about that? What would the grandmothers say?

When they talk about situations that went well or when conflict escalated, what kind of questions could help to slow this down? What could be the effect of slowing down?

Chapter 12

Change

An epilogue

Introduction

The aim of therapy and counselling is change. Even if not every problem is resolved change means that people can move forward together again. Change is a complex phenomenon. Looking back at a successful therapeutic process everyone feels satisfied about, it is often difficult to know what made clients behave differently, relationships improve and people feel reconnected with one another. Things have changed, but why? For various reasons it is a difficult question to answer. In this chapter we propose a systemic view of change and address factors that contribute to change in general and specifically in systemic therapy. We refer to topics discussed in previous chapters.

A multitude of influences

In interpersonal exchanges a multitude of interactions and meanings occur. In day-to-day life sudden or big events can happen that turn life as it is upside down: someone meets a new love or feels devastated when the partner is leaving the relationship; someone is promoted at work or a serious conflict at work ends up in being dismissed; people have debts or solve financial problems; people fall ill, loved ones die. Smaller events have an influence too. Some changes happen unnoticed and slowly, others incredibly fast. Because people's lives are complex and multi sided, when change occurs, many of life's processes intertwine without knowing exactly what and how the change happened. Consequently the influences between what happens in the clients' lives and what happens in the therapeutic sessions are manifold. People are influenced by a continuous stream of interactions and influence these in turn. Watzlawick and Beavin-Bavelas (2009) wrote that communication in the wider sense of the word is not something we *do*, but something we *participate* in, are part of. Clients indicate for instance that a particular word or a sentence uttered by a therapist made them think. Or that the joint conversation with the grandparents has set something in motion while the therapist felt it was not the greatest session. What practitioners do or

DOI: 10.4324/9781003272038-12

say has meaning and is given meaning. The meaning itself is outside the therapist's control and can differ between clients. And the intention of the professional's words and actions does not necessarily generate the hoped-for effect on the clients. In the first session the therapist may aspire to map the client's problems and hopes. That inventory can have immediate unintended effects and alter views, meanings or interactions (Midori Hanna & Brown, 2018; Reijmers, 2014c; Vetere & Dallos, 2003). Even before the start of a therapeutic trajectory changes may have already started. People who talked with others about their problems may notice this effected change. They have looked for explanations and solutions, perhaps by speaking with others, reading something in the paper or a magazine, browsing the internet or watching something on TV. All this can lead to change. After a conversation with friends a man decides to finally bite the bullet and leave his partner. A woman reads an article about burn-out and recognises what could explain her sleeping problems; she decides to take sick leave.

What contributes?

Even though the question of what or who contributes to change remains difficult to answer, there has been considerable research into factors that correlate with change processes. Wampold has carried out extensive research into factors contributing to positive treatment outcomes (Wampold, 2001; Wampold & Imel, 2015). He makes a distinction between general and specific factors. General factors are common for all treatment modalities while specific factors are part of a particular type of treatment, model or approach. His research shows that common factors have a bigger impact on the outcomes of treatment than specific factors. While his research mainly focussed on individual treatment, the results appear to be applicable to systemic treatment (Loots et al., 2014; Sprenkle & Blow, 2006).

Common factors

Client factors, the alliance, positive expectations and therapist factors are recognised as the common factors for all treatment models.

Client factors are two-fold: client traits and supportive factors in their environment. Client characteristics include how clients approach life, whether they have the ability to reflect and take action. Supportive factors surrounding the client are unique and diverse, such as a new job, the help from an aunt, a special encounter or a new school where things are much better.

A *good working relationship* or *alliance* appears to be an essential context for change to happen. A therapeutic alliance consists of three elements: a solid connection, consensus about the approach and goals of treatment and sufficient safety. A good alliance is instrumental to successful therapy.

Positive therapy outcomes strengthen the alliance in return. How the client perceives the alliance is of more importance than the therapist's perception and has a stronger correlation with change.

Expectations or hope for change is also correlated with change. Hoping for unrealistic change however could perpetuate the problems. Some clients seek help with insoluble problems or have unrealistic expectations towards a partner or a child. In those situations working with reasonable hope could be a better approach (Weingarten, 2010). Meeting with a therapist can effect change in itself but it remains unclear why. Perhaps because prior to seeking help the client felt so demoralised that taking action has a positive effect. Perhaps there is a placebo effect, similar to the proven effects of placebo medication (Duncan, 2012; Duncan et al., 2010).

Therapist factors. Therapists are all different and some achieve better results than others. Research shows that therapists are more effective when they focus on the clients and results, regularly practise deliberately what they need to improve, try things out and reflect on these experiences (Duncan, 2012). Better results are achieved when the practitioner has the ability to establish a good working alliance with clients of all walks of life. Clients who work with effective therapists feel understood, trust the professional and believe that they can help. They find the explanations offered by the practitioner for their problems plausible and fitting their persona and context including their socio-cultural values and beliefs. The effective therapist radiates hope and optimism and they convey a sense of confidence and belief in their treatment approach. The likelihood of change increases when the professional is interested in feedback and actively seeks feedback, with questionnaires for example (Lambert, 2010; Verdru & Stickens, 2009; Wampold, 2001). Clients' satisfaction appears to be a better predictor of successful therapy than the therapist's satisfaction.

What works in systemic therapy

What works in systemic therapy ought to be discussed under the heading of specific factors. However systemic therapy represents several perspectives, each with a different focus and diverse models in the field of relationship therapy and family therapy. Several authors therefore suggest focussing on the common factors of different approaches within systemic therapy rather than on their differences (Gurman & Burton, 2014; Karam et al., 2015; Sprenkle & Blow, 2006). This is based on the idea that practitioners need to adopt an integrated and personalised systemic approach with attention for common factors.

Another common factor additional to the alliance is situating problems within a relational and contextual perspective. This implies looking through 'the systemic lens', disrupting dysfunctional patterns, encouraging new connecting patterns and expanding or changing the treatment system or setting when needed, with attention for who is not physically present and for the wider network (Karam et al., 2015).

The importance of creating a therapeutic alliance with multiple persons has been a recurring theme in this book. We also described how in individual conversations or in sessions with partners, parents or family members problems are relationally and contextually framed so they may be perceived differently. In conversations with partners or families the therapist has an opportunity to not only experience the existing relationships but to participate and intervene as well (Gurman & Burton, 2014). In other chapters we highlighted how the systemic practitioner can attend to people who are absent and can invite them if necessary, and how to include loved ones, significant others or professionals in the therapy. Changes in setting contribute to change as well; often the focus shifts and other topics come to the fore (Van Daele, 2014).

The therapist

A therapist who works with multiple people in the sessions is usually more pro-active than in individual conversations. This can be quite a transition and uncomfortable for practitioners who are mainly trained in individual therapy. The relationship between the therapist and the clients is different too. The most important relationship is not the exclusive and protective relationship between therapist and client, but the mutual relationships between family members, partners or other people involved. Irrespective of the therapeutic setting the practitioner needs to be able to attune and have empathy for the various orderings of the clients. This requires taking the time and slowing down the conversation to allow for the exploration of each person's ideas about the problems and what solutions have been considered. The therapist looks for a collective starting point and helps in the process of considering who ought to be present in the session and which setting offers opportunities for change. The practitioner needs to be able to lead, interrupt clients occasionally, make alternative suggestions and introduce exercises. The therapist's validation, feedback, interpretations, suggestions, opinions and tasks are considered meaningful and contribute to a positive working alliance. It makes everyone feel that the professional is making an effort to think along with them and to help them (Loots et al., 2014; Miller et al., 2010). When talking with multiple people in one setting it is crucial that the therapist can manage emotional intensity. They need to be able to respond to conflicts that arise on the spot and to tensions and strong emotions from one or more family members. They need to be capable of calming clients and containing harmful interaction sequences.

This requires the therapist to have developed a systems framework and approach that matches their personality and they feel comfortable with. Their approach needs to have the flexibility to connect with a variety of people who live in different family constellations, have different backgrounds and differ in terms of gender, socio-economic and cultural backgrounds. And last but not least the systemic practitioner has to be mindful of the difference between what they believe 'is the matter', what is 'helpful to the client' and 'what the client believes is happening' (Midori Hanna & Brown, 2018; Savenije et al., 2014). When hypotheses appear unworkable or don't fit the client, the therapist has to be able to abandon these. This touches on the pragmatics of systemic help or in other words noticing what works. They adopt an attitude of 'discovery' together with the client and guided by their feedback.

Purposeful

Partners family members and significant others may have differing opinions and views of the problems and what needs to change. Even when they agree that they're dealing with a relationship, parenting or personal problem, their hopes for change can differ significantly. Parents may agree that their son is having problems, but the mother believes this is due to her husband not supporting her in the parenting while the father believes that the problems have occurred because his wife is too tolerant and inconsistent. A mother believes her son is having problems, but for the father it is not a big deal. He thinks that his wife always sees problems because of her background. The mother doesn't feel heard by her husband and wants this to change. Their son is of the opinion that his parents urgently need therapy to work on their relationship. The people in a family's network can support or reject particular perspectives. The neighbour whom the family is close to is on father's side, the son's friends are convinced that his view is the right one, while the mother's concerns are supported by the school.

Problem definitions and hopes for change are polyphonic. There are always varied levels of consensus about the goals for change. When clients with their own orderings of the problems and solutions access professional help, the polyphony is expanded with the therapist's voice and professional framework. Systemic help consists of continuously attuning different perspectives and meanings. Having a starting point everyone agrees enough with can be helpful. This could be a shared view of the problems, the hopes for change, what therapy might look like or what needs to be addressed and with whom. This can but doesn't always include the formulation of a specific goal. Regardless professional help is always goal-directed. This does not necessarily result in achieving those goals despite what is happening inside and outside the therapy. Change can arrive unexpectedly and unforeseen and cannot be predicted beforehand. That change cannot be imposed externally is an important systemic principle. Goal-directed help is a process and implies a continuous attuning between all involved about the direction, the topics and the effectiveness of the help and how to do the work together.

Different for everybody

Change can happen in various areas and is not necessarily the same for partners, family members or involved others. Something could change in meaning or at the level of interactions. Those two aspects are intertwined and influence each other. Change doesn't happen simultaneously for all family members. One partner can experience a change, but the other doesn't, or they experience a change in different areas. For example parents notice that things are better with the children and they're working better together as parents, but their partner conflicts remain. A young person may feel better at school but doesn't see any change at home, while the parents have the impression that a lot has changed at home. Change can be partial or uneven or its effect is less positive than expected. The therapist needs to remain alert about how change affects everyone and the mutual relationships, because change can have different effects and these differences have an effect as well.

When to finish?

The ending of therapy can depend on the organisational context. Perhaps only a limited number of sessions are available and the therapy needs to stop after five to ten sessions. In other cases closing the therapy is related to the changes made. The agreed goals or other goals have been achieved. Even when goals have been partially achieved, clients may feel confident they can manage together again and therefore close the therapy. Feedback questionnaires can inform when to end therapy, for instance when the client has been indicating more frequently that things are better. Miller (Miller et al., 2010) found that therapy outcomes can deteriorate when therapy takes too long. Behaviour too can indicate that the end of therapy is near: the client attends less frequently, bigger gaps between sessions don't appear to be problematic or in sessions the client just gives a run-down of how things are. Dilemmas associated with when and how to finish therapy are integral to the therapeutic process but receive little attention in practice and in the literature. Carr (2012) lists four processes as part of ending (successful) therapy: 1) decrease the frequency of the conversations; 2) discuss the changes: what has changed, what contributed, how robust are the changes?; 3) discuss fears around relapse and the client's plans if this were to happen; 4) frame the ending of therapy as a phase in the relationship rather than the end. The latter is important to avoid clients feeling abandoned when therapy stops. Carr makes a few suggestions here: make a follow-up appointment, give clients a 'voucher' for one or more sessions if needed, or agree to phone calls. The final session usually takes on a ritual character. Children are given a certificate (White & Epston, 1990) or clients and therapist decide on a shared ritual (Midori Hanna & Brown, 2018; Savenije & van Lawick, 2014). In the latter case clients and therapist often revisit the therapeutic trajectory:

what went well, what didn't go so well. Sometimes presents are exchanged. Ending therapy may be harder when clients don't return because they were dissatisfied. Some clients are eager to continue even when the therapeutic goals have been achieved. Therapy is discontinued at times because of lack of change. However painful as part of their continuous learning process the therapist has to reflect on why this happened, with or without the clients.

In conclusion

People expect that a professional can assist them in achieving desired changes. Although information is available about which factors contribute to change, this does not answer the question what effects change. Change is a vague and complex process. This is due to a multitude of influences at play and the complexity of the question. Common factors have been identified in research with substantive samples but cannot predict for individual situations. Does this mean that the factors and considerations described in this chapter are insignificant? Absolutely not, but they do not explain change. Change cannot be planned; change remains a mystery. Perhaps the systemic therapist can accept such a humble attitude towards change yet remain hopeful as conveying hope is one of the factors that contribute to change.

Exercise

What have been significant changes in your life? Which contexts and persons have contributed or supported these change processes?

Which contexts influence you, your relationships and your life? Presently do you have a need for change? In which contexts? Who and which relationships could contribute to change?

References

Ackerman, N. W. (1966). *Treating the troubled family*. Basic Books.

Alan, J. (2004). Mother blaming: A covert practice in therapeutic intervention. *Australian Social Work*, *57*(1), 57–70.

Alblas, N. (2005). Settingkwesties: Gebruik van settingwisselingen als therapeutisch instrument. In E. Reijmers, L. Cottyn, & M. Faes (Eds.), *Spelen met werkelijkheden: Systeemtheoretische psychotherapie met kinderen en jongeren* (pp. 120–136). Bohn, Stafleu & van Loghum.

Alink, L., van IJzendoorn, R., Bakermans-Kranenburg, M. J., Pannebakker, F., Vogels, T., & Euser, S. (2012). *Kindermishandeling in Nederland Anno 2010: De Tweede Nationale Prevalentiestudie mishandeling van kinderen en jeugdigen* (2nd ed.). Casimir.

Alon, N., & Omer, H. (2006). *The psychology of demonisation: Promoting acceptance and reducing conflict*. Routledge.

Anderson, H. (1997). *Conversation, language and possibilities: A postmodern approach to therapy*. Basic Books.

Anderson, H., & Goolishan, H. A. (1988). Human systems as linguistic systems. *Family Process*, *27*, 371–393.

Andersson, M. (2016). When you say: 'it's not sickness, it's love', there will be a powerful change of context. In I. McCarthy & G. Simon (Eds.), *Systemic therapy as transformative practice* (pp. 419–432). Everything is Connected Press.

Andolfi, M. (2016a). *Multi-generational family therapy: Tools and resources for the therapist*. Routledge.

Andolfi, M. (2016b). How to give voice to children in family therapy. In M. Borsa & P. Stratton (Eds.), *Origin and originality in family therapy and systemic practice* (pp. 143–168). Springer.

Asen, E., & Scholz, M. (2010). *Multi-family therapy: Concepts and techniques*. Routledge.

Asen, E., Tomson, D., Young, V., & Tomson, P. (2004). *Ten minutes for the family: Systemic interventions in primary care*. Routledge.

Baars, J., & van Meekeren, E. (Eds.). (2013). *Een psychische stoornis heb je niet alleen: Praten met families en naastbetrokkenen*. Boom.

Baert, D. (1990). 'Geen wonder met zo'n ouders': Over sociale perspectieven en opvoeding. *Systeemtheoretisch Bulletin*, *8*, 215–235.

Bak, M., Domen, P., & van Os, J. (2017). Psychiatrie ontward. In M. Bak, P. Domen, & J. van Os (Eds.), *Innovatief leerboek persoonlijke psychiatrie: Terug naar de essentie* (pp. 11–18). Bohn, Stafleu & van Loghum.

Barnett, O., Miller-Perrin, C. L., & Perrin, R. D. (2005). *Family violence across the lifespan: An introduction* (2nd ed.). Sage Publications.

Bartelink, C. (2018). *Dilemmas in child protection: Methods and decision-maker factors influencing decision-making in child maltreatment cases.* Proefschrift Rijksuniversiteit Groningen.

Bateson, G. (1972). *Steps to an ecology of mind.* Chandler.

Bateson, G. (1979). *Mind and nature: A necessary unity.* Fontana.

Baucom, D. H., Belus, J. M., Adelman, C. B., Fischer, M. S., & Paprocki, Ch. (2014). Couple-based interventions for psychopathology: A renewed direction for the field. *Family Process 53*(3), 445–461.

Beach, S. R. H., & Whisman, M. A. (2012). Affective disorders. *Journal of Marital & Family Therapy*, *38*(1), 201–219.

Beckers, W. (2017). Netwerkversterking als antigif voor de strijd bij hoog conflicten na scheiding. *Systeemtheoretisch Bulletin, 34*, 277–295.

Berg-Nielsen, T. S., Vikan, A., & Dahl, A. A. (2002). Parenting related to child and parental psychopathology: A descriptive review of the literature. *Clinical Child Psychology and Psychiatry*, *7*(4), 529–552.

Bertrando, P. (2007). *The dialogical therapist: Dialogue in systemic practice.* Karnac.

Boeckhorst, F. (2003). *Duivelse spiralen: Werkboek voor meervoudig-systemisch denken in de sociale psychiatrie.* CGNet Warnsveld.

Boeckhorst, F. (2014). Behandelcontext. In A. Savenije, M. J. van Lawick, & E. T. M. Reijmers (Eds.), *Handboek systeemtherapie* (2nd ed., pp. 163–177). de Tijdstroom.

Bolt, A. (2017). *Het gezin centraal: Handboek voor ambulant hulpverleners.* SWP.

Bolt, A., & van der Zijden, Q. (2015). *1 gezin 1 plan. Handboek voor de praktijk.* SWP.

Bom, H., & Wiebenga, E. (2017). Verbindend gezag: Naar een nieuwe vorm van autoriteit gebaseerd op principes van geweldloos verzet. *Tijdschrift Voor Psychotherapie*, *43*(4), 1–18.

Bongaerts, B. (2014). In goede en kwade dagen. Over partnerrelatietherapie en psychopathologie. *Systeemtheoretisch Bulletin, 32* (1), 39–54.

Bongaerts, B. (2016). Over grote en kleine herstelverhalen: Zoeken naar mogelijkheden met aandacht voor beperkingen. *Systeemtheoretisch Bulletin, 34*, 11–34.

Bongaerts, B. (2017). Waar is de liefde in therapie? *Systeemtheoretisch Bulletin, 35*, 25–42.

Boscolo, L. & Bertrando, P. (1996). *Systemic therapy with individuals.* Karnac.

Bredewold, F. & Tonkens, E. (2021). Understanding successes and failures of family group conferencing: An in-depth multiple case study. *The British Journal of Social Work*, *51*(6), 2173–2190.

Breunlin, D. C., & Jacobsen, E. (2014). Putting the 'family' back into family therapy. *Family Process*, *53*(3), 462–475.

Brinkgreve, C. (2004). *Vroeg mondig, laat volwassen* (6th ed.). Augustus.

Brinkgreve, C. (2012). *Het verlangen naar gezag: Over vrijheid, gelijkheid en het verlies aan houvast.* Atlas Contact.

Brok, L. J. M. (1990). De verwijzer: Collega, cliënt of blok-aan-het-been. *Systeemtherapie*, *2*, 109–125.

Burck, C., & Daniel, G. (1995). *Gender and family therapy.* Routledge.

Burnham, J. (2012). Developments in social GGRRAAACCEEESSS: Visible-invisible and voiced-unvoiced. In I.-B. Krause (Ed.), *Culture and reflexivity in systemic psychotherapy: Mutual perspectives* (pp. 139–163). Karnac.

Buurma, D. (1999). *Family play genogram*. Play Therapy Press.

Byng-Hall, J. (1995). *Rewriting family scripts: Improvisations and systems change*. Guilford Press.

Carr, A. (2012). *Family therapy: Concepts, process and practice* (3rd ed.). Wiley & Sons.

Carter, B., & McGoldrick, M. (2004). *The expanded family life cycle: Individual, family and social perspectives*. Allyn and Bacon.

Castelijns, P. (2016). Welke plek krijgen ervaringsdeskundigen in een team? *Systeemtheoretisch Bulletin, 34*, 34–48.

Cecchin, G. (1987). Hypothesizing, circularity and neutrality revisited: An invitation to curiosity. *Family Process, 26*(4), 405–413.

Cecchin, G., Lane, G., & Ray, W.A. (1992). *Irreverence: A strategy for therapists' survival*. Karnac Books.

Cecchin, G., Lane, G., & Ray, W.A. (1994). *The cybernetics of prejudices in the practice of psychotherapy*. Karnac Books.

Chasin, R., & Roth, S. (1990). Future perfect, past perfect: A positive approach to opening couple therapy. In R. Chasin, H. Grunebaum, & M. Herzig (Eds.), *One couple, four realities: Multiple perspectives on couple therapy* (pp. 129–145). The Guilford Press.

Choy, J. (Ed.) (2005). *De vraag op het antwoord- systemische interventies voor conflicten in organisaties*. NISTO Publicaties.

Colapinto, J. A. (1995). Dilution of family process in social services: Implications for treatment of neglectful families. *Family Process, 34*(1), 59–74.

Colijn, S. (1995). Het slechte(n) van een ivoren toren: Psychotherapie en cultuurverschillen. *Systeemtherapie, 7*(3), 125–137.

Cooklin, A., Miller, A., & McHugh, B. (1983). An institution for change. *Family Process, 22*(4), 453–468.

Cornelis, J., van Oenen, F. J., & Bernardt, C. (2014). Systemisch werken in een psychiatrische context. In A. Savenije, M. J. van Lawick, & E. T. M. Reijmers (Eds.), *Handboek systeemtherapie* (2de druk, pp. 717–731). de Tijdstroom.

Cottyn, L. (2005). Veerkracht bevorderen bij ouders die ook psychisch ziek zijn. *Systeemtheoretisch Bulletin, 23*, 103–122.

Cottyn, L. (2008). Een dynamische visie op gezin. *Systeemtheoretisch Bulletin, 26*, 191–212.

Cottyn, L. (2009). Conflicten tussen ouders na scheiding. *Systeemtheoretisch Bulletin, 27*, 131–161.

Cottyn, L. (2012, May 31). *Onmogelijk met zulke ouders! Als positief kijken naar ouders in het gedrang komt*. Lezing Rino groep, Congres *Ouders! wat moet je er mee?* Reehorst Ede.

Cottyn, L. (2021). *Complexe scheiding: Uit de maalstroom van conflict. Een systemische gids voor hulpverleners*. Interactie-Academie VZW.

Coyne, J. C. (1985). Toward a theory of frames and reframing: The social nature of frames. *Journal of Marital and Family Therapy, 11*(4), 337–344.

Davolo, A., & Fruggeri, L. (2016). A systemic dialogical perspective for dealing with cultural differences in psychotherapy. In I. McCarthy & G. Simon (Eds.). *Systemic therapy as transformative practice* (pp. 111–125). Everything is Connected Press.

De Cock, M. (2008). Collaboratief werken met gezinnen binnen de gedwongen hulpverlening. *Systeemtheoretisch Bulletin, 26*, 163–190.

de Jong, P., & Berg, I. K. (2002). *Interviewing for solutions*. Brooks/Cole.

De Mol, J. (2011). Waarom broers en zussen zo verschillend zijn... twintig jaar later. *Systeemtheoretisch Bulletin, 29*, 261–330.

De Mol, J., Reijmers, E., Verhofstadt, L., & Kuczynski, L. (2018). Reconstructing a sense of relational agency in family therapy. *Australian & New Zealand Journal of Family Therapy, 39*(1), 54–66.

de Regt, A. (2014). Maatschappelijke ontwikkelingen. In A. Savenije, M. J. van Lawick, & E. T. M. Reijmers (Eds.), *Handboek systeemtherapie* (2de druk, pp. 57–69). de Tijdstroom.

De Shazer, S., Dolan, Y., Korman, H., Trepper, T., McCollum, E., & Kim Berg, I. (2021). *More than miracles. The state of the art of solution-focused brief therapy.* Routledge.

De Sterck, S. (2017). Directief en sturend werken is ook steunend: Hulp bieden aan jonge plegers en hun ouders in tijden van crisis. *Systeemtheoretisch Bulletin, 35*, 191–205.

de Swaan, A. (1981). The politics of agoraphobia: On changes in emotional and relational management. *Theory and Society, 10*(3), 359–385.

de Swaan, A. (1988). *In care of the state. Health care, education and welfare in Europe and America.* Oxford University Press.

de Vogel, V., de Vries Robbe, M., Bouman, Y. H. A, Chakhssi, F., & de Ruiter, C. (2013). Innovatie in risicotaxatie van geweld. *Gedragstherapie, 46*, 107–118.

De Vos, J. (2012). Systeemtherapie en psychiatrische diagnoses... aparte werkelijkheden? Over diagnoses en unieke verhalen. *Systeemtherapie, 24*, 204–219.

De Wachter, D. (2014). *Liefde, een onmogelijk verlangen?* Lannoo.

Decraemer, K., & Cottyn, L. (2017). Een tanker verandert langzaam van koers: Externaliserende conversaties met ouders en hun netwerk bij hoog-conflict na scheiding. In S. Vermeire, & J. Sermijn (Eds.), *Wegen naar her-verbinding. Narratieve, collaboratieve en dialogerende praktijken* (pp. 206–217). Interactie-Academie VZW.

Decraemer, K., & Reijmers, E. (2017). Systeemtherapie. In J. Spaans, J. Rosmalen, Y, van Rood, H. van der Horst, & S. Visser (Eds.), *Behandeling van somatisch onvoldoende verklaarde lichamelijke klachten* (pp. 417–430). LannooCampus.

Dehue, T. (2014). *Betere mensen: Over gezondheid als keuze en koopwaar.* Atlas Contact.

den Otter, J. Verschuur, F., & Schell, P. (2009). Assertive community treatment ook voor jeugd? *Tijdschrift Sociale Psychiatrie, 89*, 15–21.

Denborough, D. (2008). *Collective narrative practice: Responding to individuals, groups, and communities who have experienced trauma.* Dulwich Centre Publications.

Dickerson, V. C., & Zimmerman, G. (1995). A constructionist exercise in anti-pathologizing. *Journal of Systemic Therapies, 14*, 33–45.

Diekmann, M. (2005). Scheiden en verbinden met 'een taal erbij'. *Systeemtherapie, 17*, 68–82.

Duncan, B. L. (2012). *On becoming a better therapist.* American Psychological Association.

Duncan, B. L., Miller, S. D., Wampold, B. E., & Hubble, M. A. (Eds.). (2010). *The heart and soul of change: Delivering what works in therapy.* American Psychological Association.

Dunn, J., & Plomin, R. (1991). Why are siblings different? The significance of differences in sibling experiences within the family. *Family Process, 30*, 271–283.

Ekholdt, M. (2016, January 15). *Interview with Elspeth McAdam. Protecting interview* [Video]. *YouTube.* https://www.youtube.com/watch?v=A6gHd4FyzxA

Emmelkamp-Keizer, M., & Aptroot, E. (2014). Seksualiteit. In A. Savenije, M. J. van Lawick, & E. T. M. Reijmers (Eds.), *Handboek systeemtherapie* (2de druk, pp. 381–391). de Tijdstroom.

Enzlin, P., & Pazmany, E. (2006). Wanneer lust verwordt tot last… over de invloed van chronische aandoeningen op partnerrelaties. In L. Migerode, & J. van Bussel (Eds.), *Als liefde alleen niet volstaat* (pp. 154–172). Lannoo.

Faes, M. (2014). Narratieve partnerrelatietherapie. In A. Savenije, M. J. van Lawick, & E. T. M. Reijmers (Eds.), *Handboek systeemtherapie* (2de druk, pp. 455–467). de Tijdstroom.

Faes, M. (2016a). Geweld in paren: Werken met de veiligheidslandkaart. *Tijdschrift Klinische Psychologie, 46,* 12–17.

Faes, M. (2016b). Lichaam, beweging en doen in partnerrelatietherapie. *Systeemtheoretisch Bulletin, 34,* 139–155.

Falicov, C. (2004). Training to think culturally: A multidimensional comparative framework. *Family Process, 34,* 373–388.

Falicov, C. (2012). Immigrant family processes: A multidimensional framework. In F. Walsh (Ed.) *Normal family processes* (4th ed., pp. 297–323). Guilford Press.

Falicov, C. J. (Ed.). (1988). *Family transition: Continuity & change over the life cycle.* Guilford Press.

Flaskas, C, Mason, B., & Perlesz, A. (Eds.). (2005). *The space between: Experience, context and process in the therapeutic relationship.* Karnac.

Flaskas, C. (2016). Relating therapeutically in family therapy: Pragmatics and intangibles. *Journal of Family Therapy, 38,* 149–167.

Flaskas, C., & Perlesz, A. (Eds.). (1996). *The therapeutic relationship in systemic therapy.* Karnac.

Fondelli, T. (2007). Aan de slag met de diagnose 'autisme'. *Systeemtheoretisch Bulletin, 25,* 113–129.

Fredman, G. (1997). *Death talk: Conversations with children and families.* Karnac.

Fredman, G. (2007). Preparing ourselves for the therapeutic relationship. Revisiting 'hypothesizing revisited'. *Human Systems, 18,* 44–59.

Fredman, G. (2004). *Transforming emotions: Conversations in counselling and psychotherapy.* Whurr Publishers.

Freedman, J., & Combs, G. (2015). Narrative couple therapy. In A. S. Gurman, J. L. Lebow, & D. K. Snyder (Eds.). *Clinical handbook of couple therapy* (5th ed., pp. 229–259). The Guilford Press.

Freeman, J., Epston, D., & Lobovits, D. (1997). *Playful approaches to serious problems.* W. W. Norton & Company.

Friedli, L. (2009). *Mental health, resilience and inequalities: How individuals and communities are affected.* World Health Organisation.

Gergen, K. J. (Ed). (2015). *An invitation to social construction* (3rd ed.). Sage.

Gerlsma, C., Karsen, J., & Sleurink, K. (2012). Gezinsinteracties als risicofactor in een forensisch psychiatrische context. Over de betekenis van expressed emotions. *De Psycholoog, 47(10),* 39–47.

Gil, E. (2015). *Play in family therapy* (2nd ed.). The Guilford Press.

Goffman, E. (1974). *Frame analysis.* Harvard University Press.

Goldner, V. (1985). Feminism and family therapy. *Family Process, 24,* 31–48.

Gottman, J. M., & Silver, N. (2015). *The seven principles for making marriage work.* Crown Publishers.

Govaerts, J. M., & Splingaer, G. (2014). Gezinsontwikkelingsperspectief. In A. Savenije, M. J. van Lawick, & E. T. M. Reijmers (Eds.), *Handboek systeemtherapie* (2de druk, pp. 295–308). de Tijdstroom.

Groen, M., & Lawick, J. van (2009). *Intimate warfare. Regarding the fragility of family relations*. Routledge.

Gualthérie van Weezel, L., & Jong, C. de (2014). Ernstige ziekte. In A. Savenije, M. J. van Lawick, & E. T. M. Reijmers (Eds.), *Handboek systeemtherapie* (2de druk, pp. 705–717). de Tijdstroom.

Gupta, A., & Blumhardt, H. (2016). Giving poverty a voice: Families' experiences of social work practice in a risk-averse child protection system. *Families, Relationships and Societies*, *5*(1), 163–172.

Gurman, A. S. (2015). The theory and practice of couple therapy. In A. S. Gurman, J. L. Lebow, & D. K. Snyder (Eds.), *Clinical handbook of couple therapy* (5th ed., pp. 1–19). The Guilford Press.

Gurman, A. S., & Burton, M. (2014). Individual therapy for couple problems: Perspectives and pitfalls. *Journal of Marital and Family Therapy*, *40*(4), 470–483.

Habekotté, F., & Reijmers, E. (2014). Narratief perspectief. In A. Savenije, M. J. van Lawick, & E. T. M. Reijmers (Eds.), *Handboek systeemtherapie* (2de ed., (pp. 309–325). de Tijdstroom.

Haley, J. (1963). Marriage therapy. *Archives of General Psychiatry*, *8*, 213–234.

Haley, J. (1971). Family therapy: A radical change. In J. Haley (Ed.), *Changing families* (pp. 272–284). Grune & Stratton.

Haley, J. (1976). *Problem solving therapy*. Jossey Bass.

Haley, J. (1979). *Leaving home: Therapy with disturbed young people*. McGraw-Hill.

Hamels, J., & Nichols, T. L. (Eds.). (2007). *Family interventions in domestic violence. A handbook of gender-inclusive theory and treatment*. Springer Publishing Company.

Hare-Mustin, R. T. (1978). A feminist approach to family therapy. *Family Process*, *17*, 181–194.

Hare-Mustin, R. T., & Marecek, J. (1988). The meaning of difference: Gender theory, postmodernism and psychology. *American Psychologist*, *43*, 455–464.

Harris, P. B., McBride, G., Ross, C., & Curtis, L. (2002). A place to heal: Environmental sources of satisfaction among hospital patients. *Journal of Applied Social Psychology*, *32*, 1276–1299.

Hawley, D. R., & de Haan, L. (1996). Toward a definition of family resilience: Integrating life-span and family perspectives. *Family Process*, *35*, 283–299.

Hedges, F. (2005). *An introduction to systemic therapy with individuals: A social constructionist approach*. Palgrave McMillan.

Hillewaere, B. (2006). Werken met de mogelijkheden van cliënten en gezinnen met behulp van kernkwadranten en genogrammen. *Tijdschrift Voor Psychotherapie*, *32*, 161–177.

Hillewaere, B., & LeFevere de Ten Hove, M. (2006). Narratieve en oplossingsgerichte toepassingen bij genogrammen: Samen hoopvolle perspectieven creëren. *Systeemtherapie*, *18*, 69–88.

Hochschild, A. (1989). *The second shift*. Avon.

Hoeymans, N., Melse, J. M., & Schoemaker, C. G. (Eds.). (2010). *Gezondheid en determinanten. Deelrapport van de volksgezondheid toekomst verkenning 2010 van gezond naar beter*. RIVM-rapport nr. 270061006. RIVM.

Hooley, J. M. (2007). Expressed emotion and relapse of psychopathology. *Annual Review of Clinical Psychology*, *3*, 329–352.

Huijser, E. (1984). Emancipatie van de vrouw en gezinstherapie. In F. Boeckhorst, Th. Compernolle, J. Hendrickx, & A. van der Pas (Eds.), *Handboek gezinstherapie*. Van Loghum Slaterus.

Hurst, M. (2011). Professional judgement in the assessment of risk: Is there a role for systemic practice? *Journal of Family Therapy*, *33*, 168–180.

Hydén, M., Gadd, D., & Wade, A. (Eds.). (2016). *Introduction to response based approaches to the study of interpersonal violence*. Palgrave Macmillan.

Ilfeld, F. W. (1977). Current social stressors and symptoms of depression. *American Journal of Psychiatry*, *134*, 161–166.

Imber-Black, E. (1988). *Families and larger systems. A family therapists guide through the labyrinth*. Guilford Press.

Jackson, D. D. (1965). Family rules: Marital quid pro quo. *Archives of General Psychiatry*, *12*, 589–594.

Jakob, P. (2006). Bringing non-violent resistance to Britain. *Context*, *84*, 36–38.

Jakob, P. (2018). Multi-stressed families, child violence and the larger system: An adaptation of the nonviolent model. *Journal of Family Therapy*, *40*, 25–44.

Jensen, P. (2007). On learning from experience. Personal and private experiences as context for psychotherapeutic practice. *Child Clinical Psychology and Psychiatry*, *12*(3), 375–384.

Jessurun, N. (2010). *Transculturele vaardigheden voor therapeuten: Een systeemtheoretisch behandelmodel*. Coutinho.

Jessurun, N., & Warring R. (2018) *Verschillen omarmen. Transcultureel systemisch werken*. Coutinho.

Johnson, S. (2004). *The practice of emotionally focused therapy. Creating connection*. Routledge.

Jones, E., & Asen, E. (2000). *Systemic couple therapy and depression*. Karnac.

Karam, E. A., Blow, A. L., Sprenkle, D. H. & Davis, S. D. (2015). Strengthening the systemic ties that bind: Integrating common factors into marriage and family therapy curricula. *Journal of Marital and Family Therapy*, *41*(2), 136–149.

Kaufmann, J. C (2009). *Gripes, the little quarrels of couples*. Polity Press.

Kiecolt-Glaser, J. K., & Newton, T. L. (2001). Marriage and health: His and hers. *Psychological Bulletin*, *127*, 472–503.

Klijn, W. J. L. (1991). *Systeemtaxatie in beweging: Behandelcontext en het gebruik van psychomotorische en creatieve technieken bij gezinsdiagnostiek en gezinsbehandeling in de geestelijke gezondheidszorg*. Swets en Zeitlinger.

Klijn, W. J. L. (2006). Gaat geel in blauw veranderen? *Systeemtherapie*, *18*, 16–33.

Laing, R., Phillipson, H., & Lee, A. (1966). *Interpersonal perception*. Perennial Library.

Lambert, M. J. (2010). "Yes, it is time for clinicians to routinely monitor treatment outcome". In B. L. Duncan, S. D. Miller, B. E. Wampold, & M. A. Hubble (Eds.), *The heart and soul of change: Delivering what works in therapy* (pp. 239–266). American Psychological Association.

Lange, A. (2014). Systeemtherapie en onderzoek, de stand van zaken. In A. Savenije, M. J. van Lawick, & E. T. M. Reijmers (Eds.), *Handboek systeemtherapie* (2de druk, pp. 110–128). de Tijdstroom.

Laqueur, H. P., Laburt, H. A., & Morong, E. (1964). Multiple family therapy. *Current Psychiatric Psychotherapies*, *4*, 150–154.

Larner, G. (2015). Ethical family therapy: Speaking the language of the other. *Australian and New Zealand Journal of Family Therapy*, 36, 434–449.

Lebow, J. (1997). The integrative revolution in couple and family therapy. *Family Process*, *36*, 1–18.

Lemmens, G., Eisler, I., Migerode, L., Heireman, M., & Demyttenaere, K. (2007). Family discussion group therapy for major depression: A brief systemic multi-family group intervention for hospitalized patients and their family members. *Journal of Family Therapy*, *29*(1), 49–68.

Lewis, K. G. (1989). The use of color-coded genograms in family therapy. *Journal of Marital and Family Therapy*, *15*, 169–176.

Loots, G., Escudero, V., Sermijn, J., Jiraskova, K., & Lenaerts, P. (2014). Procesonderzoek. In A. Savenije, M. J. van Lawick, & E. T. M. Reijmers (Eds.), *Handboek systeemtherapie* (2de druk, pp. 129–139). de Tijdstroom.

Luyens, M., & van Steenwegen, A. (2014). De derde in de relatie. In A. Savenije, M. J. van Lawick, & E. T. M. Reijmers (Eds.), *Handboek systeemtherapie* (2de druk, pp. 391–401). de Tijdstroom.

Madsen, W. C. (2007). *Collaborative therapy with multi-stressed families* (2nd ed.). Guilford Press.

Madsen, W. C., & Gillespie, K. (2014). *Collaborative helping. A strengths framework for home-based services*. Wiley & Sons.

Mason, B. (2019). Re-visiting safe uncertainty: Six perspectives for clinical practice and the assessment of risk. *Journal of Family Therapy*, *41*(3), 343–356.

Matt, J., & Weeda, F. (2008, December 10). *Eerst de kinderen weghalen, en dan de ouders horen*. NRC.

McAdam, E. (2002). Boven verdenking en buiten gevaar. Interview met gezinnen met vermoeden van seksueel misbruik. *Tijdschrift Voor Familietherapie*, *8*, 195–215.

McCarthy, I. C. (1995). Women, poverty and systemic family therapy. In I. C. McCarthy (Ed.), *Irish family studies: Selected papers* (pp. 181–199). Family Studies Centre.

McGoldrick, M. & Hardy, K. (Eds.). (2008). *Revisioning family therapy. Race, culture and gender in clinical practice* (2nd ed.). Guilford Press.

McGoldrick, M., & Gerson, R. (1985). *Genograms in family assessment*. W. W. Norton & Company.

McGoldrick, M., Gerson, R., & Shellenberger, S. (1999). *Genograms: Assessment and intervention* (2nd ed.). W. W. Norton & Company.

Meerdinkveldboom, J., Kerkhof, A., & Rood, I. (2019). *Handboek suïcidaal gedrag bij jongeren* (3th ed). Boom.

Midori Hanna, S., & Brown J. H. (2018). *The practice of family therapy. Key elements across models* (5th ed.). Taylor & Francis Ltd.

Miller, S. D., Hubble, M. A., Duncan, B. L., & Wampold, B. E. (2010). Delivering what works. In B. I. Duncan, S. D. Miller, B. E. Wampold, & M. A. Hubble (Eds.), *The heart and soul of change. Delivering what works in therapy* (2nd ed., pp. 421–429). American Psychological Association.

Minuchin, S. (1974). *Families and family therapy: A structural approach*. Harvard University Press.

Minuchin, S. (1998). Where is the family in narrative family therapy? *Journal of Marital and Family Therapy*, *24*(4), 397–403.

Minuchin, S., & Fishman, H. C. (1981). *Family therapy techniques*. Harvard University Press.

Minuchin, S., Montalvo, B., Guerney, B. G., Rosman, B. L., & Schumer, F. (1967). *Families of the slums: An exploration of their structure and treatment*. Basic Books.

Monk, G., Winslade, J., Crocket, K., & Epston, D. (Eds.). (1997). *Narrative therapy in practice. The archaeology of Hope*. Jossey-Bass Publishers.

Mous, J. (2014). De stoelendans. *Systeemtheoretisch Bulletin, 32*, 97–114.

Mumford, D. J., & Weeks, G. (2003). The money genogram. *Journal of Family Psychotherapy, 14*(3), 33–44.

Nagtegaal, W., & van Stratum, N. (2017). Drukte in de therapiekamer: Een ontmoeting van meerdere werelden. *Systeemtherapie, 29*, 87–100.

Neeleman, A., & Bout, J. (2014). Parengroepstherapie. In: A. Savenije, M. J. van Lawick, & E. T. M. Reijmers (Eds.), *Handboek systeemtherapie* (2de druk, pp. 481–495). de Tijdstroom.

Neyens, K. (2017). Van weerstand naar werkrelatie. Contact maken met forensische jongeren. *Systeemtheoretisch Bulletin, 2*, 155–173.

Nichols, M., & Schwartz, R. (2006). *Family therapy: Concepts and methods*. Pearson Education.

Nieuwpoort, J. (2006). De synergie van co-therapie, een therapievorm waarbij waarlijk samenwerken van belang is. *Systeemtherapie, 18*, 5–16.

Nieweg, M. R., & de Rooy, K. M. (1992). Parallelprocessen tussen team- en gezinssysteem in (semi) residentiële kinder- en jeugdpsychiatrie. *Systeemtherapie, 4*, 3–14.

Nuyts, K. (2012). Eigen kracht conferenties. *Welwijs, 23(2)*, 10–13.

Olthof, J. (2018). *Handbook narrative psychotherapy for children, adults and families*. Routledge/Karnac.

Omer, H. (2011). *The new authority: Family, school and community*. Cambridge University Press.

Omer, H. (2021). *Non-violent resistance: A new approach to violent and self-destructive children*. Cambridge University Press.

Omer, H., & Lebowitz, E.R. (2016). Nonviolent resistance: Helping caregivers reduce problematic behaviors in children and adolescents. *Journal of Marital and Family Therapy, 42*(4), 688–670.

Omer, H., Steinmetz, S., Carthy, T., & Schlippe, A. von (2013). The anchoring function: Parental authority and the parent-child bond. *Family Process, 52*, 193–206.

Omer, H., & Wiebenga, E. (2015). *Geweldloos verzet in gezinnen. Een nieuwe benadering van gewelddadig en zelfdestructief gedrag van kinderen en adolescenten* (2de ed.). Bohn, Stafleu & van Loghem.

Östman, M. (2008). Interviews with children of persons with a severe mental illness: Investigating their everyday situation. *Nordic Journal of Psychiatry, 62*, 354–359.

Papp, P., Scheinkman, M., & Malpas, J. (2013). Breaking the mold: Sculpting impasses in couples' therapy, *Family Process, 52*, 33–45.

Parkinson, L. (2019). Wider perspectives in family mediation: An ecosystemic approach. *Australian and New Zealand Journal of Family Therapy, 40*(1), 62–73.

Pearce, W. B., & Cronen, V. E. (1980). *Communication, action and meaning: The creation of social realities*. Praeger.

Penn, P. (1985). Feed forward: Future questions, future maps. *Family Process, 24*, 299–310.

Perel, E. (2006). *Mating in captivity: Reconciling the erotic and the domestic.* Harper Collins.

Perel, E. (2017). *The state of affairs: Rethinking infidelity.* Harper Collins.

Peters, R. F. (1999). Redefining Western families. *Marriage and Family Review, 28*(3), 55–66.

Reerink, K. (2010). *De invloed van de inrichting van de spreekkamer van een psycholoog op de cliënt. Een onderzoek naar de effecten van omgeving op de zelfonthulling van de cliënt* [Masterthesis, Universiteit Twente, Faculteit Gedragswetenschappen Consument en Gedrag].

Reijmers, E. (1999). Systeemtheorie en psychopathologie. *Systeemtherapie, 11*, 214–232.

Reijmers, E. (2014a). Individuele systemische therapie. In A. Savenije, M. J. van Lawick, & E. T. M. Reijmers (Eds.), *Handboek systeemtherapie* (2de druk, pp. 595–605). de Tijdstroom.

Reijmers, E. (2014b). Ontwikkelingen in theorie en praktijk. In A. Savenije, M. J. van Lawick, & E. T. M. Reijmers (Eds.), *Handboek systeemtherapie* (2de druk, pp. 26–43). de Tijdstroom.

Reijmers, E. (2014c). Systemische diagnostiek. In A. Savenije, J. M. van Lawick, & E.T.M. Reijmers (Eds.), *Handboek systeemtherapie* (2de druk, pp. 187–199). de Tijdstroom.

Reijmers. E. (2007). Samenspel. Introductie op het thema. *Systeemtheoretisch Bulletin, 25*, 101–112.

Reijmers, E., & Cottyn, L. (2014). Communicatieperspectief. In A. Savenije, M. J. van Lawick, & E. T. M Reijmers (Eds.), *Handboek systeemtherapie* (2de druk, pp. 259–272). de Tijdstroom.

Reijmers, E., Cottyn, L., & Faes, M. (eds) (2005). Spelen met werkelijkheden: Systeemtheoretische psychotherapie met kinderen en jongeren. Bohn Stafleu van Loghum.

Rivett, M., & Street, E. (2009). *Family therapy: 100 key points and techniques.* Routledge.

Rober, P. (2002). Some hypotheses about hesitations and their nonverbal expression in family therapy practice. *Journal of Family Therapy, 24*, 187–204.

Rober, P. (2005). The therapist's self in dialogical family therapy: Some ideas about not-knowing and the therapist's inner conversation. *Family Process, 44*, 477–495.

Rober, P. (2009). Relational drawings in couple therapy. *Family Process 48*(1),117–133.

Rober, P. (2014). Het kind betrekken in de gezinstherapeutische sessie. In A. Savenije, M. J. van Lawick, & E. T. M. Reijmers (Eds.), *Handboek systeemtherapie* (2de druk, pp. 523–535). de Tijdstroom.

Rober, P. (2017). *In therapy together. Family therapy as a dialogue.* Palgrave Macmillan.

Rowe, C. L. (2012). Family therapy for drug abuse. Review and updates 2003-2010. *Journal of Marital & Family Therapy, 38*, 59–81.

Rynes, K. N., Rohrbaugh, M. J., Lebensohn- Chialvo, F., & Shoham, V. (2014). Parallel demand-withdraw processes in family therapy for adolescent drug abuse. *Psychol Addict Behav, 28*(2), 420–430.

Satir, V. (1972). *Peoplemaking.* Souvenir press.

Satir, V. (1983). *Conjoint family therapy.* Science and Behavior Books.

Satir, V. (1988). *The new peoplemaking.* Science and Behavior Books.

Savenije, A., van Lawick, M. J. & Reijmers, E. T. M. (Eds.). (2014). *Handboek systeemtherapie* (2de druk). de Tijdstroom.

Savenije, A. (2014a). Cultuur. In A. Savenije, M. J. van Lawick, & E. T. M. Reijmers (Eds.), *Handboek systeemtherapie* (2de druk, pp. 69–85). de Tijdstroom.

Savenije, A. (2014b). Families met pubers en adolescenten. In A. Savenije, M. J. van Lawick, & E. T. M. Reijmers (Eds.), *Handboek systeemtherapie* (2de druk, pp. 535–549). de Tijdstroom.

Savenije, A., & van Lawick, J. (2014). Methoden en technieken. In A. Savenije, M. J. van Lawick, & E. T. M. Reijmers (Eds.), *Handboek systeemtherapie* (2de druk, pp. 223–259). de Tijdstroom.

Scheinkman, M. & DeKoven Fishbane, M. (2004). The vulnerability cycle: Working with impasses in couple therapy. *Family Process, 43*(3), 279–299.

Scheller-Dikkers, S. M. (1998). Waar woorden tekortschieten. *Systeemtherapie, 10*, 157–173.

Schuurman, M., & Mulder, C. (2011). *Eigen kracht-conferenties bij gezinnen in de regio Amsterdam: Wat levert het op? Resultaten van onderzoek.* Kalliope Consult/Antropol.

Seikkula, J., & Olson, M. E. (2003). The open dialogue approach to acute psychosis: Its poetics and micropolitics. *Family Process, 42*, 403–418.

Selvini Palazolli, M. (1985). The problem of the sibling as the referring person. *Journal of Marital and Family Therapy, 11*(1), 21–34.

Selvini Palazolli, M., Boscolo, L., Cecchin, G., & Prata, G. (1980b). Why a long interval between sessions? The therapeutic control of the family-therapist supersystem. In M. Z. I. Andolfi (Ed.), *Dimensions of family therapy* (pp. 161–169). Guilford Press.

Selvini Palazolli, M., Boscolo, L., Cecchin, G., & Prata, G. (1980a). Hypothesizing-circularity-neutrality: Three guidelines for the conductor of the session. *Family Process, 19*(1), 3–12.

Sheinberg, M., & Brewster, M. K. (2014). Thinking and working relationally: Interviewing and constructing hypotheses to create compassionate understanding. *Family Process, 53*, 618–639.

Sheinberg, M., & True, F. (2008). Treating family relational trauma: A recursive process using a decision dialogue. *Family Process, 47*, 173–195.

Shotter, J. (2011). *Getting it: Withness thinking and the dialogical… in practice.* Hampton Press.

Sillevis, C. (2011). Signs of safety: Een reis op weg naar veiligheid in het gezin. *Pedagogiek in Praktijk, 63*, 15–19.

Simons, M. (2017). Vrouwenopvang: Indirect en gezinsgericht werken aan veiligheid. *Systeemtheoretisch Bulletin, 35*, 231–244.

Smeltzer, M. (2007). Onopgemerkt leed. Over partnerrelatietherapie wanneer sprake is van autisme. *Systeemtheoretisch Bulletin, 25*, 131–144.

Splingaer, G. (2014). Het ontwikkelingshuis. Een kijk op de co-evolutie van kinderen en gezinnen. *Systeemtheoretisch Bulletin, 32*, 13–37.

Sprenkle, D. H. & Blow, A. (2006). Common factors and our sacred models. *Journal of Marital and Family Therapy, 30*(2), 113–129.

Stith, S. M., McCollum, E. E., Amanor-Boadu, Y. & Smith, D. (2012). Systemic treatments for domestic violence. *Journal of Marital and Family Therapy, 38*(1), 220–24.

Suddaby, K., & Landau, J. (1998). Positive and negative timelines: A technique for restorying. *Family Process*, *37*, 287–298.

Tilmans-Ostyn, E. (1990). Het creëren van therapeutische ruimte bij de analyse van de hulpvraag. *Kinder- en Jeugdpsychotherapie*, *16*, 203–221.

Timimi, S. (2014). No more psychiatric labels: Why formal psychiatric diagnostic systems should be abolished. *International Journal of Clinical and Health Psychology*, *14*, 208–215.

Tjin A Djie, K., & Zwaan, I. (2007). *Beschermjassen: Transculturele hulp aan families*. van Gorcum.

Tomm, K. (1987a). Interventive interviewing: Part I. Strategizing as a fourth guideline for the therapist. *Family Process*, *26*, 3–13.

Tomm, K. (1987b). Interventive interviewing: Part II. Reflexive questioning as a means to enable self-healing. *Family Process*, *26*, 167–184.

Tomm, K. (1988). Interventive interviewing: Part III. Intending to ask lineal, circular, strategic, or reflexive questions? *Family Process*, *27*, 1–15.

Trip, H. (1995). Kliniekcontext en gezinscontext in strijd. *Systeemtherapie*, *7*, 64–76.

Turnell, A., & Essex, S. (1999). *Signs of safety: A solution and safety oriented approach to child protection casework*. Norton.

Turnell, A., & Essex, S. (2006). *Working 'denied' child abuse: The resolutions approach*. Open University Press.

Van Daele, M. (2014). Settingwisseling. In A. Savenije, M. J. van Lawick, & E. T. M. Reijmers (Eds.), *Handboek systeemtherapie* (2de druk, pp. 605–615). de Tijdstroom.

van Dam, L., Heijmans, L., & Stams, G.J. (2021). Youth initiated mentoring in social work: Sustainable solution for youth with complex needs? *Child Adolescent Social Work Journal*, *38*, 149–155.

van Dam, L., & Verhulst, S. (2016). *De JIM-aanpak: Het alternatief voor uithuisplaatsing van jongeren*. Boom.

Van den Berge, L. (2001). *Materie en identiteit*. Interactie-Academie vzw.

Van den Berge, L. (2011). Beelden van ouderondersteuning: Van infantilisering naar een rijke opvatting van zorg. *Systeemtheoretisch Bulletin*, *29*, 243–260.

van der Pas, A. (1994). *Handboek methodische ouderbegeleiding. Deel I ouderbegeleiding als methodiek*. Ad Donker.

van der Pas, A. (2003). *A serious case of neglect: The parental experience of child rearing. Outline for a psychological theory of parenting*. University of Chicago Press.

van der Pas, A. (2014). Ouderschap: Een systemisch multiversum. In A. Savenije, M. J. van Lawick, & E. T. M. Reijmers (Eds.), *Handboek systeemtherapie* (2de druk, pp. 495–510). de Tijdstroom.

van der Veen, H. C. J., & Bogaerts, S. (2010). *Huiselijk geweld in Nederland: Overkoepelend synthese rapport van het vangst-hervangst slachtoffer en daderonderzoek 2007-2010*. WODC.

van Lawick, J. (2014). Geweld. In A. Savenije, M. J van Lawick, & E. T. M Reijmers (Eds.), *Handboek systeemtherapie* (2de druk, pp. 659–673). de Tijdstroom.

van Lawick, M. J., & Bom, H. (2008). Building bridges: Home visits to multi-stressed families where professional help reached a deadlock. *Journal of Family Therapy*, *30*, 504–516.

van Lawick, J., & Savenije, A. (2014). Basisbegrippen. In A. Savenije, M. J. van Lawick, & E. T. M Reijmers (Eds.), *Handboek systeemtheorie* (2de druk, pp. 203–222). de Tijdstroom.

van Meekeren, E., & Baars, J. (2013). Het eerste contact en basisvaardigheden. In E. van Meekeren, & J. Baars (Eds.), *Een psychische stoornis heb je niet alleen. Praten met families en naastbetrokkenen* (pp. 163–192). Boom.

van Oenen, F. J., Bernardt, C., & van der Post, L. (2007). *Praktijkboek crisisinterventie: De kunst van het interveniëren in moeilijke behandelsituaties in de spoedeisende psychiatrie en psychotherapie*. de Tijdstroom.

van Oenen, F. J., Cornelis, C., & Bernardt, B. (2012). Consensusgericht systemisch interviewen en interveniëren: Een systemisch 'goed genoeg' pakket voor hulpverleners in de psychiatrie. *Systeemtherapie, 24*, 63–81.

van Oenen, F. J., van Deursen, S., & Cornelis, J. (2016). Uw wens is mijn gedachte. Over rolkeuze en verrassing in het afstemmingsproces. *Tijdschrift Voor Psychotherapie, 42*, 336–352.

van Os, J. (2003). Is there a continuum of psychotic experience in the general population? *Epidemiologia e Psychiatria Sociale, 12*, 242–252.

van Os, H., & Boerma, N. (2015). *Heilige en onheilige families*. Balans.

van Ramshorst, G. (2004). Samenspel: Samenwerking van systeemtherapeut en vaktherapeut bij gezinsdiagnostiek en gezinsbehandeling. *Systeemtherapie, 16*, 132–149.

Van Reybrouck, T. (2012). De kracht van dialoog. *Systeemtheoretisch Bulletin, 30*, 109–127.

Vansteenwegen, A. (2014). Communicatie en interactie: Directieve relatietherapie. In A. Savenije, M. J. van Lawick, & E. T. M. Reijmers (Eds.), *Handboek systeemtherapie* (2de druk, pp. 425–433). de Tijdstroom.

Varese, F., Smeets, F., Drukker, M., Lieverse, R., Lataster, T., Viechtbauer, W., Read, J., Van Os, J., & Bentall, R. (2012). Childhood adversities increase the risk of psychosis: A meta-analysis of patient-control prospective-and cross-sectional cohort studies. *Schizophrenia Bulletin, 38*, 661–671.

Verdru, H., & Stickens, N. (2009). Op welke manier kan het meten van verandering in de psychotherapie ons iets bijbrengen? *Systeemtheoretisch Bulletin, 27*, 163–183.

Verhaeghe, P. (2014). *What about me? The struggle for identity in a market-based society*. Scribe Publications.

Verkuyten, M. (1999). *Etnische identiteit: Theoretische en empirische benaderingen*. Het Spinhuis.

Vermeire, S. (2015). Over theezakjes, suikerklontjes en koffielepeltjes... *Systeemtheoretisch Bulletin, 33*, 91–108.

Vermeire, S. (2017). Tienerterreur. *Systeemtheoretisch Bulletin, 35*, 173–189.

Vermeire S., & Bracke, S. (2007). Gewrongen tussen vertrouwen en verantwoordelijkheid. *Systeemtheoretisch Bulletin, 25*, 41–59.

Vermeire, S., & Van den Berge, L. (2021). Widening the screen: Playful responses to challenges in online therapy with children and families. *Journal of Family Therapy, 43(2)*, 329–345.

Vetere, A., & Dallos, R. (2003). *Working systemically with families*. Routledge.

Visser, M., & van Lawick, M. J. (2021). *Group therapy for high-conflict divorce. The 'No kids in the middle' intervention programme*. Routledge.

von Bertalanffy, L. (1968). *General system theory: Foundations, development, applications*. George Braziller.

Vroon, P. (1997). *Smell: The secret seducer*. Farrar, Straus & Giroux.

Walsh, F. (2006). *Strengthening family resilience*. Guilford Press.

Wampold, B. E. (2001). *The great psychotherapy debate: Models, methods and findings.* Erlbaum.

Wampold, B. E., & Imel, Z. I. (2015). *The great psychotherapy debate: The evidence for what makes psychotherapy work* (2nd ed.). Routledge.

Watzlawick, P., & Beavin-Bavelas, J. (2009). Some formal aspects of communication. In W. A. Ray, & G. Nardone (Eds.), *Paul Watzlawick: Insight may cause blindness and other essays* (pp. 71–84). Zeig, Tucker & Theisen.

Watzlawick, P., Beavin, J., & Jackson, D. (1967). *The pragmatics of human communication.* W. W. Norton & Company.

Watzlawick, P., Weakland, J., & Fisch, R. (1974). *Change: Principles of problem formation and problem resolution.* W. W. Norton & Company.

Weakland, J. H. (1983). Family therapy with individuals. *Journal of Systemic Therapy, 2,* 4–19.

Weingarten, K. (2010). Reasonable hope: Construct, clinical applications and support. *Family Process, 49,* 5–25.

Whitaker, C., & Malone, T. (1953). *The roots of psychotherapy.* Blakiston.

White, M. (2007). *Maps of narrative practice.* W. W. Norton & Company.

White, M., & Epston, D. (1990). *Narrative means to therapeutic ends.* W. W. Norton & Company.

Wiggerink, J., & Vogel, M. (2017). *Signs of safety. Databank effectieve interventies huiselijk en seksueel geweld.* Movisie.

Wiggins Frame, M. (2001). The spiritual genogram in training and supervision. *The Family Journal: Counselling and Therapy for Couples and Families, 9*(2), 109–115.

Wilson, J. (2007). *Child-focused practice.* Karnac.

Wilson, J. (2017). *Creativity in times of constraint. A practitioner's companion in mental health and social care.* Karnac.

Yücel, M. (2013). *Yucelmethode. Bouwen aan herstel: Visueel en krachtgericht werken aan problemen van individuen en systemen.* Stichting Rehabilitatie.

Index

For Product Safety Concerns and Information please contact our EU
representative GPSR@taylorandfrancis.com
Taylor & Francis Verlag GmbH, Kaufingerstraße 24, 80331 München, Germany

9 781032 223117